PSYCHOLOGICAL MAN

*the text of this book is printed
on 100% recycled paper*

PSYCHOLOGICAL MAN

Edited by Robert Boyers

HARPER COLOPHON BOOKS
Harper & Row, Publishers
New York, Evanston, San Francisco, London

Contents

Preface

BY ROBERT BOYERS AND ROBERT ORRILL

This is a thoroughly revised edition of a volume published by the quarterly SALMAGUNDI (number 20, Summer-Fall 1972). That earlier collection included in its 248 pages the first version of a new work by Philip Rieff entitled "Fellow Teachers," a work which has itself undergone extensive revision and elaboration and which was published independently by Harper and Row late in 1973. A small excerpt from that book is all our present collection can claim.

Now Rieff is clearly the commanding presence in this volume, as he was in the earlier periodical version, and thus we have had a major task in 'replacing' the 80-page text of "Fellow Teachers." In a sense, of course, nothing can possibly replace it, but we've fleshed out the volume with a number of items that will surely be useful to students of Psychological Man, and essential for students of Rieff's theory of culture. The present volume, then, contains a whole range of materials originally included in the SALMAGUNDI issue, as well as the following: a chapter from Rieff's *The Triumph of the Therapeutic*, a brief excerpt from the book edition of *Fellow Teachers*, Norman O. Brown's consideration of "Fellow Teachers," and Leszek Kolakowski's provocative critique of the Freudian theory of culture. The selections from Rieff stand well enough on their own, but clearly we hope they will encourage careful examination of his books in their totality. The Brown item is a strange and compelling homage, tense with ambivalence and precisely the sort of prophesy Rieff has warned us about. The Kolakowski, more elaborate than the other additions, doesn't address Rieff by name, and there is no doubt that Rieff would make many of the same criticisms of the Freudian theory of culture that Kolakowski articulates so decisively. At the same time, the essay takes an alternative approach to issues covered by Rieff and, like the selection from Michel Foucault especially translated for this volume, represents an implicit critique of Rieff's categories.

Fellow Teachers opens with a question addressed to the editors of this volume. Could it be, Rieff asks, that we erred in our understanding of his writings, and somehow imagined him a "herald" of psychological man? Failing to recognize his commitment to a patient and positionless hermeneutics, did we take him to be an advocate of his ideal type? Did we suppose that he desired to promote when, in truth, he cared only to analyze? Such misgivings, though we believe them to be without foundation, do not require a lengthy reply—as Rieff indicates at the close of his letter/book, so far as the matter stands between ourselves, he hopes to have forestalled an exchange of "views". But a disclaimer of a general sort, which we addressed earlier to readers of SALMAGUNDI, should now be extended to those coming to these essays for the first time. We trust that none will assume that our intention in offering this collection, devoted to the study of human nature in its contemporary appearance, is either to proclaim or denounce a particular character type. The spirit of the enthusiastic messenger does not stir within us. Rather, and this is ambition enough, we have attempted to put together a volume of serious discourse which provides a variety of approaches to this vital problem of culture.

As we have noted, this volume as it now stands contains only a pertinent selection from Philip Rieff's work, but it is our conviction that Rieff's writings, presently studied in detail by only a few, eventually will find acceptance as the single most penetrating effort of cultural analysis produced by an American in recent times. This is a large claim not casually made. As Rieff himself would be the first to point out, our age gives and retracts such tribute with extraordinary ease, finding its protection against any binding debt in the attitude of knowing cynicism in which it offers all and nothing. We know that we cannot escape suspicion. We do not try to do so. Rieff's reputation finds its only sure support in his own writings, and we hope only that this book supplies a context in which the study of that body of work can begin.

The Impoverishment of Western Culture*

BY PHILIP RIEFF

*We are very often obliged, for therapeutic purposes,
to oppose the super-ego, and we endeavor to lower its
demands. Exactly the same objections can be made
against the ethical demands of the cultural super-ego.*
—Freud, *Civilisation and Its Discontents*

The higher dividends are essentially symbolic in nature. They are, in Freudian terms, the cultural equivalents of dividends which might be experienced more directly—if only a culture could stand the strain of immediate satisfactions. By setting a limit on the functional value of the higher dividends for most men, Freud declared that the religious question, in its inherited form, as a self-abnegation achieved with moral artistry, was no longer worth asking. This total rejection of the religious question gives even Marxism a pious look. By such a rejection psychoanalysis contributes to that symbolic impoverishment which is the only poverty a culture, as distinct from either a society or an individual, may suffer.

Wealth may define a status, or enhance a role, in the social system. Analysis may supply the energy an ego needs to strengthen its control over the deceits lodged in the unconscious by the failing means through which salvation was purchased, in the inherited culture. Both affluence and analysis may be viewed, especially in the United States, as intimations of successor modes to a culture defined by its particular symbolic of inner ordinances. Where those inner ordinances become subject to diagnostic control, as themselves conducive to suffering, there are forceful symbolisms operating against that culture itself. Of course, to suggest the relief of suffering by diagnosing the failure of the inner ordinances is no revolutionary departure from the way successor symbolics always have struggled for cultural ascendancy—except when

* Chapter two of *The Triumph of the Therapeutic*.

that successor symbolic was unable to offer a superior set of ordinances. But this describes the modern condition. The emergent symbolic is radically different from its predecessors.

Heretofore, the saving arrangements of Western culture have appeared as symbol systems communicating demands by stoning the sensual with deprivations, and were thus operated in a dynamically ambivalent mode. Our culture developed, as its general technique of salvation, assents to moral demands that treated the sensual part of the self as an enemy. From mastery over this enemy-self there developed some triumphant moral feeling; a character ideal was born. Every man was thus born twice, the second time as a creature aspiring to a moral artistry trained by deprivations. In sum, the classical character ideals were all personifications of a release from a multitude of desires.

Not only our Western system but every system of integrative moral demand, the generative principle of culture, expressed itself in positive deprivations—in a character ideal that functioned to commit the individual to the group. Culture was thus the establishment and organization of restrictive motives. Men engaged in disciplines of interdiction. The dialectic of deprivation and remission from deprivation was in the service of those particular interdicts by which a culture constituted itself. The analytic attitude does contain a certain time-element of asceticism, but it points toward a character ideal that is in principle anti-ascetic and therefore revolutionary if viewed from perspectives formed in the inherited moral demand system. The dialectic of perfection, based on a deprivational mode, is being succeeded by a dialectic of fulfillment, based on the appetitive mode.

The analytic attitude is a doctrine developed for the private wants of private men, and shifts with the individual. In trying to describe this doctrinal aspect of psychological manhood, it appears to me as an anti-doctrine, one that dismisses the therapeutic compulsions of all doctrines as ultimately ineffective. Psychological man takes on the attitude of a scientist, with himself alone as the ultimate object of his science. If the analytic therapy has been effective, the therapeutic learns to keep in touch with the options around which the conduct of life might be organized; ideally, all options ought to be kept alive because, theoretically, all are equally advisable—or inadvisable, in given personal circumstances. Not all homosexuals ought to be cured, nor should all stabilities, which may be achieved painfully and at great cost, be disturbed because of the pain that accompanies their achieve-

ment. Life is individual. Well-being is a delicate personal achievement, and only a vulgarization of the analytic attitude would permit
easy or general judgments on any such achievement. No analyst or
trained student of the painful ambiguities that have contributed to
some individual sense of well-being would be so foolish as to tamper
with it—so long as it works. Since no firm social standards for treatment have yet been erected, some grave ambiguities persist regarding
the question of just who should be treated. There may be a kindness
that is neurotic, if it develops out of unconscious compulsions, and a
cruelty that is normal, if it is freely and consciously determined upon.
So far as sainthood is determined by unconscious and uncontrolled
motives, it is neurotic; so far as sinning, as usually understood, is determined by conscious and rational choice, it is normal. One difficulty with the criteria of rationality and consciousness is that Eich-
mann, for instance, might well be considered quite without need of
treatment. He knew what he was doing; indeed, he wanted to be a
great success in his career. Freud was honest enough to discover that
there was no inherent relation between normality and the norm, such
as had been established, in the age of political and religious man,
through the mediating myth that there were natural laws. The
analytic attitude has discovered no natural harmony of goals, no hierarchy of value inscribed upon the universe. Confronted by the equality of choice, the individual could resort to the analytic attitude in
order to limit the folly of being drawn too far outside the protective
management of his own pleasures.

To reserve the capacity for neutrality between choices, even while
making them, as required by this new science of moral management,
produces a strain no less great than choosing itself. The analytic capacity demands a rare skill: to entertain multiple perspectives upon
oneself, and even upon beloved others. A high level of control is necessary in order to shift from one perspective to another, so to soften the
demands upon oneself in all the major situations of life—love, parent-
hood, friendship, work, and citizenship. Such conscious fluidity of
commitment is not easily acquired. In fact, the attainment of psychological manhood is more difficult than any of the older versions of
maturity; that manhood is no longer protected by a fantasy of having
arrived at some resting place where security, reassurance, and trust
reside, like gods in their heavens. The best one can say for oneself in
life is that one has not been taken in, even by that "normal psychosis,"
love.

Freud understood the dangers inherent in a situation in which the precious individual was vulnerable to the charge that his life had become meaningless. In answer, he asserted that no fresh access of doctrine could for long decrease that vulnerability. In such cases, the individual merely built his neurosis the more deeply into his character, hiding it behind some unstable equilibrium of faithful action. All such action systems of faith, with the neurotic factor as the mediating agent, brought more grief than relief to the modern individual in search of a cure for himself. Freud could not enter deeply enough. The internalities, being weak, had sickened, where they had not (to the betterment of the patient) died. The old therapies of action, based upon some saving truths (and authoritative institutions), no longer relieved the individual of the most oppressive of his tensions—those developing in his own private circles of love and friendship. For these therapies were based on now ineffectual attempts to bring the individual far out of himself, into some relation with an order of institutions that underwrote his sense of well-being. With the decline of a civilization of authority, the therapeutic requirement shifted toward an action which would take place, first, within the circle of personal relations; after this first level of private re-education had been successfully negotiated, the public life could then in time be altered. A new kind of community could be constructed, one that did not generate conscience and internal control but desire and the safe play of impulse. From this *pneuma* pulsing through the intimate world of friendship and love, the next culture gives signs that it will emerge— a culture that would not oppose the self but express more fully its varieties.

Dichotomies between an ultimately meaningful and meaningless existence belong to the eras of public philosophies and communal theologies. Ecologically, this transitional civilization is becoming one vast suburbia, something like the United States, populated by divided communities of two, with perhaps two junior members caught in the middle of a private and not always civil war; in relation to these intimate, though divided, communities of two, the public world is constituted as one vast stranger, who appears at inconvenient times and makes demands viewed as purely external and therefore without the power to elicit a genuinely moral response.

In the time of public philosophies and social religions, the great communities were positive. A positive community is characterized by the fact that it guarantees some kind of salvation to the individual by virtue of his membership and participation in that community. That

sort of community seemed corrupt to the economic man, with his particular version of an ascetic ideal tested mainly by self-reliance and
personal achievement. The positive community was displaced, in social theory, by the neutral market. Now, in the middle of the twentieth century, the market mechanism appears not so much corrupt as a
fiction to psychological man, with his awareness of how decisions are
made in the social system. In order to participate self-protectively in
the manipulative and acquisitive game, psychological man builds his
tight family island, living for the remainder of his time in negative
communities. But these collections of little islands surrounded by
therapeutic activities, without any pretense at a doctrine of salvation,
are themselves infected by the negativity of the larger community and
become manipulative arenas themselves, rather than oases of escape
from the larger arena.

The indefinite prolongation of psychoanalytic therapy is itself a
form of membership in the negative community. Positive communities were, according to Freud, held together by guilt; they appear attractive only now, in distant retrospect, but the modern individual,
faced with the necessity of merging his own life into communal effort,
would have found them suffocating. Instead, the modern individual
can only use the community as the necessary stage for his effort to
enhance himself—if not always, or necessarily, to enrich himself.

In one certain way, the therapeutically inclined individual resem-
bles his predecessor, the ascetic. That resemblance can be best
sketched historically.

Once launched into some activity, conceiving of himself as an instrument of God's will, the ascetic did not stop to ask about the meaning of it all. On the contrary, the more furious his activity, the more
the problem of what his activity meant receded from his mind. In
time, the Western ascetic ceased cultivating his doctrinal imagination.
For a time, perhaps for a century, the sheer intensity of his action carried him along to greater power and prosperity; the atrophy of doctrinal imagination caused only mild alarms. But, in the nineteenth
century, there were signs of trouble all over this failing ascetic culture.
Questions were being raised, at first by literary men; symptoms were
being observed, by all manner of men.

The most congenial climate for the training of the therapeutic has
been in a waning ascetic culture like that of Protestant America. It is
specially true of this Calvinist culture that it proved a breeding ground
for remissive equivalents to the original ascetic motives in which the

emphasis is on retraining for a fuller activity and not on the achievement of some new general meaning. One permitting condition for this therapeutic successor to the ascetic was already present in the assumption of the Protestant activist that the will, or motive, of his God was unsearchable and His ways quite inexplicable, so that they could not be understood by any human standard. To meet the demands of the day was as near as one could come to doing the pious thing, in this—God's—world. To trouble about meaning was really an impiety and, of course, frivolous, because futile. For the question of meaning, therefore, neither the ascetic nor the therapeutic type feels responsible, if his spiritual discipline has been successful. The recently fashionable religious talk of "ultimate concern" makes no sense either in the ascetic or in the therapeutic mode. To try to relate "ultimate concern" to everyday behavior would be exhausting and nerve-shattering work; indeed, it could effectively inhibit less grandiose kinds of work. Neither the ascetic nor the therapeutic bothers his head about "ultimate concern." Such a concern is for mystics who cannot otherwise enjoy their leisure. In the workaday world, there are no ultimate concerns, only present ones. Therapy is the respite of every day, during which the importance of the present is learned, and the existence of what in the ascetic tradition came to be called the "ultimate" or "divine" is unlearned. Those remote areas of experience are brought up only in order to be put in their proper place, as dead events and motives rather than as the models for events and motives of the present life. Analytic therapy is thus a form of re-education; Freud specifically called it that. It is re-education so far as it eliminates those symptoms through which the patient has tried, mistakenly, to resolve the contradictions in his life.

Therapeutic re-education is therefore at once a difficult and yet modest procedure. It teaches the patient-student how to live with the contradictions that combine to make him into a unique personality; this it does in contrast to the older moral pedagogies, which tried to re-order the contradictions into a hierarchy of superior and inferior, good and evil, capabilities. To become a psychological man is thus to become kinder to the self as a whole, to the private parts of it as well as to the public ones, to the once inferior as well as to the formerly superior. While older character types were concentrating on the life task of trying to order the warring parts of the personality into a hierarchy, modern pedagogies, reflecting the changing self-conception of this culture, are far from egalitarian: it is the task of psychological man to develop an informed (i.e., healthy) respect for the sovereign and unresolvable basic contradictions that make him the singularly complicated human being he is.

Freud's most important ideas finally may have less to do with the repression of sexual impulses (which explains neither the past discontents of our civilization nor the present ones), than with ambivalence. It is their capacity to reverse feelings that is the human problem and hope. What hope there is derives from Freud's assumption that human nature is not so much a hierarchy of high-low, and good-bad, as his predecessors believed, but rather a jostling democracy of contending predispositions, deposited in every nature in roughly equal intensities. Where there is love, there is the lurking eventuality of hatred. Where there is ambition, there is the ironic desire for failure. Although he wishes not to know it, a sore loser may be sore mainly because he almost won and is reacting against his wish to lose. Psychoanalysis is full of such mad logic; it is convincing only if the student of his own life accepts Freud's egalitarian revision of the traditional idea of an hierarchical human nature.

Yet, although Freud had proclaimed this major revision in the Western self-image, he was himself sentimentally attached to the old hierarchical assumption. On the one hand, he analyzed the damage done by this hierarchical structuring of human nature into pejoratively toned "higher" and "lower" categories—indeed, it was precisely this damage that he made it his business to mend. On the other hand, he hoped that somehow, despite the near equality of our warring emotions, reason would cleverly manage to reassert itself, despite its congenital weakness—not in the high and mighty way preached by Plato and his Christian successors but in a modest, even sly manner that would alternately dazzle and lull the more powerful emotions into submission. This way actually demands, it seems, the kind of character ideal we have called the "therapeutic" in order to contrast it with the more rigid character ideal produced by the moral demand systems preceding modernity. In the age of psychologizing, clarity about oneself supersedes devotion to an ideal as the model of right conduct.

We can now understand better why Freud was an inveterate finder of double meanings, even of some that may not be there; why the latent makes sense only as it contradicts the manifest; why the aggressive movement behind the friendly gesture needs the complement of the friendly gesture. For thus Freud succeeded in challenging simplicity, in particular moral simplicity. He encouraged a tolerance of what used to be called, in general, the "low," just as he encouraged a new respect for the young, for the deviant, and for the shocking. There was about Freud a calm anticipation of the unexpected that subverted the expectations of a life based on older schemes of an authoritative, set, hierarchical order of conduct.

On the institutional level, the Freudian analysis reduced most obviously the hierarchical order of the family and, moreover, of the "head" of the family. This reductionism applied specially to the position of the father. In the European context, the father appeared also as the personification of all those heights of repressive command from which, Freud decided, the rules of the moral game should no longer effectively be handed down. Much as he admired the Moses-figures in our culture, Freud considered their techniques of exercising authority too costly.

A tolerance of ambiguities is the key to what Freud considered the most difficult of all personal accomplishments: a genuinely stable character in an unstable time. Yet, just this rare and fine capacity, rejecting as it does the value of ignorance, encourages an equally dangerous attitude when viewed from the perspective of the instability of the times: namely, an attitude of deliberate acquiescence. Being able to recognize the equivocations of which behavior is composed need not, however, mean their encouragement.

Nevertheless, there is a sound basis for what are otherwise hypocritical objections to the immorality of interpretation with which Freudians rip away the façades of moral action. Hypocrisy is a precious thing in any culture. Like reticence, it may help build up those habits of avoidance that swerve us from honest, but head-on, collisions with one another. Nothing in psychoanalytic therapy encourages immoral behavior. The immorality of interpretation aims merely at revealing moralized compulsions behind even the most correct and apparently straightforward behavior. This means that psychoanalysis discourages moral behavior on the old, self-defeating grounds—out of what is now called a *sense* of guilt rather than guilt.

To help us distinguish between guilt on the one hand and a sense of guilt on the other, between responsibility for an offense committed and fantasies about offenses intended or merely imagined, seems a moral as well as a therapeutic aim. To suffer from scrupulosity is, after all, a well-known perversion of moral ambition, even according to the most elaborate of our established casuistries. But psychoanalysis is more than a mere scrutiny of handwashing. Freud went more deeply than that. His ambition to exhaust the sense of guilt by clinical exposures of all details may be dangerous, as he himself realized, to the life of a culture that is on the defensive. If a self-trained casuist gets along better by resolving his guilt into a sense of guilt, then he is the healthier for that resolution. This is a vulgar and popular misinterpretation of Freud; but there is something about the presuppositions of psychoanalytic therapy that encourages just such misinterpretations. A man can be made healthier without being made better—rather, morally worse. Not the good life but better living is the therapeutic standard. It is a popular standard, not difficult to follow, as Americans, despite Freud's wish to make it difficult, were the first to recognize in any significant number.

Americans no longer model themselves after the Christians or the Greeks. Nor are they such economic men as Europeans believe them to be. The political man of the Greeks, the religious man of the Hebrews and Christians, the enlightened economic man of eighteenth-century Europe (the original of that mythical present-day character, the "good European"), has been superseded by a new model for the conduct of life. Psychological man is, I suggest, more native to American culture than the Puritan sources of that culture would indicate.

The therapeutic as an American type has outgrown his immediate ancestor in one clear sense, for both Socrates and Christ taught economic man to be at least slightly ashamed of himself when he failed to sacrifice the lower capacity to the higher. Freud is America's great teacher, despite his ardent wish to avoid that fate. For it was precisely the official and parental shams of high ideals that Freud questioned. In their stead, Freud taught lessons which Americans, prepared by their own national experience, learn easily: survive, resign yourself to living within your moral means, suffer no gratuitous failures in a futile search for ethical heights that no longer exist—if they ever did. Freud proclaims the superior wisdom of choosing the second best. He is our Crito, become intellectually more subtle than the sick and old Socrates, who was still foolish enough to justify his own death sentence rather than escape from the prison of his own inhibitions about the sanctity of the state, which he mistakes for his father. Freud appeals to us because his wisdom is so cautious. Surely he is not to be blamed for living at a time when the inherited aspirations of the Greek, Christian, and Humanist past had gone stale, when both Athens and Jerusalem, not to mention Paris, Oxford, and the Italian Renaissance cities, have become tourist spots rather than shrines of pilgrims in search of spiritual knowledge. With no place to go for lessons in the conduct of contemporary life, every man must learn, as Freud teaches, to make himself at home in his own grim and gay little Vienna.

The alternatives with which Freud leaves us are grim only if we view them from the perspective of some past possibility, as though we were either political or religious men. Assuming that these character ideals are, in Freud's terms, regressive, the grimness is relieved by the gaiety of being free from the historic Western compulsion of seeking large and general meanings for small and highly particular lives. Indeed, the therapy of all therapies, the secret of all secrets, the interpretation of all interpretations, in Freud, is not to attach oneself exclusively or too passionately to any one particular meaning, or object. There is discernible in those who practice professionally the analytic attitude, that is, in the psychoanalysts themselves, a certain cultivated detachment and calm that is perhaps the highest expression of that individualism to which De Tocqueville first referred. In the most intimate of modern relations, the psychoanalytic transaction between analyst and patient, one of the members of that unique community of two must remain an almost total stranger to the other; only if the analyst draws a veil across his own life does he maintain his therapeutic effectiveness. In turn, the patient must learn how to draw the veil properly around himself. To accomplish this, he needs to develop the full power and liberty of his emotions, without paying the price of fixing them too firmly on any object or idea. This he is taught by the experience of ending his relation of intimacy to the analyst himself. Here, again, is the ascetic ideal, shorn of any informing goal or principle; thus divested of the need for compulsive attachments, the ascetic becomes the therapeutic. With Freud, individualism took a great and perhaps final step: toward that mature and calm feeling which comes from having nothing to hide. The individual need no longer keep a safe distance from the mass of his fellows. In therapy, developed as a social process, he will be so trained that vulnerability is minimized. To live on the surface prevents deep hurts. With Freud, Western man has learned the technical complexity of externalizing his inwardness, and has been able at last to usher out that crowd of shadows urging him to turn inward, so as to live in the bright, sober light of the present, where, ideally, the moment is always high noon. This is not isolation, for it is no longer confining. Nor is it a participation mystique, for the participatory action has nothing self-abnegating about it. Rather, the social therapy is liberating, rendering all objects of commitment instrumental to the therapeutic process itself. Such a clear-cut externalization as suggested here could characterize a culture developed far more highly than our present one. Doctrinal intimations along these lines are dealt with in the second half of my book.

To be truly free and yet social means to cultivate detachment as opposed to alienation. The therapeutic, even in erotic action, can do without attachment—indeed, he can do with and do without it, simultaneously, for relations that are too near and too fixed may lead to symptoms that destroy the capacity of an individual to live out his own life in ways of his own choosing. This is not to say that to live thus, detachedly, implies an absence of erotic company, or even an absence of the erotic manner. On the contrary, the therapeutic treats love instrumentally. He is likely to be more circumspect and better behaved than his ascetic forebear, who was subject to mood fluctuations between wild passion and *accidie,* due in part to the rigid system of controls and overburdened devices of release. With a shift in the system, giving greater amplitude to the releasing devices, the subject personalities are likely to develop a more measured, calculated capacity in the use of their spontaneity.

Freed from all suspicions of divinity, psychological man can continue to work efficiently in all kinds of institutions, but without permitting his feelings to be entrapped by institutional service. The ascetic was limited, and often broken, in his organizational usefulness by a naïve dedication to principle. It was as if man were made to be used by the organization, rather than the organization made to be used by man. For this character ideal of an autonomous man, using but unused, Americans already have put vulgar understandings of the analytic anti-symbolic to full use.[1]

There is a sense in which culture is always at one with the social system. In a society with so many inducements to self-interest, "self-realization" seems a noble and healthy end. The least valuable competitive position is to be self-defeating. The therapeutic cannot conceive of an action that is not self-serving, however it may be disguised or transformed. This is a culture in which each views the other, in the fullness of his self-knowledge, as "trash." Freud used the word to summarize his general opinion of people. But, the question remains: How to discipline the "trash"? To be liberated from renunciatory character ideals by the analytic attitude might give the

---

[1] Certainly, this was done without Freud's intention or approval. Representing Freud as a prophet of non-culture contradicts his own highest intentions.

"trash" (Freud's term) too much liberty to do its worst, whereas in the older system the "trash" would not do its best. One may think, therefore, an ethic of perfection to be more prudent, even on Freud's own assumptions about the human animal, than an ethic of tolerance.

Yet, probably the ethic of tolerance is the one more appropriate and safe for use in the age of psychological man. It is the ethic of a wayfarer rather than that of a missionary; it is the ethic of a pilgrim, who, out of his experience, became a tourist. Unfortunately for culture and good taste, the salesman cruelly parodies the preacher without being able to help doing so, for cultural history has allotted to the salesman the rhetorical style of a missionary. Freud distrusted that style, even in medical missionaries—or, more precisely, in missionaries of a non-saving medicine; he himself never tried to "sell" his doctrine, as now many of his successors have done, to their indubitable gain, with the nostrums known as "self-realization" and/or "self-fulfillment." What would suit the therapeutic ideal better than the prevalent American piety toward the self? This self, improved, is the ultimate concern of modern culture. If this culture develops further along lines indicated here, and if the social order moves in a parallel line, toward wider distribution of plenitude, then that general condition of detachment which prevents religious outburst and political revolution may well be established. Finally, even world government may come—with universal indifference as its cultural predicate.

Every culture is an institutionalized system of moral demands, elaborating the conduct of personal relations, a cosset of compelling symbols. Every culture is thus safely strapped to its functions. Its mode of integration defines also its limitations. For an individual to engage in a self-therapeutic effort, which must either ignore or contradict the meanings by which his character was molded, suggests either that the therapy must fail or that the culture is in the process of a change as to its control mechanism.

Thus, analyzing the analytic attitude, we may conclude, quite tentatively, that the American culture is in a remissive phase of transition to a new system of moral standards. Assuming this, the best strategy for the polemicists of the therapeutic, no less than for the ascetic, may be the playing of a waiting game: the former can use the analytic attitude to militate against renewals of the moral demand system, while the latter may seek to encourage renewals.[2] The power of the analytic attitude rests on the assumption that its proper exercise can cut off revitalization movements of the classical moral demand system. It was Freud's thought that no moral demand system could ever again compel at least the educated classes to that inner obedience which bound men to rules they themselves had made but then could not change except at the expense of spirit, far beyond the usefulness of such rules to the continuance of cultural achievement. The waiting game has thus become the permanent strategy of the contending polemicists. It remains to be seen which side is waiting in vain—that which hopes for a vital faith or that which places its hopes in vitality itself.

The revolution of rising expectations is a major weapon in the warfare of the therapeutic against the ascetic. After all, there is something to the notion that the rich—even the rich Communists—cannot take their respective religion too seriously. Even now, the rich Marxists must stave off the fanatics from poor Marxist countries. Comfort is the great social tranquilizer. This, in fact, sums up the revolutionary attitude of the rich and psychoculturally educated in the United States nowadays. Symbolic impoverishment ceases to be a problem precisely because the rich have found functional equivalents for a system of compelling moral demands, in analysis and in art, which may be said to be a mode of self-reverence. The old form of culture criticism, to the effect that our plenitude of things lies wasting and useless in a desert of belief, thus becomes irrelevant, being based on the outmoded assumption that a moral demand system must be hard and unyielding like the Sinai desert in order to be effective. On the contrary, Freud's theory was that, under present and foreseeable conditions, only a yielding demand system—more prudent than principled—would be capable of sustaining itself.

When combined with the analytic attitude, affluence may be the alternative to questionable renewals of religion, taking the form of excessive moral demands, by which this culture has been regularly carried away in the past. Educated as they are, the rich have no need

---

[2] There is a widespread hope among the more thoughtful and committed American Christian clergy that the Negro agitation will serve, providentially, to revitalize the moral demand system in the white American culture. Of course, there are religious motives among the Negroes. But the national good demands that they be educated up to the post-religious level of the whites as quickly as possible, if further civil disorder is to be avoided. Moreover, the Negro demand is for nothing less than what "integration" implies: their fair share of the national substance.

of religious renewals. In classical cultures, an ascended class had to justify itself before those below in the social structure. But the culture revolution of our time has eliminated this need for class- as well as self-justification. Nevertheless, those below still seek to emulate the ascendant social class, without being convinced of its superiority. And just as the rich have lost their idea of superiority, so have the poor lost their idea of religion. Poverty is no longer holy; the poor, insofar as they are educated in the new doctrine, have no motive for projecting onto society a new set of strict moral demands that might infuse society with the kind of impetus needed to end symbolic poverty.

According to my reading of the past psychohistorical process, members of an ascending class would mobilize their spiritual energies by representing themselves as the carrier of new moral demands. This is the classic way in which, for example, the Puritan revolution occurred. Finally, after the revolutionary releasing phase had passed, the ascending class would use the symbol system as a control device; the same symbols that once justified its revolutionary attacks on the culture served later as control devices for the preservation and expansion of the system of moral demands the ascending class had first established for itself.

In time, every revolutionary renewal of moral demands appears to exhaust itself. The ascending class would take on some of the dominant characteristics of the class it replaced. Revolutions end in some form of restoration. Thus, a revival of faith comes to its end, as a rule, in a remissive establishment. In this perspective, the price of revivalist revolutions will always appear too high. And by this rationalization the system of moral demands as such is cast into doubt. What is at stake, in this elaboration of the theory of ambivalence, is the Western capacity for mounting new moral demands as inherently superior to those established minimally and sanctioned in the past.

It follows from this interpretation that the present struggle between the United States and the post-Stalinist Soviet Union is based on their being in different phases in the psychohistorical process, a difference which may be further resolved when both would understand that they share the same cultural aims. Both issue from the assumption that wealth is a superior and adequate substitute for symbolic impoverishment. Both American and Soviet cultures are essentially variants of the same belief in wealth as the functional equivalent of a high civilization. In both cultures, the controlling symbolism has been stripped down to a belief in the efficacy of wealth. Quantity has become quality. The answer to all questions of "what for?" is "more." The faith of the rich has always been in themselves. Rendered democratic, this religion proposes that every man become his own eleemosynary institution. Here is a redefinition of charity from which the inherited faith of Christianity may never recover. Out of this redefinition, Western culture is changing already into a symbol system unprecedented in its plasticity and absorptive capacity. Nothing much can oppose it really, and it welcomes all criticism, for, in a sense, it stands for nothing.

Observations on The Therapeutic *

BY PHILIP RIEFF

It is out of a highly differentiated society, spheres of action separate, none subject to the same interdicts, and all to fewer, that the therapeutic has been born. This ideal type is free, in the first place, because he can live his life among authorities so long divided that none can assert themselves strongly even in their own sphere—quite the contrary of Durkheim's quasi-syndicalist hope. There is, however, something new about the therapeutic: a conclusive freedom, all interdicts evaginated, so highly surfaced that none can survive. Why should the therapeutic feel anything deeply when he can exhibit his sensibilities? The contemporary man of feeling is equipped with a hidden weapon, his pseudo-sensibility; he demands, he appeals, he does whatever needs to be done, under whatever slogan, to assert himself. A slogan is an unrooted saying. Slogans are the language of a radically contemporary people. The American language has become a grab-bag of slogans. This massive abnormality has become the norm.

Living on his surfaces, as he does, the therapeutic is an acutely sensitive man; it is only deep down that he has learned to be less vulnerable. I was struggling toward this point in a passage from *The Triumph of the Therapeutic* of which you reminded me in your interpretative paraphrase of it during our exchange:

> With Freud, the individual took a great and final step toward that mature and calm feeling which comes from having nothing to hide. To live on the surface prevents deep hurts.

It takes a certain genius to survive the deepest hurts. Freud favored asking less of people, most of whom are not moral geniuses or any other kind. Most of us cannot transform our hurts into anything that does not hurt (ourselves or others) more. A true culture imposes cer-

* Reprinted from Rieff's *Fellow Teachers*.

tain limits on itself; it does not ask ordinary men to make extraordinary renunciations. But in a true culture, a genius is not considered a criminal, nor is criminality honored as genius. Life is not confused with Art. Terribilità should remain an aesthetic, not a political, capacity; it rightly belonged to Beethoven and Michelangelo, in their work, not to the condottieri, or Hitler, in theirs. An extraordinarily rare talent does not emerge in transgressions; rather, in works of art, or science, that control their own spheres with full interdictory force, called 'form.' Within its culture, every art work constitutes a system of discrete limits, each a paradigm of how a culture works; none are sovereign beyond themselves. A universal culture is a contradiction in terms. We Jews of culture are obliged to resist the very idea.

Confusing spheres, modern aspirants to freedom from all authority have produced a parody terribilità in all spheres. Our re-educated classes, rich consumers of everything available, are scarcely competent to perform the most elementary decencies—yet they are urged to fulfill themselves, as if each were a Beethoven, perhaps a little deaf to his own music and in need of some third-ear hygiene. Freud called psychoanalysis a 're-education.' In our own time, post-Freudian, everything new is a re-education; mind fawns over mindlessness and tries to find fancy names for it. So the therapeutic teaching of transgressive behavior confuses art and life, rare genius and common faith, public life and private. Encounter-group teachings, for example, mainly by therapists of the revolutionary rich, follow the precedent set by the technological radicalism of those same rich in their earlier scramble: for more.

That the opposing sides of the American scene, deviants and straights, are both suspicious of authority, is mainly the fault of what passes for authority in our nation; the officers themselves are so often inferior persons that their offices cannot conceal the absence of any reference beyond themselves to a presiding presence. Modern revolt has no authority and is all the more dangerous because there is no authority against which to revolt; we are stripping politics to its barest form, struggle for power after power, violence. What Mills called 'savagery' and 'barbarism' scarcely applies so well to his notion of static societies as it does to our own dynamic one. We and our students shall have to be reminded that "discipline, that is, perfect co-operation, is an attribute of civilization," not of mass rationalization. Mill tells us that to be capable of discipline in great things, "a people must be gradually trained to it in small."[1] Such training cannot be politicized without inverting the meaning of discipline, from civilization to barbarism—from a not-doing of what is not to be done to a routine doing of precisely that.

Presences have never been encouraged to preside—now less than ever before. The therapeutic has no presence. It is impossible to revolt against him. All revolution worthy of the name has been against authority, giving rise to a new presiding presence, without which authority cannot exist; for example, Jews cannot exist without the Mosaic presence (as Freud understood, in making his attempt at a resolutive interpretation of the Jewish historical character). Suppose, however, there is no authority—only power and its theatrical affects? How can there be a crisis of authority? Among our reflective sorts, there is much fashionable talk of crisis, of our times of trouble. I doubt the gravity of the crisis, not least for all the crisis talk; the time seems to me less gravely troubled than some others. What can 'trouble' mean if our society is growing cultureless, without presiding presences and a public order of meaning? Guilt is much overestimated as a working force in the new society, usable mainly as a tactic toward its continuing dissolution. During a year in Germany, I met precious few guilty people. My German friends were having an authentically good time. My American friends seem equally guiltless, although they throw up their hands regularly as if aghast at their sense of guilt. I think they are playing games. To feel guilt takes a certain submission to authority. There can be no transgressive sense without someone (and his theory) to transgress.

No guilt is true except as it subserves the interdicts. Guilt is false, 'neurotic,' as Freud taught us to call it, when it subverts the interdicts. Far from separating crime and morals, the radical psychologizers treat certain kinds of crime as (politically) virtuous; in the name of 'humanization,' false guilt subverts the interdicts by proclaiming that everything human is permitted. The radical psychologizers have greatly increased the incidence of false guilt because culture cannot tolerate such direct openings of possibility. Our politicized therapists are the sickest people among us—and our most liberated. Their quest for health has generated an acute dis-ease, 'Liberation,' the latest mockery of all god-terms, including the pagan.

We professors of the present have in stock a large supply of god-

---

[1] John Stuart Mill, "Civilization," *The Westminster Review*, Nos. V and XLVIII (April 1836), p. 3.

terms and can conjure orders galore, from the grab-bag of things past, passing and to come. Precisely in the age of the therapeutic, the dead gods cannot rise from their graves. None are alive; any may be talked up, for an occasion, if the talkers like to drop those kinds of names. Our god-terms mock their ancestors, the gods, in one special respect: no god-term worth using can be merely heuristic, a device for extending intellectual reach. God-terms must have binding authority, compelling not merely intellectual interest but also suspicion of that interest. Our God can only reveal as he conceals himself; ask that, concealment with every revelation, and you have understood why the major questions must always continue as if unanswered.

Without concealments, revelations yield none of those compromises which make life tolerable. Imagine the length of the casualty list when a universal publicity reveals everything to all, at once, when nothing is handed down slowly, in generational dances of time. Sociology awaits its theorists in the classic style. Since the positivist takeover, in the first third of the nineteenth century, my discipline has tried too hard to remain permanently advanced, young enough to produce an endless barrage of originalities. Such youthfulness and originality—trendiness, some call it—are fatal to the life of the mind. Violent excursions toward death and perverse behavior are occupations most fit for the young, when they will not think through what their predecessors have thought. To leave the great past unremembered is to be lost in the howling present; then the best an intellectual can do is shoot off his mouth.

When the god-terms lose their inhibiting dynamic, then they become protean. ('Protean man' does not descend from the god Proteus. He has no descent, and therefore no existence.) The barbarian who is emerging, stuffed with tactical advice culled from the ages, can hop from order to order, committing himself, as in modern marriage, to a serial monogamy that is massively polygamous. ('But I'm always true to you, darlin', in my fashion'—what is the name of that old hymn? I will not remember. Was it: 'A Mighty Fortress,' as Erikson believes?) To say this barbarian is universally faithless is only to say that no character becomes authoritative in him. Only cultureless societies can exist without presiding presences. No presence can preside when all are subject to abandonments quick as their adoptions. Our passionate truths are so provisional, they move so quickly with the electrified times, that none can prepare us to receive them deeply into ourselves, as character; they do not become compelling in their interdicts but endlessly attractive in their remissions. Where creeds were, there therapies will be. Our new way, re-education, is an unlearning. What, then, have we to teach?

It is as the typical creature of a cultureless society that I have imagined the therapeutic. I do not imagine him as a serious man. Seriousness is a state of possession by god-terms, even to the negation of justified violence in their defense. Serious attacks on authority must breed new authority. In the therapeutic, I imagined someone who takes nothing seriously. Of course, a therapeutic can resonate empty militancies that signal an acceptance of their emptiness. Opposing this experimental life, in which all god-terms can be taken lightly, rather as heuristic devices, there can be only a culture of militant, opposing truths—god-terms that are interdictory before they are remissive and thus to be taken seriously because humans will oppose the interdicts with all their wits. (To take a god-term seriously, however, is not to be without humor; on the contrary, as I have said, no justification worth calling to mind ever sets it at rest. What may be taken lightly is not the god-term, but oneself. Luther called this the joy of the faithful.) A culture of truth opposing self—what culture is, understood sociologically—abides experimental lives only in its own service; thus, for example, monasticism, which opposed the corporate self-glorification of the church, served culture. Except through institutional services, before they harden into further glorifications and false guilt, experiment belongs in the laboratory and to art, most rarely to publicized individuality. Our continuous publicity for experimental living predicates that totalitarian disorder of which fascist movements gave one premonitory flash. I shall return, below, to the important point, that, as Mussolini grasped, fascism is not a creed but an opportunity.

Now I am in position to answer the question for which you prepared me before our interview (perhaps the result of our happy misunderstanding): whether the coming of the therapeutic is to be welcomed insofar as he is free from any need of a common faith. With this emergent type, you ask, will we be delivered from the nightmare history of the last half-century, and spared its mass brutalities? No; I suspect we will not be spared. Violence is the therapy of therapies, as Dr. Fanon, the political psychiatrist, suggests. There is less and less to inhibit this final therapy, least where the most progressively re-educated classes seem ready to go beyond their old hope of deliverance, from violence as the last desperate disciplinary means built into the interdicts, as punishment, to violence as a means toward a saving indiscipline, as self-expression. Geniuses of this saving indiscipline roam the college circuit, selling their guidance toward a cultureless society, without interdicts deeply installed.

Which cadre of putative guides to the new freedom will you follow: our rationalizing functionaries[2] or our functional irrationalizers?[3] Never mind: they will meet at the end of their roads. The functional irrationalizers are well on their way to becoming our next rationalizing functionaries. Both cadres will produce endless therapies. With the end of authority, no violence will be illegitimate. Rather, as they destroy the civilities basic to cultured society, the brutalities of direct action will be differently understood. Victims are being taught their complicity, their role, in brutal acts. Let every actor play his variable part, without indignation—except when indignation promotes the part. The new society already has the look, both in America and in the Soviet Union, of a hospital-theatre—in contrast to the old society, which had the look of a church. The successor to our failed credal organizations will not be another credal one, not even Marxist, which names the last major credal effort to reorganize western society; we shall be dominated by anti-creeds and think ourselves free.

Our own culture has taken form in credal organizations. Priesthoods and intelligentsias are but two of the forms credal organization, ancient and modern, may take. However, the defense of it, implicit in my theory of culture, does not make me an advocate of some earlier credal organization. In particular, I have not the slightest affection for the dead church civilization of the West. I am a Jew. No Jew in his right mind can long for some variant (including the Party)[4] of that civilization. Its one enduring quality is its transgressive energy against the Jew of culture; those transgressions have been built so deeply into the church-organized interdicts that they survive even now, after the main interdictory motifs of Christendom are dead. Christian trans-

---

[2] E.g., engineers, social and material, of control.

[3] E.g., therapists of release.

[4] But, see, on the concept 'political religions,' my remarks on functionalism, pp. 187-188. I doubt that the Party, which Gramsci saw as the Prince of this world, can be understood as a 'secular' (i.e. successor and functional) equivalent of the Church. Indeed, I doubt that penetrative thrust inheres in the concept 'secularization.' We can do better without 'secularization.' The concept obscures interdictory-remissive shifts of indirective content. Secularization specially encourages false homotonalities, an ease of transitions that may falsify true oppositions: as between pastors and professors, for example—as if becoming a Professor really does express in another form (perhaps up-dated, superior because up-dated) earlier religious aspirations.

gressions are still so vital that the recent well-publicized statements of Christian remorse are likely to be a condition of further transgression, as the Jews continue to resist their assigned roles and, worse gall, refuse to disappear into the universalist future 'Man.' The gospels were not good news; the ungospeled present has its supremely pleasant feature, the death of the church—or, less pleasant, its conversion into naively therapeutic institutions, hawking a few antique graces to ornament our triumphant gracelessness. A contentless faith in 'faith' is but one of the rather noisy rhetorics of commitment to movement—any movement—that characterize the superego turned against itself, against inhibition and for action. As in space science, so in the new reforming amorality, to be distinguished from the old Reformation morality, the count-down slogan is "All systems go."

I, for one, am not keen on being where the direct action is; there brutality and the horror of total politics, uninhibited by any presiding presence, will be. One necessary thing that we inactivists, we academic men, suspicious of all politics, have to teach our students is how not to invest in the nostrums of direct action now being hawked. It is our duty to protect and nurture, in our academies, a few enclaves within which to practice an inhibiting subtlety, to think in something like late Jamesean sentences.[5] If we are not allowed indirections, slowly ordered, if we must serve some program, one side or another, then the academy has no unique service; it is least fit of all institutions to take stands or rationalize them. The more directly political it becomes, the more certainly the university must commit itself to shifting positions, in the endless war for advantage, and so destroy its intellectual integrity. To resist endless politicizing is made more difficult when politics and therapy merge in fancies of a student culture opposed to study. Yet,

[5] Then, after James, we may graduate to Proust, who grasped Chardin, master of the ordinary and of still-life. Prepared by Chardin, Proust could grasp Vermeer, master of that little patch of yellow wall and, more profoundly, of the ordinary moment, quietly revealed. To receive Vermeer's revelation is to become quiet oneself. Looking at a Vermeer, Proust saw how inhibiting are the supreme subtleties and how hierarchical, orderly, beautifully precise and commanding those subtleties are. This praise is not for old Art. Modern art can be equally inhibiting. It is mere ignorance, parading as traditionalism, to praise the formalities of a Raphael, or the eighteenth-century painters, while dispraising the formalities of modern painting, which begin with Cézanne (to whom Roger Fry makes the best introduction, still, I think) and continue, through Braque, to our best contemporaries in painting. But exclude—from my canon, at least—those talented impresarios (e.g., Duchamp) of a constantly innovative art who, as innovators, lead what is tantamount to a campaign for the abolition of art. Duchamp's *ready-mades* intend that 1) everything is pleasurable: 2) because the pursuit of pleasure can be totally democratic, everything is art. This is cultural egalitarianism with a vengeance, first against art itself.

despite the erotic incitements on campus, some of our students remain ardent to be students.

The threat to study is double: not only from masses of students who do not study, but from faculty who will not teach. By their gurus and Research paymasters, the collegiate young are being re-educated before they have been educated. From our collegiate ranks, the therapeutic will appear a re-educated man, one who can conquer even his subtler inhibitions; his final know-how will be to irrationalize his rationality and play games, however intellectualized, with all god-terms in order to be ruled by none. In their moral modesty, therapeutics will be capable of anything; they will know that everything is possible because they will not be inhibited by any truth. Far more destructively than earlier interdict-burdened character types, the therapeutic will be the warring state writ small;[6] he may be even cannier, less sentimental, stronger in ego, shifting about his principles and his impulses like so many stage props.

Of one condition that could make him less capable of brutality, the therapeutic, conqueror of his feeling intellect, is likely to be incapable: *inwardness,* the quality of self-concealment. That has become, as Kierkegaard predicted, an aberrancy. The growth of this aberrancy is linked to the mistaken idea, held by both rationalists and sentimentalists, of an autonomous inner man. What is referred to as 'inner' and 'autonomous' expresses responses of obedience to interdictory-remissive predicates that are as complex before as after they are taken in as character.[7] Cultures are constituted by interdictory contents, and their remissions, in multiform cults. Few of those cults are recognized in their multiformity, now that all have been overwhelmed by the cult of personality. Within those cults we are free to choose among authority

[6] On this small matter, see *Fellow Teachers,* pp. 152-153, footnote 99.

[7] E.g., Jewish moral demands have a complex *We-They* order that, when taken into character, are not entirely defensive, according to my judgment. *I-Thou* is too pure a symbol to cope with the interdictory-remissive dynamic of *We-They,* in the ordinary life of Jews. The *and* between Buber's primary word, *I-Thou,* signifies, for him, an "act of pure relation" which, in its 'purity,' comes too near that emptying-out of revelation and its credal order characteristic of nineteenth-century idealism before it led toward its counter, the anticredal order of our time. I suspect a language in which "Man receives, and he receives not a specific 'content' but a Presence, a Presence as power." That sounds to me like the late Protestant emptying-out of the interdicts, by a too general affirmation. Historically and sociologically, in this way, 'Meaning' is anything but assured. Quite the contrary of Buber's vision, mine is that nothing can any longer be meaningful when 'Man' receives a 'Presence' without "specific 'content.'" [Cf. Buber, *I And Thou,* trans. Ronald Gregor Smith (Edinburgh, 1937), pp. 109-110 *et pass.*]

relations; authority generates, as culture, its indispensable interior
flexibility.

A student once revealed to me the new cultic untruth, from within
which there will be dispensed an unprecedented flexible exteriority:
"We are going to be—we all have to be—'up front,'" she said. I
gleaned from her the idea of a human who exposes himself completely
and reveals nothing. She was training to be a therapist—welfare work
and all that— mainly with clients released from psychiatric hospitals.
Almost all her clients were already 'up front,' she said. How glad I
was for her; she had found her vocation—not as a director of conscience, but as a semi-official tactician of outwardness. My one-time
student, who scarcely understood a word I said or wrote, could be
easily imagined as a functionary, herself in permanent therapy, in the
coming total welfare state.[8] What every state can best use are empty
people, without the gift of self-concealment. Beyond the concealed
life, opposing it as once our souls (and then our historical neuroses)
opposed therapy, lies the kind of naked life in which everything is exposed and nothing revealed. How we moderns love to undress. So I
imagine the political order of therapeutics, for whom all uniforms will
fit perfectly and none are to be reverenced. My ideal type is no idola-
tor, not even when standing in front of the mirror. Rather, there he
will appear in his most revealing disguise, as a comic figure.

[8] Nietzsche wrote, in 1886, of my student and her social welfare teachers: "It is
almost always a symptom of what is lacking in himself when a thinker senses
in every 'causal connection' and 'psychological necessity' something of constraint,
need, compulsion to obey, pressure, and unfreedom; it is suspicious to have such
feelings—the person betrays himself." How have we Americans lost our suspicion
of this type? How have we developed our tremendous apologetics for those who
"do not wish to be answerable for anything, or blamed for anything, and owing
to an inward self-contempt, seek to *lay the blame for themselves somewhere else*"
[Nietzsche's italics]? How well Nietzsche understood the intellectualized varieties
of this type, with their contempt for inwardness. "When they write books, [they]
are in the habit today of taking the side of criminals; a sort of socialist pity is their
most attractive disguise" [Nietzsche, *Beyond Good and Evil*, trans. Walter Kauf-
mann (New York, 1966), p. 29]. Here is prophecy, which most often takes the
form of forewarning. The type Nietzsche imagined rare in 1886, is common today
in our universities and bureaucracies.

The Psychoanalytic Theory of Culture

BY LESZEK KOLAKOWSKI

We all know how deeply Freud's thought ploughed up European culture and in what varied forms it blossomed over all the realms of humanistic work and artistic creation. Each of us can certainly say that he is, to a certain extent, "under the influence" of Freud's writing. But what does this really mean? Anyone with a command of basic philosophical culture can say that he is "under the influence" of Plato, Pascal, or Descartes and similarly of Nietzsche and Wittgenstein. No definite essence of my thinking is apprehended in autobiographical intimations of this kind. What I have in mind is rather that the reading of these philosophers opened up to me new possibilities of inquiry, new ways of looking at the world, and new poles of philosophical exploration which I would certainly not have discovered by myself. This kind of reception is characteristic of philosophical culture, in contrast to the cumulative way in which scientific discoveries operate in civilization. Freud's thought too has radiated according to the schema of philosophy, and not according to the schema of science; that is, it has given rise to theories and works which recall the original model in practically no individual point, but which nevertheless derive genetically from it, since they continue the same line of interest. The Freudian heterodoxies (side by side with which—as usually happens in philosophy—there has for quite a long time been a current rigorously faithful to the original schemata) have rejected the theory of Oedipal traumatisms, and the main key to the study of neuroses, psychical defense mechanisms, and their cultural functions. They have, however, retained the line of investigation initiated by Freud; that is, the search in human behavior for hidden motives connected with the desire to overcome conflicts between contradictory strivings, the clash of which has come about as a result of infantile traumas. An investigatory intention formulated in such general terms obviously fails to grasp what is most distinctive in Freud; but even though it fills his schemata with other contents, it can be regarded as a continuation of the same work.

The objections raised against the Freudian theory of culture can be reduced to four groups: 1. speculativeness, that is, the fact that it cannot be subjected to a procedure of verification; 2. its clashing with the explanations recognized by both ethnologists and anthropologists on the basis of empirical data (this has concerned especially the key problem of the genesis of totemism and taboo); 3. the internal contradiction in its conception of culture as the organ and, at the same time, as the enemy of instinct; and 4. its undesirable educational or moral consequences. It is clear that objection 1. is not compatible with objection 2.

I propose to consider the first, the third and the fourth objections. The first one includes, among others, the following observations: a. Freud arbitrarily transfers the schemata of the individual defense and compensatory mechanisms to collective behavior, reconstructing the history of culture on the basis of an invalid deduction from individual psychology to history; b. Freud creates an explanatory schema which, like all historiosophies, is suitable for universal application; that is, one so formed that there are no imaginable facts which contradict it; his schemata do not fulfill the conditions of "invertibility." The supposed genetic explanation is thus in reality a collection of arbitrary interpretative rules based on philosophical assumptions, and it falsely pretends to be a reconstructional hypothesis open to verification.

I regard both these objections as valid.

I should like for a start to take an example of psychoanalytic interpretation. The example relates to the history of philosophy and has the advantage that it concerns a universally known case; namely, the doctrine of Descartes. The eminent historian of philosophy Lewis S. Feuer has attempted to interpret Cartesianism genetically in the classical Freudian schemata. In summary, this explanation is presented as follows:

Cartesianism is founded on four principles: 1. the theory of the *bête-machine*; 2. recognition of the uncertainty of the existence of the world and acceptance of God as guarantor of its existence; 3. the ontological proof; and 4. *cogito ergo sum*. In the author's opinion, all these principles can be explained as autotherapeutic measures, designed to overcome the fear and the feeling of guilt connected with Oedipal traumatisms in childhood and to fortify the threatened ego. It is known that Descartes, who lost his mother in early childhood, was on cool terms with his father, who took a second wife and to whom Descartes probably bore feelings of dislike and grief arising from his sense of rejection. Thus his theory of animal automatism is an antitotemistic projection of his relationship to his father as a soulless and callous being (Freud does in fact assert that children transfer their relationships with their parents to animals). On Baillet's evidence, Descartes also liked to visit a slaughterhouse, where he made anatomical observations on the slaughtered beasts. This anatomical interest was, however, only the rationalization of a desire for revenge on animals— the totemistic bearers of father features. In this way, the doctrine and tastes of Descartes coincide in a common genesis: a repressed patricidal tendency.

The concealed patricidal desire, however, releases a sense of guilt and a fear energy which, in Descartes, assumed at first the self-destructive form which the act of doubting his own existence constituted. The *cogito*, that is, the absolute affirmation of his own existence, represents the conquest of fear and the channeling of self-aggressive energy in an extroverted direction, turning it outwards, against philosophical and religious tradition. In this way, the *cogito*, linked into the ego's defense mechanism, brought the philosopher the desired cure.

The same infantile fear and the same feeling of guilt lie at the roots of the theory which, from uncertainty about the existence of the world, moves to an affirmation of its existence by means of a truthful God. In childhood, contact with parents precedes contact with things; thus his mother's death and his father's loss of interest were for Descartes, as it were, a severing of his link with the world, which became uncertain and afforded no sense of security. Descartes's whole youth is a search for a substitute for his family (service in the Dutch Army and in the struggle against the Catholic Spanish, which was a struggle against his own superego; the seeking of contacts with secret societies; and at the same time, the constant hiding away from people and the frequent changes of abode rationalized as a desire for peace and quiet). In his original fear that God was perhaps a deceiver, Descartes expressed his relationship with his father. This whole complex was abreacted in the image of a truthful and perfect God-Father, who permits us to re-establish the lost link with the world and to direct the fear energy outwards in the form of a program of conquering nature.

The ontological proof similarly makes for the mitigation of the feeling of guilt born of repressed patricidal desires. The very method of procedure of this proof has as its background the neurotic belief in the immense power of thought ("I think God, therefore God must exist"; in the neurotic's criterion of truth, it is a question of reconciling the image of the world with one's own emotional states). And if we find the ontological proof in other seventeenth-century philosophers (Spinoza, Leibniz), then this fact is explained rather by the general situation of the time: all the revolutionary scholars of the age were devoured by a sense of guilt in view of their own revolt against the inherited religious tradition, and they all mitigated its traumatic effects by believing in the indispensable existence of God, against whom they had, as it were, committed a crime.

I have chosen this example because it is perfectly constructed according to Freud's classical schema, and at the same time it seems to me representative of psychoanalytic explanation. It is worth noting how insignificant such interpretations are from the point of view of the tasks which the historian of philosophy sets himself and how doubtful their interpretive value is.

First, we notice at once that the repressed patricidal desire (assumed in premise as a universal phenomenon, and not put forward as a hypothesis confirmed by the example of Descartes—because this desire is obviously not directly accessible in the life or utterances of the philosopher) is ideally suited to explain all mutually contradictory philosophical doctrines. In actual fact, if both a critique of traditional religious beliefs—even though carried to the point of atheism—and an affirmation of the indispensable existence of God can be explained by the same schema (if I am an atheist, then my atheism is patricide committed in thought by projection of a father image onto the divine being; and if I assert that the existence of God is analytically necessary, then I unconsciously desire to rid myself of a feeling of guilt for the intended patricide), then this schema reveals its own sterility by the mere fact of its universal applicability. It is obvious that, if Descartes had not created the theory of the *bête-machine*, but had instead (like Gassendi) assumed that animals have souls, the same reasoning could be reproduced: by his spiritualization of animals, Descartes was attempting to make good an unconscious desire with regard to his father, whom he condemned for his soullessness, and to mitigate the feeling of guilt arising out of this condemnation. His doubts about the existence of the world are the result of traumatic infantile fears which severed the contact of the philosopher-to-be with the world of things; but his affirmation of the existence of the world is explicable by reference to the same source; that is, as an auto-therapeutic measure overcoming a neurotic de-realization of being. In this way, both the solipsism and the strict realism, and both the atheism and the uncompromising faith in God are explained identically: a realist is a man who has succeeded in conquering his neurotic fear, which is just what a solipsist does not know how to overcome; atheism is a projection of patricidal desires, while belief in God compensates for the feeling of guilt deriving from these desires, etc. We have here a typical case of alleged explanation by circumstances which, though not directly accessible, perfectly explain all imaginable situations examined and which, in view of this, are about as valuable in the process of explanation as an explanation of events by reference to the inscrutable will of God: if misfortune befalls me, then clearly God is punishing me for my sins, for he is just; if fortune smiles on me, then most certainly God's kindness is at work. In precisely the same way, the defense mechanisms of the ego are able to explain genetically any acts of cultural creativity.

Second, deriving the presence of the ontological proof in other philosophers of the same epoch from a sense of guilt consuming the souls of the scholars in revolt against the religious heritage strikes one by its incoherence in comparison with an explanation specifically relating to Descartes. We know that the ontological proof recurs through the centuries in different versions, in the most varied philosophers, sometimes in men of whose biographies we know little. One can obviously declare that all of them—from Anselm to Wolff—suffered similarly from a feeling of guilt—which we know about *a priori* on the basis of the Freudian doctrine—and mitigated its consequences in similar ways; in the same way, all critics of this proof—from Gaunilo and Thomas Aquinas to Kant and Russell—will turn out, by force of an equally arbitrary decision, to be men who have not succeeded in conquering their patricidal desires. If, however, in the case of Descartes, we refer to a projection of father characteristics into God, then it cannot at the same time be asserted that, in the case of Leibniz and Spinoza (whose God, as is well-known, not only lacks any father characteristics, but expresses a radical and deliberate rejection of all anthropomorphisms), the revolt against God constituted the original source of the arousing of fear energy. Put another way: it cannot be maintained that the image of God is the projection of a father figure and that, at the same time, the conflict with God may be the original source of trauma.

Third, the fruitlessness of the interpretation cited is likewise obvious from the fact that the doctrine examined must be broken down into a multiplicity of assertions, each of which individually is reduced to its psychological genesis—always the same one; the unity of Descartes's philosophical intention can no longer be grasped—it can be apprehended only as a unity of personality because of his childhood complexes; what is specifically philosophical in Cartesian metaphysics must remain remote and *fundamentally* inapprehensible. The continuity of culture likewise ceases to exist: coincidences of philosophical doctrine (and similarly, for example, styles in painting, or literary movements, or religious formations) will be fortuitous coincidences of the psychological situations of their creators. Philosophical categories relating to cultural entities cannot be meaningful, questions of the filiation of ideas cannot be posed, and inquiries into the sense of the components of culture in the framework of greater units become pointless —in a word, psychoanalytic explanation replaces all other forms of interpretation, since it is allegedly a complete genetic reduction of the phenomenon. . . . Ever the same forms of traumas, defense mechanisms, fixations, and regressions will at any time explain for us equally well the metaphysics of Aristotle, the painting of Rembrandt, the sermons of Christ, the poetry of Rilke, everything. No differentiation of culture is possible; all creativity is amalgamated in its psychological derivation, based on an arbitrarily devised schema.

A Freudian might perhaps reply that the genetic explanation does not block the way for other explanations, and that we can therefore interpret Cartesianism as a kind of depth auto-therapy on the part of the philosopher and, independently of this, discuss his metaphysics on its merits—its logical construction, for instance, its probative value, or the historical conditions in which it arose. Such a reply, however, would not carry the power of conviction. If every thought of Descartes is fully explicable by its psychological functions, and if my own attitude to the Cartesian construction is also fully explicable in the same manner, I have no way, when I reflect on culture, of getting out of the prison into which my own infantile past casts me. Imprisonment in the traumas of childhood is universal, and it also remains when I manage to abreact this damage—for the act of abreaction is rooted in them in the same way. It is impossible to break the curse of original conflicts; there is no cognitively privileged situation. Whatever I do as a philosopher—whether I am a blasphemer or a mystic, a solipsist or a materialist, a Thomist or a Nietzschean—I will always be explained in my activities by the same mechanisms.'

The interpretations of cultural phenomena proposed by Freud are cognitively barren because they make it impossible to understand the specific nature of any realm of culture and the fundamental conceptions of any of its historical formations; they are mystifying in their claims to empirical justification, for they are in reality based on arbitrary metaphysical assumptions. They are also risky as methodological propositions, for they tend to be easily satisfied with one key which is known in advance to fit all doors equally well, and to be arbitrary in their description of the facts (the Freudians, for instance, insist that Luther hit upon the idea of his reform while sitting on the toilet; this interpretation fits into the image of anal fixation which can allegedly be detected in Luther's character and in his theology, and it is based on his use of a certain expression which is by no means unambiguous and which by no means compels one to assert that a toilet was anywhere involved).

Freud's obstinacy in seeking out monistic schemata which explain equally well all contradictory aspects of human behavior is evident in all phases of his doctrine. It is easy to perceive on what slender foundations the theory of the Oedipus complex is based in its first variant, contained in the *Traumdeutung* (if we leave aside the letters to Fliess at the time of Freud's self-analysis), and how easily suited it is to universal application. In the famous chapter which analyzes dreams about the death of people near and dear, we find the following construction: Censorship is slackened during the dream, but it is still active; it permits repressed infantile desires for the death of the father or other relatives to manifest themselves, but it does not permit the dreamer to take delight in their death and substitutes a misleading satisfaction in the form of a "regular" emotional reaction; that is, one consistent with the demands of the consciousness; if, however, dreams occur in which the death of people near and dear leaves the dreamer in a state of indifference or even gives him satisfaction, then this means that the imaginative content of the dream "really" relates to other situations than those directly contained in the dream. In other words, in the first case, the imaginative content is consistent with the

hidden will of the Unconscious, but the emotional content is inadequate and derives from the pressure of censorship, while conversely, in
the second case, the emotional content is adequate to the situation imagined, but this situation is distorted in the anecdote of the dream. It
is not difficult to observe that, in interpretations of this kind, where the
interpreter—the oneirocritic—can juggle arbitrarily with the meaning
of the images and emotions experienced during the dream, there is no
fear that any imaginable dream might fail to confirm the assumed
hermeneutic system; the fact that, after ten or fifteen years, Freud
modified his theory under the influence of investigations into the
dreams of front-line soldiers—which in time gave birth to the theory
of the two mutually limiting instincts, the libido and the death instinct—has secondary sources; that is, sources not connected with the
logic of the doctrine, which, with such instruments of manipulation,
could successfully absorb into its schema arbitrary phenomena from
the same sphere. And the presence of the Oedipus complex itself,
which was next to afford a key to the overall interpretation of the
dynamics of personality development, to general anthropology, historiosophy, and the theory of culture, is based on the observation of childhood envies of father or mother and on the perception that the Oedipus myth would certainly not have enjoyed such success over so many
centuries if it did not appeal to the essential desires present in every
one of us. It may be asked whether equal success has not been the lot
of the legend of Orestes, who, instead of unconsciously killing his father and unconsciously marrying his mother, consciously killed his
mother and consciously made love to his sister. The Freudian may,
of course, say that, in the Orestes legend, the mother is a substitute
for the sister and the sister a substitute for the mother, or offer some
other arbitrarily devised interpretive version, for he has unlimited possibilities to manipulate the representations of persons, situations,
senses, and emotions, in order to arrive at an interpretation which fits
the accepted schema. This is no exaggeration. Anyone who has read
Jones's well-known book on Hamlet knows that, in wanting to kill his
uncle in revenge for his father's death, Hamlet really wanted to kill
his father for whom the uncle—his father's murderer—was a substitute. The unconscious infantile attraction to his mother in turn led
Hamlet to turn his affections to Ophelia, who was the character opposite of the criminal queen. There is no need to add that, in Freudian
doctrine, an incestuous drive towards the mother is also superbly con-

firmed when a man directs his love to a woman who reminds him of his mother. In this way, the schema proves absolutely infallible and fits every case which the imagination can suggest to us. Jones appears at the same time not to notice at all that the possibility of an exact analysis of the unconscious content and the childhood traumas of a fictitious literary figure (for he is examining the Oedipus complex in Hamlet, not only in Shakespeare, whom he moreover drags into his interpretation, not in the least hampered by the lack of biographical information about him) hardly affords evidence in favor of the theory he professes, but rather *against* it, for it demonstrates the absence in this theory of any limitations which force it to take account of experience. Probably the greatest difficulty would be presented by a psychoanalytical explanation of the Oedipus legend itself, which no longer contains an unconscious level, since nothing in it is camouflaged and the key desires of human childhood are expressed directly; for the Freudians, Oedipus explains everything, apart from the appearance of the Oedipus myth itself.

The application of sexual characteristics to traumatic experiences in childhood and, in general, to the three phases of childhood development has been criticized so often that it is not worth entering into a discussion of this question; there are in reality, as has often been pointed out, no rational reasons for ascribing a sexual significance to elementary childish pleasures (such as sucking, eating, playing with faeces) and to the unpleasantness arising from the corresponding prohibitions, since there is no empirical fact pointing to any connection between them and reproductive activities. But it is well-known that Freud was uncompromising on this point; when, in his preface to the French translation of the *Five Lectures*, Clarapède attempted to tone down the sexual content of the category of libido and reduce it to an undifferentiated sum of driving forces, Freud raised an immediate protest against this interpretation (which was not in fact his formulation, but Jung's) and emphasized the purely sexual character of libidinal energy—which then drove Clarapède to criticize the theory.

In fact, the second Freudian theory of instincts is similarly speculative and unsupported in character. One readily notices that the binary character of the dynamic image of the psyche (the *libido* and the *Ich-Triebe* in the first phase and *Eros* and *Thanatos* in the second phase) and the triple division of static structure (the *Unconscious*, the *Sub-conscious*, and *consciousness*; later, *Id, Ego,* and *Superego*) are both maintained throughout the development of the doctrine. Freud seems to be more concerned with maintaining this quantitative relationship than with providing the schemata with real empirical support. What other reasons are there for treating aggressive tendencies as self-destructive forces working in the reverse direction? I admit that the category of the death instinct is applicable and important; that is, that various phenomena in culture and human behavior seem to indicate the presence in the psyche of dynamic death-bearing components which the human subject turns against himself. Nevertheless, the application of the same category to aggressive tendencies is an utterly arbitrary idea. Why could one not in fact declare that it is all the other way around; that is, that the drive for self-destruction is secondary and derives from the conversion of aggressive energy originally directed outwards? Or that we are dealing with two genetically independent drives? For Freud, however, this schema has a certain importance, for it emerges from all this that man, individually, is not the enemy of other men only to the extent that he is his own enemy. This is a metaphysical doctrine, which postulates an inevitable and innate mutual hostility among men and which extends to all relations between persons. Freud's catastrophic and pessimistic historiosophy has its justification in this schema, and the schema's educational influence is extremely dangerous, since all forms of aggression, especially war, are explained as indispensable manifestations of the deepest and most lasting layers of human nature. An obsessive adherence to the all-explaining *Eros-Thanatos* schema leads Freud to such plainly misguided ideas as the one contained in his treatise on negation, from which we learn that the very act of assertion in any judgment belongs to the realm of Eros, while negative judgments receive their impulse from the aggressive drive. It would follow from this that, in expressing the judgment "$2 \times 2 = 4$," I am giving vent to my libidinal energy, and that, on the other hand, when I say, "It is not true that $2 \times 2 = 5$," I am in the power of some destructive drive. It is difficult to avoid the impression that, in arguments of this sort, we are up against something in the nature of Manichean metaphysics, which makes the conflicting deities divide among themselves all the components of being and thought—a metaphysics all the more cruel for the fact that both the Freudian deities are demons, and neither of them is the bearer of a constructive power. Among misguided ideas of this sort, we must also include the interpretation of mass political movements or military organizations as consequences of a homosexual component.

I am continually emphasizing the peculiarity of Freudianism, which seems particularly dangerous and particularly barren in its effect on investigations into culture. . . . In actual fact, agreement with the genetic explanation of culture in the Freudian spirit renders any other attempts *impossible* and claims absolute self-sufficiency. Let us consider the category of sublimation as a means of explaining the mechanism of individual creativity. In this schema, creativity—artistic, scientific, philosophical, or religious—is a method of working off the destructive force of repressed desires and insoluble conflicts by releasing trapped energy and directing it into other channels. In such a generalized formula, the theory of sublimation can be useful, and attempts to transform it, that of Bachelard, for instance, are certainly rational. Bachelard, however, is answering a different question: he seeks to demonstrate that a work of art is authentic and value-creating when it grows out of its creator's struggles with his own incompletely appreciated complexes; that is, that the energy of a complex can transform itself into a culturally fruitful effort—without prejudging that the "complex" is inevitably bound up with the repression of sexual appetites, and without prejudging that the value of a work exhausts itself in its therapeutic effects on the author. Grasped in this way, knowledge of the genesis of creativity does not prevent us from ascribing to it an additional meaning related to the value of culture. Nonetheless, an interpretive direction of this kind can find no place in Freud's doctrine. For in his doctrine, sublimation is an attempt at the *substitute* and *imaginary* satisfaction of desires—the real satisfaction of which is impeded by the restrictions of culture, and which is always qualitatively defined by the same elementary aggressive and sexual tendencies. Thus, sublimational solutions are always self-deceptions, a compulsory abandonment of authenticity in favor of substitute and illusory satisfactions—like the way in which a hungry man sucks on his pipe. (The creations of sublimational effort have no other value than that related to the individual distribution of driving energies.) Fundamentally, on the basis of Freudianism, we have no possibility of considering a creative work with regard to its values in culture, since its whole meaning exhausts itself in this deceptive auto-therapy. Therefore, the criticism (especially by Catholic writers) which rebukes Freud for his complete "reduction" of culture to its function with re-

gard to elementary instinctive needs seems to me correct in its main
intention—that is, in the sense that Freud leaves no room for the
reality of any other needs than those genetically connected with pro-
creation and aggression, not even in the form of genetically secondary,
but historically self-dependent needs (as in Malinowski's philosophy of
culture). If philogenetically primary needs are at the same time the
only real needs in the progress of all human history, and if the whole
cultural superstructure does not create any autonomized spheres, but
is permanently enslaved in the service of these needs, then evaluation
of the creations of culture in their individuality is no longer "another
subject" which could be practiced side by side with psychoanalytic
explanations, but is downright impossible. Sublimation is always an
illusory solution, even if the organization of social life forces us to
seek such solutions. Furthermore, the consciousness which achieves
self-transparency, even only in the confines permitted by analytical
therapy, removes the possibility of sublimation, and therefore of creativity. Sublimational acts with full self-knowledge of their function
would be nothing but caricature (imagine Kafka first convincing himself, as a result of analytical investigation, that he was dominated by
neurotic fear because, for instance, of a castration complex, and then
deciding to work off the fear by writing *The Trial*). Since the real
satisfaction of drives is impossible, there remain the alternatives:
either we live in self-delusion, producing culture, *or* we achieve self-
knowledge and, accepting the inevitability of our frustrations and the
sufferings bound up with them, we abandon cultural creation. The
Freudian philosophy of culture does not stop at the genetic derivation
of all the spheres of culture from the same source, but in addition reduces them functionally to the same source in the individual manifestations of culture. In this sense, I am in agreement with the criticism,
once formulated by Dalbiez, that Freudianism is incapable of grasping
what is philosophical in philosophy, what is artistic in art, what is
religious in religion, and what is scientific in science—that is, that it
cannot describe the specific qualities of human spiritual values.

I should like to pose one more basic question, a decisive answer to
which would, however, demand considerably greater knowledge than
I possess of modern psychological problems. What I am concerned
with is to what extent the category of the *Id* (if we use the division
made by the later Freud) can itself be regarded as an empirical discovery. We know that the *Id* is known not directly, but only through

neurotic symptoms. The answer that we do not directly observe electrons or genes either is not a valid one, since the analogy breaks down at a key point: electrons and genes, as units of a theoretical system, are "operative" in the sense that they permit us to predict phenomena effectively. But the category of the *Id* lacks this fruitfulness, for, as Freud himself remarked, the driving forces are known only qualitatively, and it is not in our power to establish their relative quantitative distribution in the personality—in view of which, in the Freudian manner, we are able to explain symptoms *ex post*, but not to foresee them; it is moreover known in advance that every actual observation will be in keeping with the hypothesis. What then is the basis of the cognitive fruitfulness of the discovery of the unconscious mind to which Freud ascribed such great importance? What empirical reasons do we have for assuming in general the presence of an unconscious area in the psyche, and is the separation of this area from physiological impulses meaningful, or is it not a purely philosophical decision? One could reply to this that we manage to investigate the effect of subliminal stimuli, post-hypnotic suggestion, different psychosomatic reactions, ect.—that is, that the category of the unconscious mind is empirically describable. Nevertheless, there still remains the question of why the "psyche" should be included among phenomena and whether this does not simply contain a definitional convention that signifies all processes which occur with the participation of the central nervous system. In his *Outline of the Theory of Emotion*, Sartre, in a polemic with psychoanalysis, characterizes consciousness as fundamentally defined by combinations of the meanings given to its intentional equivalents (objects, situations); the unconscious mind is for him a square circle, and the motivations which man is not aware of are usually concealed by him voluntarily and arise from bad faith, from an inability to articulate these motivations—in actual fact, freely chosen each time—to himself. Someone might say that this is purely a verbal matter and not worth long discussions, and that it usually reduces itself to the scope which we confer on the word "psychological" —which we can always do arbitrarily, as long as we formulate our propositions distinctly. Disposing of the question in this way is certainly simple, but it cannot satisfy us, for both these opposed standpoints have objective links with philosophical attitudes, the conflict between which, though empirically undecidable, has real educational consequences.

In attempts to reply to this question, the following observation presents itself. The antecedents of the Freudian theory of the Unconscious are double. They are, first, the philosophical traditions which introduced the category of the Unconscious as an active but irrational and uncontrollable sphere of being, governing our conscious processes and yet completely independent of them (Schopenhauer, von Hartmann); in this conception, consciousness is a secondary rationalization of behavior the real causal conditions of which are irrational, and the Unconscious becomes a metaphysical unit rather than a separate realm of the psyche, a component of it, a "level," etc. The second tradition is formed by the common observations found in the writings of many of the moralists, especially the French moralists (La Rochefoucauld, Pascal, Bossuet, et al.), which lay bare the real springs of our behavior, totally different from those revealed and permitted by prevailing moral ideas and current views on what is proper and fitting; in these observations, it is assumed that people need not be, and more often than not are not, conscious of the motives of their own behavior—that is, that one must recognize something in the nature of a subliminal psyche which determines behavior and which is then distorted in conscious articulations according to the moral demands of the milieu. I believe that both these traditions are present in Freud's thought. Nevertheless, adherents of the doctrine of the self-transparency of consciousness in the spirit of existential phenomenology have no difficulty in accepting these common observations, but give them a different interpretation. For Sartre, a motive which we are not aware of is a motive which we do *not want* to be aware of, a motive selected voluntarily, but concealed in bad faith; consciousness is able to achieve perfect knowledge of itself, it contains nothing substantial which defies analysis, and it is a pure movement of intentionality and has no hidden depths— it is only a voluntary selected self-deception that allows it to hide its own motivations from itself. For Freud, on the contrary, the *Id* is, fundamentally, completely inaccessible, and consciousness is subject to the influence of forces which it cannot subjugate. If we compare the two diametrically opposed points of view, we arrive at the presumption that both of them are equally arbitrary philosophical constructions, but that they differ not only in the rules for using such words as 'psychological' and its synonyms, but also in merit. For Sartre, the self-transparency of consciousness is a condition of its absolute and completely unimpeded freedom; man, as a being-for-himself, precisely because he is absolutely capable of arbitrarily giving a meaning to phenomena, of creating them as units of noematic meaning, is likewise absolutely responsible for every act of his behavior in the human world and is free without restriction in the selection of his own motivations in each individual case. For Freud, the *Ego* is constrained by the pressure of the drives and of the internalized rules handed down by parental influence in the form of the *Superego,* whose considerable expanses are just as unconscious as the *Id.* The human individual is thus fettered by determinisms of the instincts and of their sedimentations settled in the course of ontogenetic development; he is endlessly the prisoner of his own childhood and, at all events, of his own past (according to Sartre, on the contrary, the past is not "given" in the form of an immutable and ready store of former facts, but is being constantly reinterpreted in the light of projects directed toward the future—thus it is not the past which determines the future, but rather the reverse). These two standpoints, I repeat, differ essentially in their educational consequences, even though they are equal with regard to their empirical support (for they are not hypotheses which interpret empirical material, but principles for understanding this material). One cannot meaningfully assert that a theory according to which the activities of the *Ego* are fatally dependent on uncontrollable forces, and another which proclaims man's absolute responsibility for his every act, differ only in verbal conventions. The presumption presents itself that, in this question, Freudianism is not in a more favorable situation with regard to its empirical foundation; rather, it is a philosophical doctrine which answers questions which cannot be decided empirically, but which must nonetheless be decided, since they determine our system of evaluation. On the other hand, the mystification of Freudianism rests on the presentation of philosophical statements as empirical hypotheses. It seems that Jung, who made the Unconscious a metaphysical category again, is more consistent than Freud on this point, since Freud persists in his opinion that his philosophy meets the rigorous demands of theories in the natural sciences.

As though it were self-evident, Freud's philosophical anthropology simply assumes man's natural hostility to man. Someone else appears to me only as a potential object of satisfaction for my sexual or aggressive tendencies. It would even seem that aggressive tendencies are a specific characteristic of man as a species (the desire for sexual satisfaction is simply a ready fact of nature, a need to release physiological tension, which, moreover, for some reason or other, as Fromm correctly observes, is allegedly not sufficiently released by mechanical means). In the whole fantastic hypothesis of the original horde, Freud takes it for granted that patricidal sons are enemies of their fathers and enemies among themselves, and that only situational coercion restrains them from aggression; in a word, Freud seems to regard it as certain that there are no endogenous checks to restrain man from acts of hostility towards others, still less any "natural conditions" which make possible a community of men. This, I repeat, is the philosophical dogma, the Hobbesian belief in the fundamental egoism of the individual life.

It would seem—and the reflections contained in *Civilization and Its Discontents* speak distinctly for an interpretation of this kind—that the antagonism of nature and culture is uneliminable from the point of view of the Freudian theory of instincts; that culture is only a repressive force in relation to the driving tendencies and a locus of substitute and illusory satisfactions, which, moreover, in their turn themselves multiply the instruments of repression; that is, create a vicious circle, where the means designed to mitigate the effects of frustration contribute to intensifying the situations which give rise to this frustration. If we were to take the schema seriously, it must be expected that the gulf between the demands of culture and the pressure of the instincts must grow in relation to the advancement of civilization, only periodically allowing the release of natural aggressiveness in acts of savage mass warfare. Similarly, there must be an increase in the part played in culture by illusory compensatory means suitable for application on a mass scale and, above all, religious beliefs. The mutual hostility of drives and cultural institutions must, I repeat, grow, since the repressed desires belong to the permanent layer of nature and since coexistence in culture is an impossibility without this repression. Nonetheless, *The Future of an Illusion* quite unexpectedly opens up a different perspective. Here, Freud declares that religious beliefs are similar to the phase of infantile neurosis which everyone goes through, but which passes off; in the same way, it is possible, and even highly probable, that mankind comes out of childhood in order to discover a rational justification of culture which dispenses with divine sanctions —that is, in order to reconcile itself to its fate. It appears impossible to reconcile these two points of view. If the perspective of reconciling oneself with one's fate were real, this would mean that mankind can abandon the satisfaction of natural desires and transform this very act of resignation into nature. In this discrepancy, we observe a typical example of the nonchalant way in which Freud transfers a category of the psychology of individual development to the history of mankind. In actual fact, the analogy with childhood neurosis is fallacious from the point of view of Freud's own doctrine, for in the case of childhood repressions (if we leave aside the later fixations, which could probably equally well befall the whole of mankind as the individual), it is a question of driving tendencies which die out by the very laws of ontogenetic development, while, in the case of the whole of mankind, it is a question of uneliminable, mature sexual and aggressive desires. Reconciling oneself to one's fate would mean either voluntarily consenting to the sufferings arising from frustration—in which case we do not know at all what living forces in man can be held responsible for this consent—or a situation which would remove the suffering without removing its sources, which in this case is an even more fantastic assumption than those of Freud himself. In the way of "normal" development, the human individual can renounce incestuous desires—if they really are a permanent component of individual psychic evolution—but it cannot be asserted that mankind could in any analogous manner renounce the drives which form an indispensable part of the behavior of the adult organism.

There is yet another contradiction present in Freudian doctrine, which has been pointed out by Malinowski. It appears in the famous story of the original horde and the patricidal sons expounded in *Totem and Taboo*. Although a critique of this story is not particularly necessary, since few people today take it seriously, it is nonetheless useful insofar as it lays bare certain unspoken philosophical premises of the doctrine. Malinowski notes that Freud ascribes to his horde features which cannot attach to it simultaneously. It is still animal, that is, entirely regulated in its behavior by the rigid demands of instinct, and at the same time it is human, that is, it assumes the presence of a cultural heritage. According to Malinowski, there is no reason why, in the animal collective, a father should have to drive out his sons, since instinct itself inclines them to reject the older generation the moment they attain maturity, nor is there any reason why the younger generation should be deprived of females or should feel hatred for its fathers. In any species, the characteristics ascribed to the horde would be lethal in their effect; thus, from a purely biological point of view, the Freudian description is unacceptable. In turn, with the assumption of a purely instinctive regulation of behavior, the rise of a feeling of guilt in patricides is inexplicable—they would have to create from nothing, suddenly and without any tradition, the abstract idea of a norm which they had violated. The genesis of the incest taboo cannot be explained on the basis of the Freudian schema, for there are no instinctive prohibitions on incest, and, on the other hand, incest is not, in Malinowski's view, reconcilable with specifically human peculiarities; that is, with the very existence of culture, which demands that the hierarchy of generations should be preserved, because the family collective forms the main instance of education and cultural inheritance; by mixing the generations and social roles, by disorganizing the feelings, incest would prevent the existence of the family as a center for the inheritance of values.

Without considering the exceptionally intricate and specialized question of the genesis of the incest taboo, I should like to comment on Malinowski's reflections only in their main point. It seems in actual fact that Freud, in *Totem and Taboo*, is trying to explain genetically the presence of the *Superego* by reference to a situation which could arise only if the *Superego* already existed previously. There are certainly factors present in animal life which inhibit acts of aggression within the species, but there is no accumulation of experience handed down over many generations, and mature individuals lose the family link with the older generation the moment parental care becomes dispensable. The internalization of parental prohibitions in the form of the *Superego* is superfluous, because mature individuals are sufficiently equipped with instincts and abilities which favor the preservation of the species. There is therefore really no reason why dissatisfied adult sons, even if they devoured their father, should carry a sense of guilt on this account. The *Superego* appears then in a totally inexplicable manner or must be assumed as given in advance, even though it is in the cannibal behavior of youth that we should in fact trace its origin. I believe that this difficulty arises in Freud's thought as a result of the more basic contradiction which encumbers the intentions of his philosophical anthropology. He would like to discover (a theoretically impossible task) the absolute genesis of humanity as a culturally organized form of existence in the purely instinctive behavior of the species and, at the same time, to recognize this same cultural form of existence as the enemy of instinctive behavior and as something to which *value* can be ascribed *in spite* of the instincts. He is endeavoring, in other words, to derive man's anti-animal qualities from his animal qualities themselves, which should lead to the assumption that the human species is a dead-end branch of evolution, doomed to extinction. Freud does not himself express this conclusion, which otherwise used to be expressed by some of the supporters of German *Lebensphilosophie*— but nonetheless only this conclusion (that, in the human species, instinct has turned against itself) could perhaps save his doctrine from the contradiction we have mentioned.

I am not, of course, asserting that the question of the absolutely original state of culture can assume a scientific form; on the contrary, I believe that it is a purely "historiosophical" question, and therefore purely philosophical and capable of being resolved only by deduction from arbitrary metaphysical principles. In this respect, Freud's doctrine is thus in no worse situation than others which answer the same question. On the other hand, it does distinguish itself by its particularly stressed claims to the status of a reconstructional hypothesis.

In this historiosophical schema, the initial assumption is the presence of a blind life force—a sort of Schopenhauerian will —which particularizes itself in individuals in the form of instinct; this force encounters the barrier of culture, which appears in a totally inexplicable manner, like a second rival deity, and from this time on mankind is doomed to the service of the two conflicting powers, since it is incapable either of returning to prehuman spontaneity or of reshaping cultural forms in such a way as to accommodate its own nature. The conflict of the individual with the collective, which presents itself to the individual mainly in the form of the police—external or internal— is a consequence of this situation, and the individual *Ego*, wedged in between the pressure of the drives and the censorship of the *Superego*, is defined purely negatively and functionally as an instrument for maintaining the balance of eternally antagonistic impersonal forces. There is an uneliminable conflict between individual desires and the stability of the social organization (social life would be best assured if there were no need to concern oneself about the good of the individual, as Freud says in *Civilization and Its Discontents*). The recognition of such a conflict does not, of course, contain any contradiction; on the other hand, there is a contradiction in the attempt to interpret culture simultaneously as a functional extension of instinct and as an antagonist of instinct. The whole complex of moral instruments regulating the coexistence of people is not, however, derived in Freud from the needs of this coexistence (there is no social contract at the source of mankind), but from the totally irrational, though casually explicable, process which arose after the murder of the father. The prohibition on killing is binding not because it was necessary for coexistence and cooperation in the collective, but because it is a result of a guilt complex arising from unfathomable reasons after the patricide. The presence of the whole of morality then has no connection with social needs; for Freud, on the other hand, culture is the source of sufferings precisely because the curbing of the drives is indispensable for "rational" reasons; that is, for the proper functioning of the collective. It is not known in what manner these two explanations can be reconciled, unless we accept the fantastic hypothesis that, for totally irrational reasons, men have adopted certain prohibitions which, by chance, subsequently proved useful in their collective life. I confess that the assumption that Jehovah simply issued the well-known commandments to Moses on Mount Sinai seems to me distinctly less irrational (and is certainly simpler) than such an interpretation.

This discrepancy—the total irrationality and fortuitousness of all culture and, at the same time, either the arbitrary recognition of it as a collection of values or the justification of it by common-sense considerations in the spirit of the *Leviathan*—is frequently encountered in Freud. An example of it is the already cited vacillation between the hope for a psychoanalytic therapy of the historical process in the *Future of an Illusion* and the ominous prognoses in his other writings. This question is more general in character and is independent of recognition or rejection of the sexual content of the original conflicts. One can, without contradiction, interpret (like Malinowski) all the institutions of culture as secondary instruments for satisfying elementary needs. One can also (like certain forms of *Lebensphilosophie*) treat culture as a manifestation of the decadence of the species, which is creating substitutes for its weakening biological efficiency. One can (like Scheler) see in it the synthesizing of independent values, which cannot be deduced from elementary needs, but which impose an ascetic discipline on these needs. But one cannot insist on the totally irrational and fortuitous character of the creations of culture and at the same time proclaim a cult of reason and spiritual creativity as independent values, and in addition indulge in melancholy reflections about the coercion of instinct in the face of the irrefutable demands of the rational coexistence of people.

The ambiguity of the practical instruction which can be justified in this situation by Freudian metaphysics is obvious, and it is pointless to argue over what educational recommendations really emerge from the internally contradictory doctrine; *ex falso quodlibet*. On the other hand, the actual question—the question of the processes of the social assimilation of Freudianism and the methods by which it is exploited in practice—is immensely interesting. For one can imagine that, since human sufferings derive mainly from a blocking of the instincts, the most proper form of moral education should rest on the removal of the cultural conditions which prevent the release of libidinal energy; thus it is not surprising that the slogan of sexual emancipation was linked up with Freudian doctrine, though it is by no means directly contained in this doctrine. But why should one not draw the reverse conclusion: since—if human civilization is to exist—we are in one way or another compelled to restrain our instincts, then effective education should aim at imposing voluntary abandonment of unsatisfied desires and also at compelling a cheerless approval for substitute and illusory satisfactions? Freud's own intention seems to me closer to the second of these alternatives, but in Freudianism as a socially operative phenomenon, the first interpretation has distinctly predominated (and is furthermore present in Marcuse too); there is nothing strange in this, for every doctrine from which, with certain manipulations, permission for sexual license can be derived, will in this spirit gain popularity, and there are many illustrations of this.

Nonetheless, the educational system of Freudianism goes considerably further and is much more complex. The American critic Richard LaPiere, the author of a book on Freudian ethics, attempts to demonstrate the destructive effects of its influence in the society of the United States. This work is written from the point of view of the conservative ideals of nineteenth century Protestant morality, with an apologia for the beneficial effects of free competition among individuals, or more bluntly (though the author does not use this expression), of the Spencerian "*survival of the fittest.*" But independently of its ideological background, his book contains many noteworthy observations. The author is of the opinion that Freud's ideal is the complete *adjustment* of the individual to the life situations he finds himself in, and that

Freudianism is a school of social irresponsibility, an apologia for a passive attitude to life, incapable of initiative, risk, and revolt. This, he maintains, emerges from the Freudian view that society imposes unnatural demands on the individual and suppresses natural organic processes in favor of artificial cycles and that the inhibition of natural needs in childhood produces maladjusted individuals; in addition, that the individual is organically incapable of self-understanding and can achieve it only with the aid of an analyst. In consequence, the education of the growing generations, dominated by the slogan "Everything for the children" and advocating a break with the authoritative model of the family, aims first and foremost at securing spiritual comfort, conditions of peace and forbearance, at protection from traumatic experiences, and, in particular, at removing the stresses connected with participation in an educational environment organized on the principle of competition. The effects are deplorable and, in part, the reverse of what was intended. An education thus planned socializes children, but it also leads them to expect that others will endlessly satisfy all their whims, thus exposing them to a considerably greater amount of frustration, trauma, and suffering in later life. On the other hand, it is effective if one wants to deprive people of their sense of the responsibility for thinking about their own lives; it always recommends the path of least resistance, and it teaches one to be afraid of risk, chance, and competition. Introduced into schools, the Freudian educational system produces passive and uncritical people; introduced into the criminal courts, it leads one to treat criminals as victims of society and gives rise to increasing forbearance, a tendency to slacken judicial sanctions, and the raising of the age of criminal responsibility; in this way, the foundations of society are exposed to the danger of disintegration (the system of psychiatric reports in the courts has led to a situation where it is necessary to prove that the criminal is responsible, for the assumptions suggest that no one is really responsible). It is furthermore not known in what way the assertion that the individual is anti-social by nature can be reconciled with the program for a society which allows individuals to satisfy their natural strivings. In LaPiere's view, the spread of this educational system in the United States corresponds to the process of disintegration of traditional bourgeois values in the conditions when the bourgeoisie takes over values once held in high regard among the working classes: stability, sense of security, and irresponsibility. The bureaucratization of industry creates a need for mediocre people rather than for enterprising gamblers. Connected with this are political paternalism and the immense extension of state power in all spheres—an extension based on the assumption that the human individual is fundamentally weak and incompetent. Freudian ethics favors these phenomena, producing people with passive characteristics, people adjusted to the processes of homogenization, where there is a continual narrowing of that margin of individual variations which determines social health and progress.

I do not need to say that I do not share the social values of the critic, whose ideal seems to be the society described in the novels of Dreiser and Sinclair. I do nonetheless share some of his observations about the harmfulness of the current reception accorded to Freudianism. In reality, if natural drives turn every human individual against others and against social institutions as a whole, then the program of making people happy by abandoning repression of the instincts would be in consequence a guideline for the destruction of civilization. But protection from traumas to the psyche as a value preferred above all others in educational processes really became widespread under the influence of the Freudians, and it is impossible not to share the fears about its fatal consequences both for the individuals themselves, who are not adjusted to the realities of life, and for the collective, which is exposed to the growing pressure of people who preserve the characteristics of capricious pre-school children—cowardly, selfish, and irresponsible. It does not, however, follow from this that the alternative model has to be the authoritarian patriarchal family. Similarly, use of the word 'adaptation' and the like can be misleading. The aim of all psychiatric therapy is adaptation in the sense of restoration of the ability to understand and coexist with others. Adaptation in the sense of a school of conformity, of smothering initiative and opposition does not seem, if one may say so, a "natural" consequence of Freudian assumptions. It is, however, a possible interpretation and one which really is used. And if, in all this, conformity is linked with a protection of asocial tendencies, then this alliance is a result of the same already noted duality which lies at the foundations of the Freudian philosophy of culture: as a bearer of instinctual energy, each human individual is by nature anti-social, but humanity, on the other hand, rests on socialization, that is, on the suppression of these energies; the educational task should be a simultaneous satisfaction of the demands of the *Id* and the demands of the *Superego*; this is clearly impossible—all that is possible is a precarious balance in which the two antagonistic forces combat one another, creating, on the one hand, a growing feeling of guilt (produced by the repressive functions of the *Superego*) and, on the other hand, a growing sense of dissatisfaction (produced by the repressed expansion of the *Id*). The program of liberation from both these sources of unhappiness cannot be carried out, for it would have to be based either on the liquidation of the *Superego* in favor of free expansion of the drives, that is, on a return to animality, on a destruction of culture and society (a chimerical task, if it were ever set, since the internalization of the process of socialization is irreversible), or on the removal of the tensions set up by the driving forces, that is, on the extermination of the species. Partial attempts to satisfy these contradictory demands can express themselves only as an educational program which combines asocial selfishness (education in protection from the traumatic effect of socializing external inhibitors) with conformity (education in fear of isolation). An educational system which produces conformist and, at the same time, capriciously selfish individuals is in actual fact the exact opposite of those values which are really necessary to mankind and which are constructive: ability to live in the community and ability to confront every situation which may arise. Education exposed exclusively to the first of these qualities always threatens to produce, in the individuals subjected to it, a fear of all initiative and an inability to criticize; exclusive orientation to the second threatens to create people incapable of understanding and compromise. Nevertheless, the power of critical opposition must not be confused with asociality, nor the ability to live in a community with conformity. The truth is that Freudian philosophical anthropology can easily be interpreted in such a way that it teaches us to understand everything in man that derives from the pressure of instinct as a hopelessly-anti-social force, and everything that is assimilated from culture as an ability to conform voluntarily. Since the *Ego* is a purely negatively defined organ for balancing the opposing forces of the two Unconsciousnesses and, as it were, the venue of their eternal conflicts, without driving forces and self-contained functions of its own, there is in actual fact no socially constructive force in the individual man; there is only the conflict between an instinct hostile to society and the police power which urges conformity. Educational recommendations which advise allowing both these possibilities to be expressed at the same time must be destructive in their consequences *for both reasons*.

Certainly, it might be said that it is difficult to blame Freud for everything that has been said and propagated in his name, or to blame him for the form of the social reception accorded to him, all the more so since the serious branches of psychoanalysis do not come within the scope of these objections. Nevertheless, we are not considering the question of Freud's "guilt." Questions of this kind in relation to people with such an enormous role in the history of culture yield little fruit. It is sufficient to note that Freudianism as a philosophy of culture is in no way theoretically secured against socially destructive interpretations, which have actually had and still do have a considerable influence in culture, that other variants of psychoanalysis have assumed the form of conscious heterodoxies or "deviations," and that Freudian philosophical anthropology literally conceived does not contain any premises permitting us, in the theory of education, to avoid the ominous either-or: freedom for anti-social instincts or resigned conformity—two possibilities between which no synthesis is possible, but only partial concessions which release opposed, but likewise socially destructive, forces.

And if someone says that a scientific theory cannot be evaluated on the basis of the social effects of its popular reception, I will reply that such a principle does not relate to purely philosophical, speculative constructions which only appear—as we have said—to legitimize themselves by an empirical origin. I do not intend to repeat here the opinions encountered in some critics of Freudianism, who say, for example, that, in general, psychoanalysis is a "disease trying to pass for a therapy" or "induced delusion" (in the clinical sense of the word). I believe simply that Freudianism as a theoretical system is a philosophical anthropology not subject to the rigors demanded of empirical hypotheses and "universal verifiability"; that it is based on value premise—as are all historiosophical or general anthropological doctrines—and that, for this reason, it is likewise subject to criticism which opposes to it, without any mystification as to its empirical legitimations, other values, values contradictory to it.

I realize, of course, that the whole spiritual culture of our times would not be what it is without Freud—not only in its dangerous tendencies and in its negative symptoms, but also in many of its fruitful and creative currents. It is obvious that extensive fields of constructive research on culture were opened up by one-sided Freudian radicalism—as if to confirm once again the Hegelian observations about the contradictions of progress. But this recognition, which I am almost ashamed to repeat and which I note only to avoid superfluous discussion, is not at variance with the point of view which I have attempted to put forward and which rejects the Freudian philosophy of culture in its entirety on grounds of content: not because it cannot be transformed into a scientific hypothesis—since every general philosophy of culture comes within the scope of this objection—and not even because it puts forward misleading claims in this sphere, but mainly in view of the fact that, in it, a description of the contradictions of culture becomes a contradiction of the description itself, and that this description is based on value premises which I regard as socially destructive. In turn, as a method of interpreting the phenomena of culture, Freudianism contributes to the impoverishment of research efforts, because it arbitrarily cuts down legitimate points of view to genetic explanations of individual phenomena always reducible to the same schema, because it makes it impossible to trace internal connections in the autonomized realms of culture and because it makes it impossible (not simply unimportant) to recognize the specific nature of the individual areas of cultural life.

None of what we have said so far contains a reply to the question of the real genesis of this doctrine and of the particular causes of its extensive influence, which certainly cannot be explained by any literary talent of Freud himself. I do not, however, intend to go into this question. I recall only the extremely suggestive treatise of Manes Sperber, who assembles everything in Freud's life-story which may explain his philosophy on the basis of private obsessions; Freud himself bore within him the injuries caused by his own unconquered past— connected with his childhood poverty, humiliations of an anti-Semitic nature, and his being brought up in a patriarchal family; he wrote, in a letter to Fliess, that he was not really a man of learning, an observer, an experimenter, or a thinker, but a man with the temperament of a *conquistador;* he would dream of making a sensational discovery which would, with one blow, compensate him for the setbacks he had suffered in all spheres—he was really constrained by his past as a child and generalized this situation into a historiosophical doctrine. His relations with other people reveal in him enormous streaks of envy, claims to exclusivity in all friendships, and superiority complexes. Sexual interests occur as a compensation for his prudish upbringing. Freud forged the moral idiosyncrasies of the Victorian age into an eternal law of civilization and, in doing so, as another critic notes, he regarded his patients—mostly middle-class Viennese Jews—with their problems and conflicts, as typical representatives of humanity. There is a doctrinaire tendency to force facts to fit assumptions evident in Freud even in the period preceding the formulation of his doctrine. When Freud forced out of a dozen hysterical young women the false confession that they had been raped by their fathers in childhood, when later, under the influence of Fliess, he withdrew this observation, which was to have been the basis for a revelational pathogenesis of hysteria, and when he finally came to the conclusion that he had himself talked his patients into making their appalling confessions, he still did not give up this line of inquiry, but reversed the model situation, constructing the theory of the Oedipus complex. This explanation seems rational. It is in fact possible that Freud's inability to assimilate his own traumas and failures—the kind that befall everyone in life in different forms— became the basis for risky generalizations and for a general theory of a human nature eternally imprisoned in the bondage of wounds suffered in childhood. (We read in the *Traumdeutung*, "The eternal and deepest essence of mankind—on the awakening of which the poet as a rule counts in his listeners—consists in the disturbances of spiritual life rooted in the period of childhood and then passing over into prehistory.") This is, however, a biographical explanation, which does not explain the unprecedented success of Freudian philosophy— unless we wish to explain it on the basis of circumstances the recognition of which presupposes prior recognition of this very philosophy; that is, the assumption that the fundamental traits of every individual biography are identical.

From the point of view of the history of ideas, Freudianism can be regarded as one of the forms of the so-called *Lebensphilosophie*, with its characteristic interpretation of "reason" and the institutions of civilization as organs of irrational forces, with its pessimistic prognosis about the fate of mankind entangled in insoluble contradictions, with its belief in the incurable conflict between individual "life" and supra-personal culture. It is, however, possible that the popular reception later accorded to Freudianism was bound up precisely with the previously discussed duality of its theoretical assumptions and with the duality of the world-view constructions which it seemed to allow. Serge Moscovici—the author of a thorough study of the soci-

ology of psychoanalysis in France—remarks that the first recipients
of the doctrine were the literary and artistic milieux, and it was considerably later—and in a totally different spirit—that psychiatrists
took it up. It must be added that these first sympathies (in the
Surrealists, for example) had a distinct ideological content: psychoanalysis was taken to be an unmistaking revolution, an attack on the
traditional values of bourgeois society and its institutions; it proclaimed the ruin of everything which this society regarded as holy,
and reduced it to its unholy and irrational genesis; it was to eradicate
the whole complex of inherited ideals, myths, and moral patterns, to
ensure intellectual and moral freedom and, at the same time, to
open up the way for the exploration of the mysterious depths which
guide man's behavior without regard to his will. The places where
psychoanalysis found social sympathies were at first the left-wing
milieux, at least the ones radically critical of the tradition of bourgeois
culture—until, on the one hand, psychoanalysis became assimilated
into American civilization and, on the other hand, became the object
of violent attacks from Communist ideology. The receptions accorded
to it thus reveal the same ambiguity which we can trace in the doctrine: psychoanalysis was received now as a slogan of emancipation
from tradition, now as a school of conformity and irresponsibility.
It is in actual fact possible that this latter conception of psychoanalysis corresponds to certain processes occurring in industrial societies; that is, those processes which increase the range of responsibility of anonymous collective institutions for the affairs of human
individuals and, at the same time, reduce—at least in the social
feeling—these individuals' margin of effective initiative in its influence
not only on general social phenomena, but also on their own life
situation. And indeed we observe that certain changes of educational
style, which the cited work by LaPiere attributes to the influence
of Freudianism, are being implemented even in those countries, like
Poland, where this influence was quite negligible.

It is at the same time worthy of note that, while the criticism in
the Communist press, which, especially in the years 1949-1952, conducted a campaign against psychoanalysis in France, was uncompromising and global in character (psychoanalysis was attacked as a
component of the ideological infiltration of America and as an instrument for the psychological disarming of the working class by a reduction of class conflicts to individual complexes; as to the content, it

was attacked as an irrationalistic and idealistic doctrine, because it proclaimed the primacy of psychological phenomena with regard to social situations, etc.), the Catholic criticism largely took as its target the philosophical assumptions of the doctrine, without questioning its therapeutic value. Moscovici demonstrates by statistical comparisons that—apart from out-and-out attacks coming from integristic milieux —the considerable majority of Catholic literature differentiates its criticisms, in the belief that psychoanalysis can be detached from Freudian metaphysics, the materialism, determinism, and biologism of which clearly cannot be reconciled with Christian philosophy. The separation of Freudian philosophy from therapeutic practice was carried out before the war (1936) in the already cited work by Dalbiez, with whom the process of the Christian assimilation of psychoanalysis began. Pius XII's speech of 1952, though warning against certain aspects of psychoanalytic therapy (the argument being that a real feeling of guilt cannot be healed by psychological means), was not so unambiguous that Catholic supporters of the psychoanalytical movement were unable to see any encouragement in it. A book by Jozef Nuttin, a professor at Louvain, seems to me characteristic of this standpoint, which aims, as the author writes, at "a constructive integration, and not a negative criticism" of psychoanalysis. The author attempts to demonstrate that faith in the irresistible compulsion of unconscious instinctual forces does not by any means follow from the observations on which psychoanalysts base themselves, but constitutes a separate metaphysical assumption, which can be rejected without any questioning of the observations themselves and without putting in doubt the category of the Unconscious as such. He also recognizes the enormous services of psychoanalysis in revealing the unknown or incompletely investigated regularities of the life of the mind, above all, in creating the developmental theory of personality. On the other hand, he opposes the doctrine which treats all forms of spiritual life as disguises of instincts attempting to mislead the vigilance of the censorship, and sees in this interpretation (rightly so, in my opinion) a purely philosophical assumption.

These questions do not, of course, relate to Freudianism as a method of studying culture, but rather to Freudianism as a component of culture. I mention them cursorily and only in order to point to the common intention of all the major currents which have come out with criticisms of psychoanalytic philosophy. This common intention is directed against the various forms of "reduction" proposed by Freud: the reduction of specifically social phenomena to their genesis in the unconscious layers of the individual psyche, or the reduction of all spiritual activity, in the sphere of the so-called higher functions, to defense mechanisms of the Ego. I have explained in what sense I accept this line of criticism as my own. I believe chiefly that the Freudian demonology of instinct, as an instrument of ideas, is dangerous in its effects. I agree with anyone who says that the dispute about determinism—in the metaphysical sense of the word—is, strictly speaking, empirically insoluble in relation to psychic phenomena. I nonetheless believe that we know what the difference is between the attitude of a man who treats himself as an object and the attitude dominated by the desire to "be a subject"; these attitudes are essentially different and can be evaluated; education toward the former or toward the latter is connected with convictions of a quasi-theoretical nature. A doctrine which teaches that we cannot truly be subjects is, from this point of view, discouraging—it teaches acquiescence in treating oneself and others as objects. And such acquiescence is what is helping to put civilization to sleep.

1967
translated by Michael Montgomery

Five Versions of "Psychological Man":— A Critical Analysis

BY JACK JONES

> Each of us, de facto, halts, is arrested, and ceases to think at a given point in a dialectical series. Some stop sooner than others. This, however, does not mean that we did not *have* *to* continue thinking. Although we stop, the dialectical series continues . . . We cut it short, but it continues to bleed within us.
>
> — Ortega y Gasset

It is somewhat prematurely that Philip Rieff has announced the emergence of "psychological man." The creature is only half-way out of the egg, and should not be counted upon too soon. At the present time, the influence of Freud's ideas is still relatively limited and superficial, especially when the world ideological situation is observed as a whole. Clearly, it is still dominated by "economic man" — especially by Marx's version, the most powerful non-psychological and in effect anti-psychological ideology of the day. Marx's direct and indirect influence has been and remains a thousand times more potent than Freud's.

Accordingly, it seems evident that any finally viable conception of "psychological man" must be defined and work in counterposition to Marxism. Otherwise, too, there are serious flaws of one kind or another in all the available psychoanalytic interpretations. Five of the more influential, including Freud's, will be reviewed here,* but it is only with social-psychological, and not with individual-psychological or clinical matters that we are concerned. It goes without saying that only a few of the more essential points can be covered, and that most of the following criticisms of Freud have been made before from one or another point of view. But the specific pattern of

---

* The sections on Freud and Rank, and some other passages of this essay, are based upon chapters in my forthcoming book *While the Temple Stands: A Depth-Psychology of Cultural Evolution.*

acceptances and rejections here leads toward a reinterpretation perhaps not without some novel features.

1) *Main Repudiations of the Freudian Legacy.* As will be often reiterated below, the most important contribution of Freudianism has been and remains its para-artistic but "scientific" insight into the past and continuing *contradiction* between natural and cultural reality. In the last, in the acculturated consciousness, there is always the factor of *repression*: there must be excluded some aspect or degree of natural-biopsychology. The idea of repression, Freud himself insisted, was "the most essential part" of psychoanalysis.[1] Almost as important, and also still valid, in my view, is Freud's belief that the contradiction between nature and culture has steadily worsened in the course of cultural evolution.

These two themes may be about the only ones that can still be accepted without reservation. Everything else in the Freudian system is at least "negotiable," and most of its other concepts will have to be greatly modified, if not altogether discarded, if the notion of "psychological man" is to be finally actualized rather than merely hypothesized.

a) Freud, in the earlier version of his pervasive dualism, saw ultimately instinct pitted against instinct: the "hunger" instinct, or instinct of "self-preservation," whose instrument was the ego, opposing the "sexual" instinct or the "libido." This implied that culture was the product of, or even "nothing but" an instinct, one or the other, or their dynamic conjunction. This view was one aspect of Freud's fundamental philosophic position, however often qualified — his biological or materialistic reductionism.

But Freud also often opposed *culture,* or the ego as the culture-bearer, to the instincts in general. And this last formula is actually far better theoretically. For culture is *not* the product of any instinct — the natural world, its instincts, or the conflicts between them cannot as such produce culture. Only the human ego can do that, through its unique ability to produce those symbolic (as distinct from natural-psychological) ideas which are the essence of the acculturated consciousness. This, as Freud saw in his own terms, rests upon the ability to consciously control and manipulate the natural biopyscho-

---

[1] *The History of the Psychoanalytic Movement.* In the *Basic Writings* (New York: Modern Library, 1938), p. 939.

logical state — *including* when necessary even the hunger or so called "self-preservative" instinct. The theoretical point is that there is a relative *independence* of the acculturated consciousness or ego, of the "superorganic" (Kroeber's phrase), from the natural biopsychological state or instincts (as later discerned by Adler and Rank, among others). It follows that the ego (and culture) cannot be reduced to the operation of any instinct.

To say this, however, is *not* also to deny the concept of repression, though it is true that many "revisionists" have done so. The ego's independence or cultural creativity must always be paid for in the coin of natural biopsychological reality.

b) Furthermore, this natural reality, aspects or levels of which must be repressed to make the cultural consciousness possible, is *not* to be reduced to the biological or sexual theme. Repression falls also, and even primarily, upon natural-*psychological* intangibles. Here and there in the texts Freud senses the presence of such intangibles, however difficult to conceptualize. He complained: "It is not easy to deal scientifically with feelings . . . I must again confess that I find it very difficult to work with these intangible quantities [qualities?]."[2] But if they are what is actually most fundamental, one has wasted precision upon the tangibles.

Neither does this second demurrer, however, affect the concept of repression itself. This last and the more profound theme has often been discredited, rather than strengthened, by the obstinate Freudian association of or reduction of it to often obviously forced and implausible biological-sexual specifics.

Unfortunately, Freud would insist, as Ernest Jones notes in his biography and standard summary of the canon, that "repression affected only sexual impulses. All other effects were secondary. He never retracted this," even though this position gave him "endless trouble."[3] Among other things, Freud was compelled to broaden the concept of "sexuality" or "libido" so far that in practice it often became equivalent to "natural biopsychological energy or functioning." This sometimes "saved the appearances" for psychoanalysis, but at the cost of perpetuating the fundamental theoretical error of materialism.

---

[2] *Civilization and Its Discontents* (London: The Hogarth Press, 1949), pp. 8, 21 ff. Hereafter CD.

[3] In *The Life and Work of Sigmund Freud* (New York: Basic Books, 1953-1957), II, p. 320; I, p. 401. Hereafter LWSF.

The alternative conception here, again, is that natural reality, what is repressed by cultural reality, is *not* reducible to the biological or sexual. The correct formula would be: cultural repression is directed against those aspects of natural biological *and* psychological functioning which are inconsistent with the elevation of human consciousness to the desired level of abstraction — of "the Idea," Hegel would say.

The progress of culture has primarily involved the progressive loss, not of quantitative or qualitative sexuality, but of natural-psychological intangibles or, more generally, states.[4] The more exact definition of these intangibles will be a prolonged task, beyond the scope of the present essay.

c) Speculation upon the events of the nursery can be safely omitted from any general interpretation of culture. For, though from the *individual's* viewpoint culture indeed begins as he first encounters it in the nursery and the family, and there absorbs as much of it as he can then absorb, this much and all the rest of the culture had been *first created* outside the family, in the adult social world. This original creating is *reproduced* in the course of infantile and familial experience, and whatever happens there cannot of itself add anything to the general cultural mode. The family is the crucible of culture only in this secondary ontogenetic sense.

For the life of an individual, the particular variations of the reproduction of a general cultural mode within a particular family are of course most significant, even decisive. But unless the individual successfully adapts to that mode, he cannot affect it and is of no concern to it one way or another. If he does so eventually adapt, he is then responding primarily to *present,* not to past, to *adult,* not to infantile, and to *social,* not to intrafamilial or merely individual needs: responding, that is, to those present adult social needs shared and abstracted from, as culture, by many individuals of widely different infantile and familial experience.

Accordingly, that which is culturally causally primary is not to

---

[4] In his often cited but still theoretically unassimilated essay, "Memory and Childhood Amnesia" (*Psychiatry,* Feb. 1947), Ernest G. Schachtel advanced a similar conception, from whose critical implications, however, he later drew back. His subsequent book, *Metamorphosis* (New York: Basic Books, 1959), though it includes and ends with the above essay, is otherwise a reversion to superficial ego-psychology, uncritically celebrating cultural "growth" out of "embeddedness" or natural reality. Schachtel here (p. xi) acknowledges the influence of Erich Fromm. This is another illustration of how helpful it would be for depth-psychology to rid itself of Marxism.

be interpreted in terms of what is causally secondary. Though Freud's method is somewhat more applicable to aspects of *individual* psychology, even there it has its limitations.

d) The "Oedipus Complex" is at best a metaphor for the general conflict between natural and cultural reality, which, again, is primarily an adult, social affair. It is not true that the frustration of the sexual or "incestuous" desire is the primary trauma in all children, still less that this is the ultimate content of adult social phenomena. As before noted, Freud so broadened the concept of sexuality that in practice it served as a metaphor for natural biopsychological functioning in general. But it is not of his sexuality that the child is deprived by progressive acculturation — rather, notwithstanding he eventually gains it biologically. Through that acculturation transmitted by the family and the school, he does, however, lose much of his former natural-*psychology*, as his consciousness becomes progressively more abstract. To this change he may react with more or less frustration and hostility, no doubt usually directed primarily against the father — but, as the child may later come to understand, the ultimate source of this frustration (insofar as it derives from the cultural norm) lies in the community, where the conflict must be ultimately resolved in one way or another.[5]

e) Freud, in trying to reduce it to the "infantile" attitude to the "father," completely missed the real import of the religious, "spiritual," or "hierophanic" factor in human nature (the last term is Mircea Eliade's useful neologism). In all psychoanalysis, it was Otto Rank who most profoundly understood what was involved in this, and to his work we now turn.

---

[5] Of course, pathologically brutal or indifferent parents may inflict on their children culturally unnecessary frustrations of one kind or another. To this the child may react with neurosis, psychosis — or, in some cases, with re-creative efforts. Only the last may (eventually) have effect upon the cultural process, which leaves aside or institutionalizes the culturally sterile reactions.

I have the greatest respect for R. D. Laing's early work on schizophrenia, but it is impossible to interpret *social* psychological problems in terms of clinical ones, and most alienations from the community — whether or not they take the form of neurosis or psychosis — do *not* end in the creative resolution. There is accordingly no such thing as "mad power," nor is madness "better," let alone "beautiful." From another point of view, Lionel Trilling has also commented upon the speciousness of Laing's later theme (*Commentary*, Sept. 1971). On the other hand, it is true that "sanity" is not in itself the answer to our common problems: in this regard it may *also* be sterile.

The contemporary attraction to "madness" might be interpreted as the 20th century variation of the 19th century romantic maneuver with tuberculosis: surely, if one is going to die, or go mad, the world will mend its ways? The Leviathan, instead, again passes by indifferently.

2) *Main Repudiations of the Rankian Legacy.* Over a decade ago, in an informal first impression of Rank (*Commentary*, Sept. 1960) I suggested that he might "turn out to have been the best mind psychoanalysis contributed to intellectual history." One might have supposed this remark to be sufficiently provocative, but it was received in sullen silence. My own opinion remains unchanged.

For some years, to accept Ortega y Gasset's phrase, the ideas of Rank continued to bleed within me. It gradually became more clear, however, that the "dialectical series" needed to be continued beyond some of the points to which Rank has advanced it.[6] But it is first necessary to apprehend something of the several ways in which Rank had gone beyond Freud.

The transitional theory of the "birth trauma," with which for decades Rank's name has been misidentified by most of the histories, encyclopedias, and commentaries, should be immediately dropped into the garbage pail. It has at best only a metaphorical relationship to Rank's later and actually characteristic ideas, of whose existence few are aware even now.

Let us first consider the aforementioned subject of Rank's more positive evaluation of the ego — or "will" as he came to call it, in this influenced by Schopenhauer, Nietzsche and Adler. To Freud himself the ego had seemed little more than the puppet of one or an opposing instinctual force. For Rank the will was the relatively autonomous master of the instincts, and in this he saw positive value. He did not deny that this mastery or culture required repression, but to him this seemed of relatively little importance. Thus at first glance it might appear that Rank's is among those ego-psychologies fundamentally uncritical of culture. Not so, however, for of this Rank was in another sense even more critical than Freud.

The normal person, in Rank's view, exercised his will in substantive confluence with that of the community; the neurotic suffered from his alienation from the community, and a consequent inability to exercise his own will in such a confluence. The creative type — which Rank often epitomized as "the artist" — in one way or another was also alienated from the communal will and faith, but was nevertheless able to exercise his own will more or less *independently*. For Rank, given alienation, the creative reaction was the

---

[6] Cf. the concluding remarks of my contribution on Rank to the *International Encyclopedia of the Social Sciences* (New York: Crowell, Collier and Macmillan, 1968). A bibliography of Rank's more significant works can be found there.

only solution, and so he often spoke of the neurotic as the "failed artist."[7]

In fact, Rank was not much interested in "normalcy," and his psychology centered on the creative man. But creativity, though of exceptional incidence, is however in one sense the "essence" of man, to which in the end normal-psychology perforce adapts itself, for recurrently the creative power has provided objective advantages in the evolutionary struggle.

Rank eventually rejected all Freudian and other attempts to explain the psychological in terms of the biological. The psychological realm was for him the irreducible level of human causality. In his final theoretical phase, he saw the basic human motive as the will to maintain one's belief in one's individual immortality (the concept will be further explained below). This belief was to this or that extent inconsistent with the belief in the *communal* immortality, and to such an extent had to be modified or surrendered to make the latter and human society possible. It was *this* conflict, between psychological intangibles, and not any conflict between instincts, or between instincts and ego, which seemed to Rank the most fundamental in human nature.

Throughout cultural evolution, he believed, men had suffered from and struggled over the contradiction between individual and collective immortality beliefs, expressed in different forms in the different cultural epochs. The artist, as defined by Rank, is he who strives through his art to actualize his *personal, individual* immortality, and does so to the extent to which the community recognizes in his art its own latent wish for the same, and accepts as art (and *only* as art) what would otherwise be ideologically anathema.

Rank's more positive conception of the ego as the creative will (at least in "essence" or potentially) is not especially difficult to understand or appreciate. It is otherwise with his much more profound

---

[7] One recognizes in the later work of Laing a partial re-emergence of and distortion of this idea. But Rank never dreamed of romanticizing alienation, neurosis or psychosis as such: he valued only the creative resolution. For Rank only this was what has been sometimes called the "authentic." However, even as concerns what is indubitably "creative" or "authentic" — whether as an individual or social phenomenon — there remain further problems of value, as some of those who use such concepts have not realized. (Indeed, Rank himself was not altogether clear as to this.) Marxism, for example, is "authentically" bad theory and politics, and yet another example of its prodigious malignancy can be seen in its acceptance by Sartre (politically speaking, perhaps the most indefatigably authentic "idiot" in Europe). In turn, it is Sartre who seems to have inspired a good part of the later Laing's social "psychology."

conception of the belief in immortality, whose critical implications and ramifications are hard to grasp theoretically; because to do so is actually more unpleasant emotionally than is reflection upon sexuality (which last Freud had misconceived to be the primary resistance to psychoanalytic theory). As Rank was aware, the natural-psychological belief in immortality is *objectively* untrue. Thus he was declaring that the *primary* human motive is not anything tangible, material, biological, economic or objective, but a psychological intangible, which was, moreover, illusory.[8] This motive or value, he thought, has been the ultimate content of all religions, all beliefs in the soul, God or other supernatural phenomena, from primitive times onward. In its sub-ideological form, it inspires art. Moreover, as Rank discerned, this faith has by no means ceased to operate upon the advent of the post-religious, rational consciousness. It then merely assumes various rational guises, and sometimes those of psychoanalytic theory itself.

By now something of the character of Rank's final ideas may have been conveyed. It is regrettable that in the past there has been so little awareness or discussion of these. In the absence of such a more solid background exchange of views, the criticism which here perforce immediately follows the defense, is in a certain sense premature.

Nevertheless, though in a less than ideal situation, it is now necessary to offer some notions as to how the value of Rank's contributions might be improved.

a) In the main, Rank's view of the ego as creative will, relatively independent of instinct, can be accepted. And yet, perhaps Freud's own concept (as modified above and below) of a tragic perennial contradiction between the created cultural and the natural reality remains equally true and relevant. The test of the first-rate psychoanalytic mind, to adapt Fitzgerald's phrase, is perhaps the ability to keep *both* ideas in mind and retain the capacity to function.

b) It seems also necessary to go beyond Rank's value-relativism. Though in this he was not completely consistent, Rank sometimes held *any* form of immortality belief to be in itself subjectively true and good. Exactly what form "does not matter . . . as long as it is

---

[8] Of course, for man too, such biological needs as "hunger" must be eventually met. But in this there is as yet nothing distinctively human. In man, who is of course partially animal, *human* psychology begins where animal psychology leaves off. Some of the ethologists have not grasped the distinction.

projection, it is helpful and therapeutic, because it is illusory."[9] "The ideologies . . . are neither true nor false — that is have no eternal validity — but change with the development of collective and individual ideas, and thus fulfill their real purpose, their extension to infinity."[10] Thus it might well appear that Rank knew no reason why any form of immortality belief, as identified with this or that individual or cultural way of life, should be preferred to another.

But, on the other hand, a different theme of Rank's work — which can be interpreted as on the whole the predominant one, though this may be debatable — is that in the *collective* form of the immortality belief there has been a progressive development *away* from the original, more natural, *individual* manifestation of that belief. The progressive decline of the latter, Rank believed, had culminated in modern rationalism, including psychoanalytic rationalism. There was thus, he felt, a contradiction between psychoanalysis as theory (which might be true) and psychoanalysis as therapy (for truth was not necessarily therapeutic).

To the whole communal cultural development, therefore, Rank, often implicitly and sometimes explicitly, opposed the will of the individual, particularly the creative artist. As concerns this issue, it seems that Rank must again be partially "re-Freudianized." The most fundamental conflict may not be between the individual and communal forms of immortality belief, but between the *more natural* and the *less natural* modes of biopsychological functioning throughout cultural evolution, though our understanding of this phenomenon is greatly improved if we then apply thereto Rank's understanding of the hierophanic factor. Thus art would express this resistance of the (relatively) natural to culture, to the prevailing cultural ideology, that is, would express the subversive re-identification of the individual soul with the more natural.   That would be the ultimate meaning of *artistic* creativity (which Rank never distinguished very clearly from creativity in general).

But when "individuality" is otherwise asserted against the community, it does not necessarily have the same meaning. Other possible meanings include: the impotence of insanity, the temporary anarchy of criminality, the successful introduction of *less* natural

---

[9] *Psychology and the Soul* (Philadelphia: University of Pennsylvania Press, 1950), p. 185. Hereafter PS.

[10] *Art and Artist* (New York: Knopf, 1932), p. 424. Hereafter AA. This work has been reissued by Agathon Press (New York, 1968).

modes of culture by innovators. Thus neither "individuality" nor "creativity" as such can serve as any absolute criterion of value. Art, on the other hand, can as above defined serve as such a criterion: the problem however is that of validating it more generally, and to this art itself cannot provide the answer.

c) Rank (like Freud and most other psychoanalytic thinkers) often tended to "reduce" objective cultural and social problems to virtual non-existence. Rank's own stress was upon "the basic importance of spiritual values as against social needs and even biological facts."[11] It is essential, however, to distinguish between what is *subjectively* most important, at least in the short run, and what may be *objectively* more important in the longer run. It does not seem that "spiritual values" are best understood as developing independently from or as always prevailing over the objective factors of cultural evolution. That is, while it is true that man has often preferred the retention of "irrational" spiritual beliefs to objective temporal advantages, and sometimes to life itself, it may yet be true that in the long run those spiritual beliefs tend to survive in the evolutionary flux *which most identify themselves with, or justify, superior objective cultural powers of one kind or another* (political, economic, military, etc.). And thus we must also consider the nature of these objective powers and their genesis, which is not "irrational" or "spiritual" alone.

d) Freud, to recapitulate, denied that any hierophanic factor actually operated in human nature, even while admitting it theologically to his own system, as "Eros" (as will be seen momentarily). Rank's recognition of both the actuality and value of that factor, and also that it was nevertheless illusory, was insofar a more profound psychological criticism than Freud's.

But Rank's particular definition may need to be reconsidered. Is it so that *all* hierophanic manifestations are explicable as derivations of the belief in *immortality*? On both theoretical and empirical grounds it is hard to believe that "the single real obstacle which freedom of the will encounters is death, which it conquers by spiritual belief." (PS, 143) Here and there Rank nominally also recognizes a second kind of soul, a "will-soul," as the will to master the temporal obstacles of life. But for Rank this other soul was only a secondary

---

[11] *Beyond Psychology* (New York: Dover, 1958), p. 119.

aspect of the more fundamental nature of the soul as the belief in immortality.

Could it be the other way around? Perhaps the soul is most fundamentally and comprehensively the natural-psychological belief in *omnipotence,* which belief would include but not be reducible to the belief in immortality. More significantly perhaps for the understanding of human psychological evolution, the belief in omnipotence necessarily encounters all sorts of *temporal* obstacles, including other human wills and souls. This modification of the concept might enable us to better relate it to those many temporal social problems to which psychoanalysis has neglected to relate.

3) *"Death-Instinctual Man"*? In his crucial 1914 essay "On Narcissism," Freud announced that the ego was also invested with sexuality or libido, and began to rework his view of the basic conflict within human nature.[12] In fact, Freud was soon to place the libido, as Eros, squarely on the side of *culture* and psychoanalysis. With this, in effect, Freud relegated to a secondary role, though he did not abandon, his own great discovery of the *contradiction* between natural and cultural reality, as this had been originally conceived.

His general sense of some fundamental and worsening conflict in things lingered, however, but now predominantly in another form. At first he surmised that a malignantly and gratuitously punitive "super-ego" — not the neessary demands of culture itself — was individually and socially the source of excessive or neurotic repression and suffering. Then this conjecture was in turn virtually swallowed up in that of the "death instinct," now identified as the main antagonist of the life instinct, Eros, culture and psychoanalysis.

There might be, he suggested, an instinctual "compulsion inherent in organic life to restore an earlier state of things . . ." — ultimately, the inorganic level, or death.[13] Turned against the environment, this "death instinct" manifested itself as the "aggressive" or destructive instinct; turned inward, it gradually destroyed the self.

But before this final vision of a cosmic duel between instincts, or "battle of the Titans" (CD, 103), most of Freud's followers, including Ernest Jones, were to balk. "No biological observation," Jones objected, "can be found to support the idea of a death instinct, one

---

[12] In *Collected Papers* (New York: Basic Books, 1959), IV, pp. 30 ff.
[13] *Beyond the Pleasure Principle* (London: Hogarth Press, 1950), pp. 47 ff.

which contradicts all biological principles." (LWSF, III, 277) in this connection, Jones even turned the Oedipal ploy against the master himself, speculating that the theory might reflect some "dread of a terrible father" (ibid., 280).

The "dread" in question was much more probably ideological (again, *adult* and *social*). The import otherwise of the death-instinctual theory was, firstly, to deflect elsewhere Freud's primary culture-critical insight; and, secondly, to introduce into Freud's system (though in a pseudo-biological form which could pass the scientific "censor"), the natural-psychological factor of hierophanic belief. Eros became the god, and Thanatos the demon of the psychoanalytic faith. These entities, of course, have only a subjective, psychological and no objective biological existence. Thus the conflict as imagined by the later Freud in reality reflected a psychological struggle between faith and disbelief in psychoanalysis itself, and also as now identified with *culture*. What we have here is *theology*, not *theory* (whereas in Rank's system the hierophanic value is always understood *theoretically*).

The exact relationship of the "death-instinct" to the "aggressive instinct" also has to be reinterpreted, but this task will not concern us here.

This late lapse of Freud into theology, concerning which he himself was somewhat uneasy, has never been accepted by the majority of psychoanalysts and by Jones himself was in effect excluded from the canon. Norman O. Brown has since tried to modify and rehabilitate Freud's conception,[14] and though he is among those relative few who have tried to grapple at the deepest level with the problem as posed by Freud, of the contradiction between natural and cultural reality, in the end Brown, for all his many trenchant observations, did not succeed in advancing the fundamental theoretical position. In general, he has accepted too uncritically far too many of the classical Freudian themes (concerning which what has been said before need not be repeated here). In particular, Brown takes the "death instinct" even more seriously than Freud did, also misconceives it as a biological reality, and also insists upon the causal primacy of infantile experience: "Everywhere, psychoanalysis must

---

[14] *Life Against Death* (New York: Vintage, 1960). Hereafter LAD, from which all citations below until further notice.

take the paradoxical position that the Child is Father to the Man" (125).

Brown's own distinctive hypothesis, however, is that an original self-traumatization of the *infant* generated "neurosis" (by Brown, as by Reich, equated with the presence of repression) and all cultural evolution since. This has been a universal "dialectic of neurosis" (12). In man, Brown says, the period of infancy under adult protection is so long and pleasurable that the child's initial exposure to harsh reality — variously equated by Brown with the separation from the body, care or protection of the mother, or the family — is invariably "a trauma from which the individual never recovers psychologically." (25) Thus the original conflict is between childish narcissism (he follows Freud in seeing this as fundamentally "sexuality") and *natural* rather than *cultural* reality. This last is the incidental and always neurotic by-product. The shock of this confrontation arouses the "death instinct" in the child, who reacts by "trying to repress his own death." (101) This, Brown thinks, was man's Original Sin, or "the first repression" which then engendered culture, for "Man aggressively builds immortal cultures and makes history in order to fight death." (101)

The striving for immortality, Brown conceives, is a "neurotic" corruption of natural, childish or animal narcissism, in which latter the life and death instincts exist in a harmonious "dialectical unity . . . Animals let death be part of life, and use the death instinct to die . . ." (100 ff.) Only man "represses death" and this inevitably also means repression of the "dialectical fusion" of life and death, and thus also of the life instincts. (103 ff.)[15] Brown thus calls for "a resurrection of the body" and the "abolition of repression." (307) The precondition of this, however, would be the *acceptance* of the death instinct. We must, he says, become "strong enough to die . . ."

---

[15] Like Freud, Brown usually reduces the natural biopsychological to the biological: "since life is of the body" repression or negation must be of "specific bodily organs." (164) Brown's secondary theme in LAD is that most cultural phenomena express "sublimated anality" (177 ff.) and he devotes much ingenuity to trying to demonstrate this. However, he does not interpret the phenomenon as caused by any actual specific disturbance of or repression of the anal function. It is rather that to the latter the causally prior trauma and fantasies of the "flight from death" tend to attach themselves (230 ff.).

But, despite Brown, the truth is probably only that for many people, anal references serve as convenient biological metaphors for that general repression of natural (and primarily natural-psychological) reality by *cultural* reality — just as primitives often use "blood" as such a biological metaphor not only for biological, but also and primarily for *psychological* "life" or faith.

(291) no longer looking upon death as an enemy, but as "a friend."
(322)

Again, what was said before of Freud's system also applies, *mutatis mutandis*, to Brown's. There is no "death instinct" nor is there any "natural" acceptance of death — animals also "flee" and "fight" death as best they can. Neither culture nor repression of itself signifies neurosis; nor does the hierophanic belief of itself produce repression, although in man it has accompanied repression. It is also present in childish "narcissism" (and also probably in that of animals), which narcissism is wrongly counterposed by Brown to its allegedly "neurotic" manifestation in adults (in *both* versions, however, hierophanic belief is *inherently* illusory). In *neither* does it have any biological ground—he who does not understand the human soul *psychologically* is doomed to re-express its existence *theologically*, and this unfortunately has been also the case with Brown, as is especially evident in his second book.

Of this in due course. Even, for the sake of argument, assuming the existence of a death instinct, Brown's system has many logical inconsistencies and for practical purposes ends in a blind alley. If it all came originally from the unusual length of human infancy, as Brown supposes, one would expect the neurosis to break out at a rather late or the terminal period of that infancy. And yet anxiety and repression seem to appear at "a very early stage . . . going back to the birth trauma." (III ff.) Why should birth, or early natural frustrations, produce neurosis, repression, culture in human but not animal infants? (This was also an objection to Rank's ephemeral birth-trauma theory.)

Assuming however that the later prolonged-infancy trauma could somehow manifest itself retroactively, or could be inherited through the genes and thus subsequently affect the human infant at an earlier stage, how can Brown's recommendation that he be "strong enough to die" be taken literally? If the infant were indeed that "strong," it would be the end of him, and if this "strength" became universal, the end of the species.

But let us suppose that we are not to understand this recommendation too literally; Brown means only the strength to accept the *idea* of death. Even assuming this to be desirable, how could one demand this "strength" from the infant, something which is in fact unknown to the animal world, is highly *unnatural* psychologically, and of which with a few exceptions even adults have been incapable until the advent of the philosophy and science of modern times? How is one to "existentialize" the infant? And yet, if we cannot, human infants would presumably continue to self-traumatize themselves, engendering repression and neurosis. Apparently the only hope—though this seems to violate the law that "the child is father to the man"— would be that in adulthood they might recover, through acquiring full "psychoanalytic consciousness" and "accepting death." The implications of this possibility will be reviewed a little further on.

Let us now finally suppose that we are not to understand the concept of "accepting death" in *any* literal sense. Brown means only to say something like "strong enough to accept the frustrations of life without illusions." But this is in fact just what most men already do, though indeed few of them without illusions. Whether *with* or *without* illusions, however, this also means accepting in practice those repressions inherent in culture. Thus it is *Brown,* among others, who cannot "accept death"—i.e. accept that man is *not* omnipotent in this latter and most crucial sense. This non-acceptance of the objective necessity of repression is one manifestation of the essentially theological and irrational character of the death-instinct concept, in every version of it. Brown's apparently rational-existential idea of "accepting death" has in reality a deeper and reverse layer of meaning—his affirmation of the possibility of abolishing the temporal factor of repression actually signifies *retention of faith* in man's *temporal* omnipotence.[16] But this is theology, not theory.

And if indeed some individual were "strong enough to die" in the sense of "abolishing repression" in himself—then, what would follow? If this were possible, then along with repression would vanish his cultural power, and he would have in effect excluded himself from cultural evolution. Assuming that he managed to survive at all, it is possible that he might find some kind of *personal* salvation, but it could be nothing more than this. It is indeed in this general direction that Brown has since moved. In his last book, the basically theological character of his system has fully surfaced.[17] He has now tacitly abandoned not only the death instinct and anal theories, but *any* theorizing in the strict sense. LB is a regression—"expectations

---

[16] The same point applies, in general, to the existentialist side of the philosophy of Sartre and his death-obsessed mentor Heidegger.

[17] *Love's Body* (New York: Vintage, 1966). Hereafter LB; from which all citations below until further notice.

were not realized . . . the continuity is fractured," as Brown puts it in his introduction — into a weird shamanistic stew of hyper-Freudian and primitive-Christian fantasies: "We go beyond Freud with Melanie Klein: the body the brothers partook of was not the body of the father, but the body of the father and mother combined." (24) There prevails throughout LB an at once rigid and reckless reduction of the adult, social, political to the biological and familial. Each social "group is to the other the breast; but, as we know from Melanie Klein, the breast is equated with the penis. Thus copulation is always oral . . . coitus is a process of mutual devouring—oral copulation, or rather, cannibalistic, and therefore combining in one act the two Oedipal wishes, parental murder and incest; and including sexual inversion, since the male member is seen as a breast sucked." (25) As for politics, "It is the specific gift of psychoanalysis to see behind these sociological abstractions the human face; and their name is fatherhood and brotherhood . . . the real question in politics is Jesus' question, Who is my father?" (9, 5) It is to be hoped that Brown does not finally decide (with Sartre) that it is Mao.

Interpreting in this "Freudian" way the Christian concept of the "resurrection of the body," to Brown "the Second Coming is the fulfillment of the first . . . The resurrection is to recur, to be fulfilled in us: it is to happen to his[Christ's] mystical body, which is our bodies, in this flesh." (213 ff.) Of course the *objective* historical significance of the emergence of Christianity — as Freud himself was well aware—was the introduction of a *higher* level of instinctual renunciation, despite the hierophanic excitation accompanying the same.[18] To suppose that with any neo-Christian (or neo-Judaic) revival it could be otherwise, is only to have again bought subjective faith at the expense of objective theory.

"To give up boundaries is to give up the reality principle." (149) And why not?, asks Brown.[19] Let us "cast [it]off; in order to begin the Odyssey of consciousness in quest of its own true body." (154) Let's not. For if this colossal engine of cultural power which we

---

[18] The *literal* sense of the bodily "resurrection" theme is actually of late *Judaic* provenance. St. Paul gave this its Christian *spiritual* meaning — in this respect as others *dephysicalizing* Judaic monotheism. Cf. I Cor. 15:44, p. 50; Samuel Sandmel, *The Genius of Paul* (New York: Schocken Books, 1970), p. 89 ff.

[19] Laing's theme of mad power to a somewhat lesser extent is paralleled by Brown: "Seduce the world to madness . . . Freedom is fire, overcoming this world by reducing it to a fluctuating chaos, as in schizophrenia; the chaos which is the eternal ground of creation." (242, 248) Once more, from this, viable creation does not *necessarily* and usually does *not* follow.

have indeed created at the expense of natural reality—of the "true body" if you like—is ever to be brought under humane control, if it is ever to be commanded, it must first be obeyed. This does not mean without the essential reservations and ulterior purposes.

4) *"One-Dimensional Man"?* In the past decade the ideas of Herbert Marcuse, a Marxist wolf in Freudian clothing, have devoured many an "international idiot."[20] In this regard, his world influence has been at least equal to Sartre's. The main pernicious theoretical effect of Marcuse's work has been to spread "Freudo-Marxism," or the misapprehension that Freud's work complements and confirms that of Marx. But the two cannot be so reconciled. Over the fundamental theoretical issues—are the contradictions in human affairs most fundamentally economic, or psychological; are they inherent or remediable?—no compromise is possible. "How long will you go on limping on two opposite contentions; if Yahweh is God, follow him, but if the Baal, follow him." (I Kings 18: 21) Consciously or unconsciously impressed by the rise of Marxism to temporal power, and by Freudianism's failure to make any comparable gains, not a few Freudians, and even some of the orthodox party, are limping between the two gods, and some are noticeably edging toward Marx.[21] (This very natural if unedifying phenomenon, is also quite evident in "Christian"—especially Catholic—leftism.)

Having spent the earlier part of his career as a Hegelian Marxist, Marcuse came belatedly to depth-psychology, it seems only because he was not quite able to digest according to Hegel and Marx the events in Russia from the thirties onward. When the devil was sick,

---

[20] For an earlier, more detailed account of Marcuse's work, here reiterated in part, see my "Herbert Marcuse and the Cunning of Revolution," in the *Michigan Quarterly Review* (spring, 1970). Cf. also my essay-review of his *Five Lectures* (Boston: Beacon Press, 1970), in *Interplay* (Nov. 1970).

[21] At the 1971 congress of the International Psychoanalytic Association at Vienna, Alexander Mitscherlich of Frankfurt called upon psychoanalysis to become politically involved. All very well in theory, but what it might mean in practice, in the present state of the art, was indicated when a lady Freudian from Brazil, very possibly under Marcuse's influence, thereafter rose to suggest that "aggression" might be the consequence, not of the "death instinct," but of the institution of private property. For a while it seems she had a pretty nice thing going, until some meanie observed that aggression was also not unknown to socialist societies. — Earlier, one had also noticed the friendly allusion by Ernest Jones to Marcuse's "thoughtful" notions. (LWSF, III, 347 ff.)

the devil a Freudian would be. Like Brown, Marcuse accepts too uncritically the greater part of Freud's biological and familial inter- pretations, including the "death instinct."[22] Given these and his own Marxism, Marcuse invades and occupies Freud's system chiefly in terms of the following arguments.

Predominantly by far, Freud saw repression as the consequence of Oedipal guilt. But here and there he also saw a rational element in repression: that is, without it men would spend all their time in the arms of Eros. No repression, no work, and society's material needs could not be met. Seizing upon this last formula, Marcuse points to the advent of automation-cybernation, which in theory might take over all or most work. His own formula: No work, no repression.

Further, he makes a distinction between "basic" and "surplus" repression. The former consists of those repressions which are actually necessary, for as Marcuse *appears* to concede, "any form of the reality principle demands a considerable degree and scope of repres- sive control over the instincts . . ." (EC, 34) Their nature, degree and scope, however, are nowhere clearly indicated by Marcuse, and for good reason, for this apparent concession is only apparent. What he really believes in is a "non-repressive civilization . . . the gradual abolition of repression" (5), both basic and surplus. Thus it turns out that the repression which is "basic" is not really repression at all, but "the privilege and distinction of man, which has enabled him to transform the blind necessity of the fulfillment of want into desired gratification," in fact, into "the human form of the pleasure prin- ciple." (35) [23]

On the other hand, and to the same superficial effect, "surplus" repression Marcuse understands as "the restrictions necessitated by social domination," which "is exercised by a particular group or individual in order to sustain and enhance itself in a privileged posi- tion." (32 ff.) Such repression, he declares, can be abolished along with the revolutionary overthrow of the dominant class. Marcuse

---

[22] Marcuse's main study of psychological theory is his *Eros and Civilization* (New York: Vintage, 1962). Hereafter EC; from which all citations below until further notice.

[23] Observe that while Marcuse (and rightly) attacks the ego-psychology of Fromm and certain others — in which the *present* factor of repression is denied or at least de-emphasized — his own ideas are no less "revisionist," though for him this repressive factor is to disappear only in the *future* revolution. Thus Marcuse is little more than Fromm futurized.

further affirms that from this elimination of scarcity and "surplus" repression there would follow a qualitatively different mode of consciousness, such as that already manifest in art, play, fantasy. This would be "non-repressive sublimation." (190) Therefore, he concludes, there is a real "prospect of a civilization without repression." (216) With this Marcuse in effect promulgated the Dogma of the Assumption of the Unrepressed Body into Marxism.

In my view, none of these ideas actually goes beyond Freud's position, and none is finally tenable.

a) The equation of repression with "work" is misleading, for human work depends upon the *pre-existence* of an acculturated consciousness, which acculturation—as Freud also really believed—is *inherently* repressive. Thus the abolition of work through automation of itself would "abolish" neither the acculturated consciousness nor repression. Moreover, an irreducible amount of work would remain, even if largely intellectual work—since some at least would have to devote themselves to tending the automation economy. Almost inevitably, they would soon emerge as the objectively most powerful, thus "dominant" class.

b) Marcuse's concept of "surplus repression" is potentially valid in one sense, though he rarely uses it in this sense. That is, as the concept that there might be such a thing as "surplus culture," too much culture, in view of the repression it inevitably costs. But what Marcuse has done is to try to absorb this theme within the *Marxist* concepts, including that of "surplus value," which are something "radically" different. The Marxists see the most fundamental conflict as economic, between the capitalist and the worker, between capitalism and socialism. This conflict, they imagine, disappears with the establishment of socialism. Marxism has no thought of any check upon cultural growth which, on the contrary, it glorifies even more unquestioningly than capitalism. The criticism of Marcuse's system must be most fundamentally the criticism of Marxism itself, but as concerns this in the present essay it is not possible to go beyond some incidental observations.[24]

c) Marcuse's third main contribution is easily dealt with. The existence of art, play and fantasy demonstrates only that *less*-repressed sublimation is possible. The latter takes place within the context of

---

[24] Somewhat more helpful in this respect may be my previous article on Marcuse, and especially my "Le Socialisme des Profundeurs" in *Esprit* (Paris, May, 1971) — English version in *Abraxas* (Southampton College, Spring, 1971).

the greater amount of repression objectively required to establish, maintain and defend whatever the general cultural mode (which artists, children and fantasts do not and cannot create).

The development of Marcuse's ideas and activities since EC has made ever more explicit that which is more implicit there—the actual dominance of Marxist over Freudian concepts in Marcuse's originally nominally "complementary" arrangement. Marcuse, however, has not formally repudiated his Freudian adventure (unfortunately, for this would clarify the true theoretical relation).

The best of his books followed a decade later.[25] By means of the interesting concept of one-dimensionality, Marcuse effectively criticized the thought and practice of all advanced industrial societies as shallow, egotistic and indifferent to their fundamental reality, which he saw as one of progressive unfreedom. In this interpretation, he then included the established socialist as well as capitalist domains, though the weight of his attack was primarily by far directed against the latter, which he characterized as also "totalitarian." Unfortunately, what might otherwise be many valuable insights into the limitations of "one-dimensional" thought and life are drawn by Marcuse into the service of Marxist theory and theology. The West may well be "one-dimensional" but it is not totalitarian, though in recent years it has become ideologically fashionable to confuse the two things, so as to make it appear that there exists no viable anti-totalitarian position. If indeed the West should ever become totalitarian, this will have been most likely the work of Marxism, considerably assisted by Marcuse (in the picture, there is at present no equivalent to the National Socialist competitive reaction).

In all versions, including Marcuse's, totalitarianism is most fundamentally an irrational, sacrificial, revolutionary phenomenon. Throughout history, revolutions have given birth to higher levels of cultural power *and repression,* which last may (after Thermidor) again prevail as the "one-dimensional" norm. The "one-dimensionality" of all established *socialist* systems, however, prevails upon a significantly higher level of repression than that of the capitalist systems, by any objective estimate.

But Marcuse refuses to make any such estimates, because the opposite relation is how it "ought to be" according to Marxist theory and

---

[25] *One-Dimensional Man* (Boston: Beacon Press, 1966). Hereafter O-DM.

theology.[26] It is in this sense, which goes deeper still than the one he intends, that we must reinterpret one of his favorite aphorisms: "That which is, cannot be true." (O-DM, 123, passim.) The remark has an implicit corollary: "That which comes to be, must always be true"—and this blind idolatry of the development of the cultural power Marcuse indeed shares with Hegel and Marx. It would be more accurately designated as "the uncritical theory." Unless "aufgehoben," in my view it may lead humanity to its final ruin, and in any case is in spirit certainly the opposite of the psychoanalytic quest.

5) *"Therapeutic Man"?* With the work of Philip Rieff, we are again on the main highway of rational theory, and it is good to be there. The first of his two books is an exceptionally intelligent and careful review of the Freudian positions; the second more fully develops his own supplementary concept of "therapeutic man." [27]

In general, FMM reaffirms the continuing validity of Freud's ideas, including those of the *inherence* of the conflict between cultural and natural reality (which Rieff wisely avoids tying too dogmatically to Freud's biological, sexual, Oedipal specifics). Unfortunately, he allows himself too many rhetorical and literary flourishes at the expense of theoretical precision (his excessive reliance on literary evidence is one aspect of this); and he often adds his own ambivalency or indecision, as concerns this or that specific issue, to Freud's. A good many of Rieff's rhetorical formulations, if taken literally, are inconsistent with others. Thus at one point Freud is said to be "the architect of a great revolt against pleasure, not for it." (FMM, 355) In another place, it is said that "Yet . . . Freud advanced the long-established assault on the repressions . . . Sexuality has shown,

---

[26] Significantly Marcuse never refers to the works of those dissidents who have actually lived under and confronted the totalitarian system, with whom he therefore can have nothing in common. They easily recognize, and some have objected to his views as neo-totalitarian. His own claim that he actually espouses "libertarian socialism" has grown less and less convincing with the passing years, and with his inability to cite any existing example of the same. In fact, of late he seems to have tacitly dropped this claim — *any* revolution he now welcomes, as also apparently one that might be led by the Communist Party, which in O-DM had been nominally included among the "totalitarian" forces. But this is only the inevitable practical consequence of the fact that his own system had never actually made itself theoretically independent of conventional Marxism.

[27] *Freud: the Mind of the Moralist* (New York: Vintage, 1961). Hereafter FMM. *The Triumph of the Therapeutic: Uses of Faith After Freud* (New York: Harper and Row, 1968). Hereafter TT.

for Freud and related figures of his century, a revolutionary potential . . ." (FMM, 373, passim.) But, as Rieff himself recognizes, Freud's *predominant* conception by far is neither "revolutionary" nor "counter-revolutionary" properly speaking — it is that of the desirability of some better *balance* between the natural and the cultural, than generally prevails in the modern world. *This* is the idea that it is profitable to consider. One can do little with the idea of Freud as either "revolutionary" or "counter-revolutionary." And the actual recent "great revolt against pleasure" is assuredly of *totalitarian* not Freudian provenance. (Such political problems are badly understood by Rieff in both books, as will further appear below.)

When, in the title of Rieff's first book, and throughout, Freud is characterized as a "moralist," the effect is again more rhetorical than exact. As in the usual sense a "moralist" is one who upholds some specific notion of right and wrong, it is doubtful if the term can be very meaningfully applied to Freud. Apart from the general commitment to rationality and science, which strictly speaking is not a moral commitment, Freud's doctrine tended toward the morally neutral, even nihilistic, as indeed Rieff recognizes (FMM, 352 ff.). Thus one of the valid criticisms of Freudianism is that in general it does *not* offer any moral guidance.

More fundamentally, however, Rieff's rhetorical imprecisions are those of theory. In the Freudian Scriptures, as in many others, support can usually be found for one or the other side of any issue. It is therefore essential to have grasped, as concerns this or that matter, which is Freud's predominant or final position. For neither he nor anyone else can finally have it both ways. On a good many issues, however, Rieff leaves Freud's as well as his own ultimate position in doubt. This may be the correct legal strategy in defense of the Freudian system, but getting *beyond* is something else. Theory progresses only as a "dialectical series" of definite positions. In this respect, Rieff's ambivalences and indecisions are retarding.

There are nevertheless in his books numerous intimations of the necessary modifications of Freud's ideas. These, if carried beyond a certain point, might have ended in the realization that finally the "appearances" could not be saved, that Freud's system, though it has indeed given us what no other can, is methodologically unsound, and most of the specific theses invalid. But at the end of FMM, we are left with the impression that Freudianism, whatever revisions may be needed, is still basically sound overall. This is not true: as also in the case of Marxism, the problem is how to get fundamentally through and beyond.

Rieff is more alert than Freud to the existence and importance of the hierophanic factor in human nature. This he usually designates as "faith," as a vaguely adumbrated phenomenological reality.[28] In fact, Rieff's own most distinctive theme, just because he takes the subject of faith more seriously than did Freud, is that the Freudian *denial* of faith goes so far in depth and scope as to be something new in the world. Psychoanalysis "is not a therapy of belief but one which instructs how to live without belief." (FMM, 334) This way of living is the "therapeutic." The concept is used by Rieff in several senses, not always clearly discriminated. It appears to mean variously 1) any ideological faith or "commitment"; 2) the psychotherapeutic use of the same; 3) the peculiar Freudian combination of unbelief with "minimum faith" (FMM, 376) — of which last again in due course. In addition, it is not always clear when by this faith in the therapeutic Rieff intends ordinary secular confidence (which may be rationally grounded), and when faith in its specific hierophanic, irrational manifestations.

In any event, it is true enough that never before Freud had the contradiction between natural and cultural reality been so sharply defined as irremediable, without hope of any final redemption. Freud's meliorism was a relatively minor and superficial theme. His predominant belief was that the burden of repression one had "to endure with resignation" (FMM, 358), through rational psychoanalytic self-comprehension and self-mastery. Psychological man, says Rieff, "aware at last that he is chronically ill . . ." has withdrawn into an internal world, "the self, in an attempt to conquer it and assimilate it to the [outer] world *as it is*." (FMM, 392, italics added). Rieff acknowledges that all this has conformist implications, but makes much of psychoanalysis's alleged ability to transform this *subjectively* into "a modest but nonetheless significant liberation . . . the successful patient has learned *to withdraw from the painful*

---

[28] In his apparent unfamiliarity with Rank's post-Freudian works, except for the psychotherapeutic treatises *Will Therapy* and *Truth and Reality* (both New York: Knopf, 1945) Rieff has plenty of company, including all three of the other psychoanalytic notables previously reviewed (although Marcuse, in his own EC, 183, does make a brief, superficial reference to Rank's AA). There are, incidentally, several allusions to Rank in Rieff's TT, none included in the index.

tension of assent and dissent in his relation to society by relating himself more affirmatively to his depths. His newly acquired health entails a self-concern that *takes precedence over social concern* and encourages an attitude of ironic insight . . ." This Rieff sees as "a distinctively intimate" defense "of the private man . . ." (FMM, 364, 362, 361 — italics added) There is "nothing at stake beyond a manipulative sense of well-being . . . the 'end' or 'goal' is to keep going. Americans, as F. Scott Fitzgerald concluded, believe in the green light." (TT, 13, 27)

a) In part because his conception of the hierophanic factor is not sufficiently precise, Rieff also does not see clearly enough its actual role in Freudian theory and therapy. As far as therapy is concerned, Freud accepted the important, even decisive role of faith, although characteristically reinterpreting it as only "transference," thus as the effect of something "real" — the "infantile" attitude toward the father or parents (Rieff, FMM, 223). Elsewhere too Rieff contradicts his own theme that psychoanalysis has no need of belief. He does write, after all, that "Freud mixed belief with theory . . .," that in Freud, faith was "stripped to a minimum faith in reason." (FMM, 336, 376)

That is the real point. *Faith in reason retains its inherently illusory, irrational character.* Thus, *despite* all his critical reservations, Freud retained an irrational element in his system, as an implicit faith that reason, at least as psychoanalysis, and sometimes even as the established rational ideology of modern civilization, would be able to cope with things. This "minimal" irrational faith had "returned as the repressed" in the Eros-death instinct concept, it was previously argued. Rieff, who wants to maintain that Freudianism is *entirely* rational — as indeed was nearly but not quite true — barely mentions the death instinct theory, or the one of civilization as progressive renunciation, in his books.[29] The eventual rejection of the death instinct theory by orthodox analysis did *not*, however, signify any final theoretical mastery of the irrational and uncritical element, but merely the amputation of the whole subject from the psychoanalytic consciousness.

Thus unbelief in Freudianism has only a *relative* significance. In the showdown, for all its critical reservations, Freudianism ended

---

[29] In TT, Rieff recognizes the theological character of the former concept, in relation to Reich's "Deadly Orgone Energy" (185) but does not refer this insight back to Freud.

as a subideology of the Western rational faith. That is also why it actually has no significantly independent "moral" counsel: it is implicitly or explicitly in the service of whatever morality may be successfully created elsewhere (potentially including that of Marxism).

b) In Rieff's version too, the notion that man or culture is a mental "illness" must be discarded for the sake of theoretical clarity. Again, such an illness exists only in the breakdown of the viability of an individual's relation to the community, and there is no such thing as a "sick" *viable* community. One can, of course, criticize such a society for being excessively repressive, or for other reasons, but this itself carries no imputation of "neurosis" or "sickness." In fact, it is such criticism itself, insofar as it is unable to prevail or maintain itself effectively, that carries the potentiality and sometimes the actuality of neurosis.[30]

Before going on to the final critical points, let us consider Rieff's last book, where the social implications of his position are most fully developed. It seems that it might have been more accurately subtitled "The Uselessness of Faith After Freud," for he asserts here that all attempts to combine therapy with faith (or as he also calls it, with "commitment") — other than in the "minimal" Freudian sense — have become impossible in modern cultural conditions, and furthermore, inconsistent with the Freudian ideal or "therapeutic." The "triumph" of this last he sees as already largely actualized, and as on the whole also desirable, since up to now historical experience has demonstrated to man that "every cure must expose him to a new illness." (FMM, 392) Rieff estimates the three most significant efforts to restore faith to modern man to be those of Jung, Reich, and D. H. Lawrence, and in TT he negatively evaluates their systems.[31]

It is Rieff's opinion that the "cultural revolution" is actually

---

[30] It is perfectly true that anyone who really does not believe in a community ideology — not necessarily the established one — is a *potential* madman. In the West, there is less explicit insistence on this point, but the Soviets, in shipping their dissenters to mental hospitals, are trying to "certify" — if not even to *induce* — that which is still (in most cases) only potential. To put it another way, they are trying to abort what is actually or potentially a *creative* reaction to ideological disillusion, trying to characterize, if not actually transform it into "mad powerlessness."

[31] Though their consideration does not fall within the scope of the present essay, an interpretation of Reich will be offered in my forthcoming book. I have in common with Rieff the detection of the spiritual or hierophanic element in Reich's "scientific" work (and in some other phenomena) but my own view of Reich is, I hope, more respectful.

taking place in the *West*. The aforementioned Freudian-reformist among other "remissive" themes are gaining the ascendancy. This is "anti-politics, representing a calm and profoundly reasonable revolt of the private man against all doctrinal traditions urging the salvation of self through identification with the purposes of the community." (TT, 243). This self-salvation is in confluence with the ideal of ever higher material standards of living, of which last Rieff also approves, rejecting as unwarranted any "suspicions" of it. "Everything conceivable can be made universally available . . The reformer asks only for more of everything — more goods, more money, more leisure; in short, more life . . . This may well be the closing time of ascetic culture in the West . . . Who will be stupid enough to lead a counter-revolution?" (TT, 243 ff.) The Communist societies too are inexorably passing on into the age of affluence, and losing their former "therapy of commitment . . . The Soviet Union and the United States are engaged in a common race to appeal to, and increase, the new-rich." (TT, 253) All this is to be welcomed, as part of the general "warfare of the therapeutic against the ascetic." (TT, 63) "It is a terrible error to see the West as conservative and the East as revolutionary. We are the true revolutionaries." (TT, 13)

c) In my own opinion, this is a profoundly misleading evaluation of the contemporary situation, deriving in part from the aforementioned erroneous theoretical positions Rieff shares with Freud, and in part from that implicit continuing faith, however "minimal," in the viability of rationality and Western civilization as they now stand, which Rieff also shares with Freud. But in this version too the faith is inherently illusory, and all of the above Freudian positions continue to bleed within him.

No "true revolution" in human history has been "remissive" in the fundamental (Freudian) sense, and this is why the Communists are in fact the proprietors of "true revolution," and the West is *not*. Since Stalin's death there has been, no doubt, a let-up in revolutionary fanaticism in Russia and East Europe, but there remains a qualitative difference and competitive relationship between the repressive norms of the totalitarian and Western societies. This is among the problems left aside by Rieff, who wants to believe that it is both possible and desirable to treat the totalitarian pressures as non-existent and simply seek one's self-salvation in that relatively hedonistic and rational way he envisages.

This attitude, which to a considerable extent indeed already prevails in the West today, is symptomatic of that "false revolution" which is characteristic of a culture in decadence. In this phenomenon, the particular general-epochal relationship between cultural reality (or repression) and natural reality does not fundamentally change, despite the many more superficial sexual, individualistic and other "remissions" which temporarily flourish at this time. These, and material plenty, do not mean "more life" in the more profound sense.[32] So far in history, such periods have always been eventually followed by a "true revolution" and its higher level of repression. To such a new historical event, we may be sure, most Freudians (along with most other people) will automatically adapt themselves; those who do not may end, "ironic insight" and all, as *patients* in the hospitals of the new order (there are perhaps already some Freudians trapped in the hospitals of Russia).[33] There and elsewhere, despite Rieff's view, the struggle for "psychological man" is not being won, but lost.

In reality, Rieff's "faithless" therapeutic of self-salvation is still too faithful, in assuming that the social problems will take care of themselves, that the human end or goal is merely "to keep going." They won't, and it isn't.

Concluding Political Intimations. Freud's original vision of psychoanalysis as a fully independent ameliorative ideology had faded by the end of the twenties. Reich, for all his follies, was the last great exponent of that vision. We have had since only a number of psychoanalytically inspired efforts, including the last three just reviewed, which have been actually *dependent* (at least in practice) upon the established ideologies of Progress and Revolution. The hour is late, but perhaps not too late for psychoanalysis to recover the independence and potential fruits of its most essential themes. These, I have argued, are that of the past and continuing *inherence*

[32] Rieff reacts negatively to the artistic criticism of the decadence, finding such works as the film *La Dolce Vita* "a bore . . . fraudulent." (TT, 254). But here, as so often, art has discerned that which should not be there according to any theory less than the most profound.

[33] Cf. the special issue "Les Opposants En U.R.S.S." in *Esprit* (Paris, juillet-aout, 1971). Subsequently, the World Psychiatric Association refused to condemn the Soviet use of psychiatry for political repression. This too has been denounced from within the left: cf. "Betrayal by Psychiatry," by I. F. Stone, in *The New York Review of Books,* Feb. 10, 1972.

and *progressive increase* of the contradiction between natural and cultural reality, after these themes have been disentangled from all those misleading specifics which hitherto have held them enthralled and powerless.

Psychoanalysis will perhaps then seek its allies among those who — usually without benefit of psychoanalytic insight, indeed, sometimes without benefit of any theoretical insight at all — are trying to cope with one or another manifestation of the primary contradiction. The new science of ecology, which has come to the fore in recent years, in this respect is revealed as psychoanalysis's natural partner.[34] Clearly ecology itself cannot supply a depth psychological comprehension of man. But an alliance between these two kinds of profundity might prove immensely fruitful, theoretically and practically. In this direction there lies the possibility of that comprehensive and "authentic" alternative to Marxism which the West lacks at present.

---

[34] Over seven years ago in *Kultura,* I had advanced this conception, together with what are now known in ecological thought as the "zero-growth" themes, in my *"Nowa Koncepcja Ideologii Pomarksistowskiej"* (Paris, Dec. 1964 - Jan.-Feb. 1965). An abridged English version appeared in the *Centennial Review* (summer, 1966).

Of late, such ideas have made rapid progress elsewhere; as these lines are written, there is an ideological scandal in England over the ecological appeal of a group of leading scientists, which has been called a second "Communist Manifesto" (the *New York Times,* Jan. 6, 1972, p. 3).

Civilized Man: A Portrait

BY E. M. CIORAN

Our determination to banish the irregular, the unexpected, and the misshapen from the human landscape verges on indecency: that certain tribesmen still choose to devour their surplus elders is doubtless deplorable, but I cannot conclude that such picturesque sybarites must be exterminated; after all, cannibalism is a model *closed economy*, as well as a practice likely to appeal, some day, to an overpopulated planet. However, it is not my intention to bemoan the lot of the man-eaters, though they are mercilessly oppressed, though they live in terror, the great losers of today's world. I grant the fact: their case is not necessarily an excellent one. Moreover they are dying out: a hard-pressed minority, bereft of self-confidence, incapable of pleading their own cause. Quite different is the situation of illiterates, a considerable group attached to their traditions and privileges, tyrannized with a virulence which is quite unjustified. For after all, is it an evil not to know how to read or write? In all honesty I cannot think so. As a matter of fact, I believe that when the last illiterate has vanished from the earth, we can go into mourning for man.

The interest civilized man takes in the so-called backward peoples is highly suspect. Unable to bear himself any longer, he busily unloads on them the excess evils which overwhelm him, urges them to sample his miseries, begs them to confront a destiny he can no longer face alone. Brooding over their good luck in not having "developed," he envies them with all the resentment of a failed desperado. What right have they to hold themselves apart, outside the process of degradation he himself has endured so long and from which he cannot manage to extricate himself? Civilization, his fabrication and his folly, seems a punishment he has inflicted on himself — now it is his turn to inflict it on those who have hitherto escaped. "Come share its calamities, be partners in my hell" — that is the meaning of his solicitude, that is the basis of his indiscretion and his

zeal. Oppressed by its discontents and even more by its "benefits,"
he will not rest until he has imposed them on those fortunately
exempt. This was his behavior even in the days when, not yet
"enlightened" nor tired of himself, he indulged his greed, his thirst
for adventure and infamy. At the height of their power, the Spaniards
must have felt oppressed as much by the demands of their faith as
by the rigors of the Church. The Conquest was their revenge.

If you try to convert someone, it will never be to effect his salvation
but to make him suffer *like yourself*, to be sure he is exposed to the
same ordeals and endures them with the same impatience. You keep
watch, you pray, you agonize — provided he does too, sighing,
groaning, beset by the same tortures that are racking you. Intolerance
is the work of ravaged souls whose faith comes down to a more or less
deliberate torment they would like to see generalized, instituted. The
happiness of others never having been a motive or principle of action,
it is invoked only to appease conscience or to parade noble excuses:
whenever we determine upon an action, the impulse leading to it
and forcing us to complete it is almost always inadmissible. No one
saves anyone; for we save only ourselves, and do so all the better if
we disguise as convictions the misery we want to share, to lavish on
others. However glamorous its appearances, proselytism nonetheless
derives from a suspect generosity, worse in its effects than a patent
aggression. No one is willing to endure alone the discipline he may
even have assented to, nor the yoke he has shouldered. Vindication
reverberates beneath the missionary's bonhomie, the apostle's joy.
We convert not to liberate but to enchain.

Once someone is shackled by a certainty, he envies your vague
opinions, your resistance to dogmas or slogans, your blissful incapacity
to commit yourself. Blushing in secret for belonging to a sect or a
party, ashamed of possessing a truth and of being enslaved by it, it is
not his acknowledged enemies he resents, those who profess another,
but *you*, the Indifferent, guilty of pursuing none. And if, in order to
escape the servitude into which he has fallen, you seek refuge in
vagueness or caprice, he will do everything in his power to forestall
you, to hold you in a thrall analogous and, if possible, identical to
his own. The phenomenon is so universal that it exceeds the realm of
convictions to encompass that of renown. Literature, as we might
expect, will afford a painful example. What writer enjoying a certain
fame does not ultimately suffer from it, enduring the discomfort of

being known or understood, of having a public, however limited it may be? Envious of his friends who loll in the comforts of obscurity, he will do his best to pull them out of it, to trouble their peaceful pride, in order that they too may be subjected to the mortifications and the anxieties of success. To achieve his ends, any tactic will seem fair. Henceforth, their life will become a nightmare: he nags them, urges them to produce, to exhibit themselves, he thwarts their aspiration to a clandestine glory, that supreme dream of the sensitive and the abulic. Write! Publish! he keeps urging furiously, shamelessly. The wretches obey, without suspecting what is in store for them. He alone knows. He lies in wait, parading their timid divagations with violence, with extravagance, with a desperate warmth, and, in order to cast them into the abyss of actuality, finds or invents for them enthusiasts, disciples, surrounding them with a throng of readers, those omnipresent and invisible murderers. The crime committed, he subsides, withdraws, gratified by the spectacle of his protégés at grips with his own shames and torments, the shames and torments well accounted for by the remark of some Russian writer: "You can go mad at the mere thought of being read."

Just as the author stricken and tainted by fame tries to spread it to those not yet infected, so the civilized man, victim of an exacerbated consciousness, strives to communicate its pangs to peoples refractory to his fragmentation. That alienation from himself which harasses and saps him — how could he permit them to reject it, to be unconcerned, to turn away? Utilizing every possible device to corrupt them, to make them resemble him and traverse the same Calvary, he will lure them by his civilization whose wonders, triumphantly dazzling, will keep them from distinguishing its possible benefits from its actual drawbacks. And they will imitate only its harmful aspects, everything that has made it a concerted and systematic scourge. Were they up to now innocuous and carefree? Henceforth they will seek to be strong and dangerous, to the great satisfaction of their benefactor, conscious that as a matter of fact they will be, following his own example, strong and endangered. He will be interested in them,, then, and will "help" them. What a relief to watch them get entangled in the same problems, entombed in the same destiny! All he asked was to make them complicated, obsessed, demoralized. Their neophyte enthusiasm for luxury and machines, for the deceptions of technology, comfort and reassure him: they swell the numbers of the condemned, add unhoped-for fellow-sufferers who can help him in their turn, taking upon themselves a part of the burden that is crushing him or, at least, bearing one that is as heavy as his own. This is what he calls "advancement," a word well chosen to camouflage both his treachery and his wounds.

Vestiges of humanity are still to be found only among the peoples who, outdistanced by history, are in no hurry to catch up. In the rear-guard of nations, untempted by enterprise, they cultivate their outmoded virtues, they make it a duty to "date." Certainly they are *backward*, and would gladly persevere in their stagnation if they had the means to do so. But this they are not allowed. The conspiracy which the "advanced" have mounted against them is too cunningly articulated to be upset. Once the process of degradation is under way, their rage at having been unable to oppose it will lead them, with the brashness of beginners, to accelerate its course, to espouse and exaggerate its horror, according to the law by which a new evil invariably prevails over an old good. And they will try to bring themselves up to the moment, if only to show the others that they too know how to decline, that in questions of downfall they can even surpass their instructors. What use is our surprise, our regret? Do we not see counterfeits everywhere victorious over essence, agitation over repose? Do we not appear to be witnessing the death-agonies of the indestructible? Every step forward, every form of dynamism, entails something satanic: "progress" is the modern equivalent of the Fall, the profane version of damnation. And those who believe in it are its promoters — in other words, all of us, for what are we but an army of the damned, predestined to the foul, to these machines, to these cities of which only an exhaustive catastrophe could rid us? Then, once and for all, our inventions would have occasion to prove their usefulness and to rehabilitate themselves in our eyes.

If "progress" is so great an evil, how is it that we do nothing to free ourselves from it without further delay? But do we really want to? Is it not rather our fate *not* to want to? In our perversity, the "best" is what we want, what we pursue: a deadly pursuit, at every point contrary to our happiness. One does not "perfect" oneself, nor does one "advance" without paying for it. Movement, we know, is a heresy; and that is precisely why it tempts us, why we fling ourselves into it, and why, irremediably depraved, we prefer it to the orthodoxy of quietude. We were created to vegetate, to prosper in inertia, and not to destroy ourselves by speed, and by hygiene, the cause of the proliferation of these bodiless and aseptic beings, of this swarm of specters where everything fidgets and nothing lives. A certain proportion of dirt being indispensable to the organism (physiology and filth are interchangeable terms), the prospect of a world-wide cleanliness inspires a legitimate qualm. We would be better off, verminous and serene, if we had kept company with the animals, wallowing beside them for millennia to come, breathing the smell of the stable rather than that of the laboratories, dying of our diseases and not of our remedies, circling round our Void and gradually sinking into it. For *absence,* which should have been a duty and an obsession, we have substituted the *event;* and every event · encroaches upon us, devours us, since it occurs at the cost of our equilibrium, our duration. The more our future shrivels, the more we let ourselves sink into what is destroying us. Our drug civilization has so intoxicated us that our attachment to it offers all the characteristics of an addiction, a mixture of ecstasy and execration. In its present form, it will finish us off, no doubt about that; as for renouncing it, freeing ourselves from it, we can do no such thing — today less than ever. Who would fly to our aid and deliver us? An Anthisthenes, an Epicurus, a Chrysippus found their own times too complicated — what would they think of ours, and which of them, transplanted to Paris, London, New York, would have character enough to preserve his serenity there? In every respect healthier and better balanced than we, the ancients might have managed without wisdom; they elaborated it nonetheless; what disqualifies us forever is that we have neither concern nor capacity for it. Is it not significant that the first modern man to have denounced, out of his idolatry of nature, the misdeeds of civilization should have been the contrary of a sage? We owe the diagnosis of our disease to a lunatic, more contaminated and scarred than any of us, to an avowed maniac, precursor and model of our own delirium. No less significant is the more recent advent of psychoanalysis, a sadistic therapeutics committed to the irritation rather than the relief of our sufferings, and singularly expert in the art of substituting, for our naive discomforts, an intricate variety.

Every need, by orienting us toward the surface of life in order to disguise its depths, confers value on what has none, on what cannot have value. Civilization, with all its panoply, is based on our propensity to the unreal, to the useless. If we agreed to reduce our needs, to satisfy only necessities, civilization would crumble forthwith. Therefore, in order to endure, it seeks to create ever new needs for us, to multiply them without end, for the generalized practice of ataraxia would involve much graver consequences for civilization than a war of total destruction. By adding to the fatal disadvantages of nature certain gratuitous ones, it obliges us to suffer doubly, it diversifies our torments, reinforces our infirmities. No need to remind us again and again that it has cured us of fear. As a matter of fact, the correlation is obvious between the multiplication of our needs and the growth of our terrors. Our desires, sources of our needs, provoke in us a constant anxiety, much more unbearable than the shudder inspired, in the state of nature, by some fugitive danger. We no longer tremble by fits and starts; we tremble without respite. What have we gained by trading fear for anxiety? And who would hesitate between an instantaneous panic and one that is permanent and diffused? Our vaunted security conceals an uninterrupted agitation which poisons every moment, those of the present as well as those to come, rendering the former null and void, the latter inconceivable. Our desires and our terrors are inextricable — lucky the man who manages to avoid either! Desires — no sooner do we experience one than it engenders another, in a series as lamentable as it is unhealthy. Let us rather apply ourselves to submitting to the world, to considering each impression we receive from it as an impression that has been *imposed,* that does not concern us, that we endure as if it were not our own. "Nothing is mine that happens to me," says the self when it is convinced that it is not of this world, that it is in the wrong universe, and that it has only one choice: between impassivity and imposture.

Committed to appearances, each desire, by forcing us outside our essence, rivets us to a new object and limits our horizon. Yet, to the degree that it grows more intense, it permits us to discover that morbid thirst of which it is the emanation. Have our desires ceased to be "natural," do they derive from our condition as civilized men? Fundamentally impure, they perturb and contaminate our very substance. Everything which adds itself to our profound imperatives is a vice, everything which distorts and confuses us without necessity. Laughter and even our smiles are vices. On the other hand, everything is a virtue that induces us to live against the grain of our civilization, everything which urges us to compromise and sabotage its course. As for happiness, if this word has a meaning, it consists in the aspiration to the minimum and the ineffectual, in the notion of *limitation* hypostatized. Our sole recourse: to renounce not only the fruit of action, but action itself, to make a rule of nonproduction, to leave a good share of our energies and opportunities unrealized. Guilty of trying to exploit ourselves beyond our means or our deserts, failures by *overexertion,* unfit for true fulfillment, reduced by tension to zero and enlarged only by exhaustion, by the dilapidation of our resources, we expend ourselves without taking into account either our possibilities or our limits. Whence our lassitude, aggravated by the very efforts we have made to habituate ourselves to civilization, to all it implies by way of eventual corruption. That nature, too, is corrupted one cannot deny; but such dateless corruption is an immemorial and inevitable evil to which we accommodate ourselves automatically, whereas the corruption of civilization, product of our creations or our caprices, the more overwhelming in that it seems accidental, bears the stamp of a choice or a fantasy, of a premeditated or arbitrary doom; right or wrong, we believe it might not have occurred, that we could have kept it from happening at all. Which only makes it even more odious for us than it is. We are inconsolable, having to endure it and to confront the subtle miseries which proceed from it, when we might have been content with those crude and, after all, endurable ones with which nature has so generously endowed us.

If we were fit to wrest ourselves from our desires, we should thereby wrest ourselves from destiny; superior to beings, to things, and to ourselves, reluctant to amalgamate ourselves further with the world, by the sacrifice of our identity we would accede to freedom, inseparable from a training in anonymity and abdication. "I am *no one,* I have conquered my name!" exclaims the man who, rejecting the degradation of leaving tracks, tries to conform to Epicurus's command: "Hide your life." These ancients are always the ones we return to when it is a matter of the art of living, whose secret two thousand years of supernature and convulsive charity have stolen from us. We return to them, to their poise and their amenity, provided we are free of that frenzy Christianity has inculcated in us; the curiosity they waken corresponds to a lowering of our fever, a retreat toward health. And we also return to them because the interval which separates them from the universe being vaster than the universe itself, they offer us a form of detachment we should seek in vain among the saints.

By making us frenetics, Christianity prepared us in spite of itself to create a civilization of which it is now the victim: did this religion not create too many needs, too many demands? Initially inward, these needs and demands were gradually corrupted and externalized, just as the fervor generating so many suddenly interrupted prayers, unable to subside or to remain unemployed, was to apprentice itself to makeshift gods and to forge symbols befitting their vacuity. Thus we were handed over to counterfeits of infinity, to an absolute without metaphysical dimensions, submerged in speed since we were not plunged into ecstasy. This panting contraption, the answer to our fidgets, and these specters that work it, this procession of automata, this parade of hallucinated zombies — where are they going, what are they seeking? What wind of madness bears them onward? Each time I tend to absolve them, each time I entertain doubts as to the legitimacy of the aversion or terror they inspire in me, I need only think of the country roads, on a Sunday, for the image of that motorized vermin to confirm me in my disgust and my dread. Use of the legs being abolished, the walker, among these paralytics behind the wheel, seems an eccentric or an outlaw; soon he will appear to be a monster. No more contact with the ground: all that sinks into it has become alien and incomprehensible to us. Cut off from every root, unfit, moreover, to mix with dust or mud, we have achieved the feat of breaking not only with the depths of things, but with their very surface. Civilization, at this stage, would seem to be a bargain with the Devil, if man still had a soul to sell.

Was it really to "save time" that these engines were invented? More deprived, more disinherited than the troglodyte, civilized man has not one moment to himself; his very leisure is feverish, oppressive: a convict on leave, succumbing to the ennui of the *dolce far niente* and the nightmare of beaches. When you have frequented regions where idleness is the rule, where everyone is good at it, you find it hard to adjust to a world where no one recognizes or knows how to enjoy it, where no one breathes. Is the being tied to time still human? Is he entitled to call himself *free*, when we know that he has shaken off every servitude but the essential one? At the mercy of the hours he feeds and fattens on his substance, he wastes and weakens himself to assure the prosperity of a parasite or a tyrant. Cunning despite his madness, he supposes that his trials and tribulations would be less if, in the form of a "program," he managed to bestow them on the "underdeveloped" peoples, whom he reproaches for not being "in the swim," by which he means drowning. In order to push them there, he will inoculate them with the toxin of anxiety and release them only when he has observed in them the same symptoms of haste as in himself. In order to realize his dream of a breathless humanity, bewildered and time-bound, he will cross continents, ever in search of new victims on whom to vent the overflow of his feverishness, his darkness. Contemplating him we glimpse the true nature of hell: is that not the place where one is condemned to time for all eternity?

Though we have conquered the universe and taken possession of it, so long as we have not triumphed over time, we remain slaves. Such victory is won by renunciation, a virtue to which our conquests make us particularly unsuited, so that the greater their number, the more obvious our subjection. Civilization instructs us how to take hold of things, whereas it is the art of letting them go that it should teach us, for there is no freedom, no 'real life' without an apprenticeship to dispossession. I seize an object, I consider myself its master; as a matter of fact I am its slave, as I am the slave of the instrument I make, the tool I use. Every new acquisition signifies a new chain, every power factor a cause of impotence. Even our talents contribute to our bondage; the man who raises himself above others is less free than they are: inseparable from his faculties and his ambitions, a prisoner of his gifts, he asserts them at the cost of his salvation. No one liberates himself if he insists upon becoming someone or something. All that we possess or produce, all that is superimposed upon our being or proceeds from it denatures us, smothers us. And our very being — what a mistake, what an injury to have adjoined it to existence, when we might have persevered, intact, in the virtual, the invulnerable! No one recovers from the disease of being born, a deadly wound if ever there was one. Yet it is with the hope of being cured of it some day that we accept life and endure its ordeals. The years pass, the wound remains.

The more complicated and differentiated civilization becomes, the more we curse the links which bind us to it. According to Soloviev, it will come to an end (which the Russian philosopher called the end of all things) in the middle of the "most refined century." This much is certain, civilization was never so threatened or detested as at the moments when it seemed best established; witness the attacks made, at the height of the Age of Reason, against its practices and prowess, against every conquest it prided itself upon. "In cultivated periods, men make it a kind of religion to admire what was admired in primitive times," notes Voltaire, hardly one, let us admit, to understand the rationale of so correct an enthusiasm. It was, in any case, during the period of the salons that the "return to nature" became a rule, just as ataraxia could be conceived only in a time when, weary of divagations and systems, minds preferred the delights of a garden to the controversies of the agora. The appeal to wisdom always issues from a civilization out of patience with itself. Oddly enough, it is difficult for us to imagine the process which brought to satiety that ancient world which, compared with ours, seems to us in all its phases the ideal object of our regrets. Moreover, compared to an unnamable present, any other age seems blessed to us. By straying from our true destination, we shall enter, if we are not there already, the century of the end, that "refined century" *par excellence* (though *complicated* would have been the better adjective) which will necessarily be the one in which, on every level, we shall find ourselves at the antipodes of what we should have been.

The evils implicit in our condition prevail over what is good; even if they were not balanced, our problems would not be solved. We are here to do battle with life and death, not to dodge them as we are urged to do by civilization, an enterprise of dissimulation, glossing over the insoluble. Because it contains no principle of duration within itself, its advantages — so many impasses — help us neither to live nor to die. Were it to succeed, seconded by a useless science, in ridding us of all our afflictions or, to entice us, in bestowing the other planets as a reward, civilization would manage only to increase our mistrust, our exasperation. The more it struts and struggles, the more we envy the ages which possessed the privilege of knowing nothing of the conveniences and the wonders it keeps showering upon us. "With bread and a little water, a man can be as happy as Jupiter," kept repeating that sage who advised us to hide our lives. Is it nonsense to keep quoting him? But to whom are we to turn, whom are we to ask for advice? Our contemporaries, those indiscreet, frustrated creatures who by deifying confession, appetite, and effort are guilty of having turned us into lyrical puppets, as insatiable as we are exhausted? The only excuse for their fury is that it derives

not from a fresh instinct or a sincere impulse but from panic in the
face of a sealed horizon. So many of our philosophers who brood,
flabbergasted, over the future are really no more than the interpreters
of a humanity which, realizing that the moments are escaping,
struggles not to think about it — and thinks about it continually.
Their systems generally offer the image and in a sense the discursive
development of that obsession. Similarly, History could solicit their
attention only at a moment when man has every reason to doubt
that it still belongs to him, that he continues to be its agent. Indeed
everything suggests that since History too escapes him, man is beginning a nonhistorical career, brief, convulsive, which relegates to the
rank of insipidity the disasters with which he was hitherto so smitten.
His degree of Being shrinks with each step forward he takes. We
exist only by retreat, by the distance we keep with regard to things
and to ourselves,. To bestir ourselves is to give ourselves up to the
false, the fictive, to practice an abusive discrimination between the
possible and the funereal. Given our present degree of mobility, we
are no longer in control of our gestures nor of our fate. Over it
presides, no doubt about it, a negative providence whose intentions,
as we approach our goal, become less and less impenetrable, since
they would be revealed without difficulty to the first comer, if he
merely designed to stop and step out of his role in order to contem-
plate, were it only a moment, the spectacle of this winded and tragic
horde to which he belongs.

All things considered, the century of the end will not be the most
refined or even the most complicated, but the most hurried, the
century in which, its Being dissolved in movement, civilization, in a
supreme impulse toward the worst, will fall to pieces in the whirl-
wind it has raised. Now that nothing can keep it from being engulfed,
let us give up practicing our virtues upon it, let us even manage to
discern, in the excesses it delights in, something exalting, something
which invites us to moderate our outrage and reconsider our scorn.
In this fashion, these specters, these automata, these zombies are less
detestable if we reflect upon the unconscious motives, the deeper
reasons for their frenzy: do they not feel that the interval granted
them is shrinking day by day and that the dénouement is taking
form? and is it not to ward off this notion that they immerse themselves in speed? If they were sure of *another* future, they would have
no motive to flee nor to flee themselves, they would slow down their

cadence and take up residence, fearlessly, within an indefinite expectation. But for them there is not even a question of one future or
another, for they quite simply have none whatever; that is the dim,
unformulated certainty, rising out of the very panic of the blood,
which they dread considering, which they seek to forget by hurrying,
by moving ever faster, by refusing to have the slightest moment to
themselves. Yet the Ineluctable which that moment masks is what
they meet by the very speed which, in their minds, should save them
from it. Of so much haste, of so much impatience, our machines are
the consequence and not the cause. It is not they who are driving
civilized man to his doom; rather he has invented them because he
was already on his way there; he sought means, auxiliaries to attain
it faster and more effectively. Not content to run, he preferred to *ride*
to perdition. In this sense, and in this sense alone, we may say that
his machines allow him to "save time." He distributes them, he
imposes them on the backward, the late-comers who may then follow
him, even outstrip him in the race to disaster, in the founding of a
universal and mechanical amok. And it is in order to assure its
advent that he strives so desperately to level off, to standardize the
human landscape, to efface its irregularities and banish its surprises;
what he wants to establish here is not anomalies but *Anomaly*,
monotonous and routine anomaly converted into a rule of conduct,
an imperative. Those who avoid it he accuses of obscurantism or
extravagance, and he will not lay down his weapons until he has
brought them into the straight and narrow path — into his own
errors. Illiterates, first and foremost, are reluctant to fall in with him;
then he will force them to learn to read and write, so that, ensnared
in knowledge, none may escape the common doom a moment longer.
So benighted is civilized man that he does not even conceive the
possibility of choosing another confusion besides his own. Divested
of the respite necessary to the exercise of irony, to which a simple
glimpse of his fate should lead him, he thereby deprives himself of
all recourse against himself. He merely becomes more deadly to
others. Aggressive and pitiable both, there is a certain pathos about
him: we understand why, seeing him inextricably distracted, we feel
a certain embarrassment about denouncing and attacking him, not
to mention the fact that it is always bad taste to abuse an incurable,
however odious he may be. But if we were deterred by bad taste,
could we make the slightest judgment on anything whatever?

Herbert Marcuse:
Toward A Marxist Hermeneutic

BY FREDRIC JAMESON

L'ainée, celle qui ne parle pas! l'ainée, ayant le
   même âge! Mnémosyne qui ne parle jamais!
Elle écoute, elle considère.
Elle ressent (étant le sens intérieur de l'esprit),
Pure, simple, inviolable! elle se souvient.
Elle est le poids spirituel. Elle est le rapport
   exprimé par un chiffre très beau. Elle est
   posée d'une manière qui est ineffable
Sur le pouls même de l'Etre.

—Paul Claudel, *Cinq grandes odes*

Herbert Marcuse's work takes the form of a commentary on Hegel
and Marx, on Freud and Schiller and aims precisely at rethinking
these earlier systems, and their consequences, in the light of the
utterly new socio-economic environment of postindustrial capitalism
which began to emerge at the end of World War II. The new
environment is one in which the possibility of eliminating poverty and
hunger definitively for the first time in history goes hand in hand with
the technical possibility of unparalleled control and total organization
in the realm of social life. It is neither a completely technological nor
a completely political development: for the purely scientific Utopias
of food from the sea and world government ring hollow, while at the
same time the older class analyses no longer seem applicable to a
situation in which there are no longer any visible "agents" of the
historical process, in which the working classes become assimilated
in their values and politics to the bourgeoisie, while the "power elite"
often seems, in comparison to the older types of ruling classes, as
much a pawn as a master of the enormous forces at its disposition.

Abundance and total control: such is the paradoxical context in
which Marcuse prepares to rethink Freud and Marx, to reevaluate
the classical opposition between individual happiness and social

organization with which they were both concerned. Indeed, his cultural reflections may be taken as a kind of ironic reversal of those of Freud in *Civilization and Its Discontents*, which posited an irreversible and unavoidable interdependency between progress in the evolution of society and unhappiness in the repressed psyche of individual man, between individual self-denial and the diversion of psychic energy for collective purposes. For Marcuse, on the other side of the great watershed of postindustrial capitalism, things no longer look quite the same, and it turns out that it is precisely increased sexual freedom, greater material abundance and consumption, freer access to culture, better housing, more widely available educational benefits and increased social, not to speak of automotive mobility, which are the accompaniment to increasing manipulation and the most sophisticated forms of thought-control, increasing abasement of spiritual and intellectual life, a degradation and dehumanization of existence. Thus it is that the happier we are, the more surely we are given over, without even being aware of it, into the power of the socio-economic system itself.

It is this feature of Marcuse's thinking which has lent renewed actuality to the ancient Platonic debate about the nature of the good: for his analysis raises precisely the problem of happiness, and forces us to ask whether people can know what is good for them, whether the social good can be judged in terms of a subjective feeling of contentment, in a world in which brainwashing and manipulation exist as everyday mechanisms. At the same time, his books have been the target of the classic objection to the trustworthiness of the philosopher king or the philosophical elite who are expected to make the ultimate judgments on the good of society in the absence of a reliable voice from the people themselves.

It seems to me, however, that the problem is most usefully posed the other way round, and that the thrust and persuasiveness, the basic unity, of Marcuse's work can best be felt if we reverse these conceptual priorities and take as his basic theme not happiness, but rather the nature of the *negative* itself. Indeed, what his discussion of Freud's instinctual dynamics has in common with his sociological doctrine, as it emerges from Marx, as well as with his tactical positions expressed in *Repressive Tolerance* and *An Essay on Liberation,* is the notion that the consumer's society, the society of abundance, has lost the experience of the negative in all its forms, that it is the negative alone which is ultimately fructifying from a cultural as well as an individual point of view, that a genuinely human existence can only be achieved through the process of negation.[1]

Thus seen, Marcuse's relationship to Adorno and the Frankfurt School becomes that of the practical to the theoretical. For where Adorno drafted the theory of negative or critical thinking (or of a "negative dialectic"), where in his essays on literature or philosophy or music he traced the effects of a weakening of the negative upon the superstructure, Marcuse's works may be thought of as explorations of the psychological and socio-economic infrastructure of the same massive historical transformation.

For we find essentially the same circumstances at work on all the levels of modern life, whether on the political or the psychological, that of action or that of contemplation. The basic development in the light of which all of Freud must be rethought is the collapse of the family, the disappearance of the authoritarian father, that is, of oppression at the level of the cellular family unit. With this liberalization, the Oedipus complex and the superego themselves are greatly weakened, so that the apparently liberated individual is at the same time denied that path toward genuine psychic individuality once offered him by the revolt against the father. The ego of modern man "has shrunk to such a degree that the multiform antagonistic processes between id, ego and superego cannot unfold themselves in their classic form. . . . Their original dynamic becomes static: the interactions between ego, superego, and id congeal into automatic reactions.

---

[1] It will be observed, perhaps, that the recent Freudian tradition has produced a position even more thoroughly critical and negative than Marcuse's, namely that of Philip Rieff, who rejects not only the dominant culture itself — rightly insisting that it is no genuine culture at all, but rather a privative element in which the older values and motives wither and disappear — but also those forces within it which oppose it and make for radical change. Rieff would thus seem to have enlarged the concept of "what is", the vision of that established order systematically to be refused and negated, to include not only the business-men, but also their enemies the students, not only the imperialists, but also the third world revolutionaries who attempt to reduce and subvert their control: his alone would therefore seem to qualify as a genuinely global negation. Yet the "plague on both your houses" only serves in the long run to reinforce those already in power, as the John Stuart Mill of *On Liberty* saw no less clearly than the Marcuse of *Repressive Tolerance*. In Hegelian terms, such total negativity proves to be indistinguishable from an affirmation of the status quo; and indeed, Mr. Rieff is a philosophical descendent of the anti-dialectical tradition of Nietzschean rather than Hegelian negation. But his ritualistic invective against the New Left betrays the contradictions inherent in the claim to diagnostic "objectivity", and shows once again that the deep unconscious forces of ideological motivation possess all the more strongly he who declares himself above them or who dares pronounce them inoperative and non-existent.

Corporealization of the superego is accompanied by corporealization of the ego, manifest in the frozen traits and gestures, produced at the appropriate occasions and hours. Consciousness, increasingly less burdened by autonomy, tends to be reduced to the tasks of regulating the coordination of the individual with the whole."[2] In much the same way, on the social level, the overt burden of societal repression and enforced sublimation is withdrawn: the older restraints, characteristic of a period of "primitive accumulation of psychic capital," have given way to "repressive desublimation," in which the society of sexual abundance encourages overt but specialized sexual activity as a way of reducing conscious unhappiness within the system, of foreclosing conscious dissatisfaction with the system, while at the same time compensating for the necessarily increased impoverishment of the environment from an emotional or libidinal point of view, a phenomenon we have described above.

On the political level, the withdrawal of the right to revolt against the father is reproduced as a disappearance of any effective possibility of negating the system in general. The weakening of the class struggle, the assimilation of the working classes into the bourgeoisie, is the objective condition for this universal neutralization; and with the extension of the media, the very content and gestures of revolt are exhausted, in the sense in which television performers speak of the "exhaustion" of their raw material through overexposure. In this sense, tolerance in our society can be said to be genuinely repressive, in that it offers a means of defusing the most dangerous and subversive ideas: not censorship, but the transformation into a fad, is the most effective way of destroying a potentially threatening movement or revolutionary personality.

Attenuation of the Oedipus complex, disappearance of the class struggle, assimilation of revolt to an entertainment-type value — these are the forms which the disappearance of the negative takes in the abundant society of postindustrial capitalism. Under these conditions, the task of the philosopher is the revival of the very idea of negation which has all but been extinguished under the universal subservience to what is; which, along with the concepts of nature and of freedom, has been repressed and driven underground by the reality principle. This task Marcuse formulates as the revival of the Utopian impulse. For where in the older society (as in Marx's classic

---

[2] Herbert Marcuse, *Eros and Civilization* (New York, 1955), pp. 90, 93-94.

analysis) Utopian thought represented a diversion of revolutionary energy into idle wish-fulfillments and imaginary satisfactions, in our own time the very nature of the Utopian concept has undergone a dialectical reversal. Now it is practical thinking which everywhere represents a capitulation to the system itself, and stands as a testimony to the power of that system to transform even its adversaries into its own mirror image. The Utopian idea, on the contrary, keeps alive the possibility of a world qualitatively distinct from this one and takes the form of a stubborn negation of all that is.

We may therefore say that for Marcuse it is the Utopian concept — "the attempt to draft a theoretical construct of culture beyond the performance principle"[3] — which henceforth, absorbing and replacing the function of art for Schiller and for the Surrealists, embodies the newest version of a hermeneutics of freedom. For Utopian thinking may be said to unite both the philosophical and the artistic impulses, at the same time that it transcends both: it is philosophy become concrete, it is art which takes as its object not products and works but life itself. The impulse of fantasy, in which alone the pleasure principle remains pure and unrepressed, now negates the existing real world, the "realistic" world, and prepares for that world a future. For Adorno had also shown, after his fashion, that the production of works of art is in our time undermined by powerful internal contradictions, and that the resulting art objects are immediately absorbed back into the immensity of what is. Now Marcuse sees in the new sensibility and the new sexual politics an application of the artistic impulse to the creation of a new life-style itself, to a concrete acting out of the Utopian impulse.

But the political limits of the new sensibility are inherent in the very notion of a hermeneutic: its political implications can only be clear when it is itself understood as a dress rehearsal of Utopia, as a foreshadowing of ultimate concrete social liberation. The immediate contingent freedoms of the new life-style must therefore function as *figures* of Freedom in general; and without this characteristic movement in them from the particular to the general which we have described above, from individual experience to that universal liberation for which the experience stands, they remain a matter of individual narcosis, of individual salvation only in the midst of the collective shipwreck. Now indeed we are in a better position to resolve

---

[3] *Eros and Civilization*, p. 144.

the traditional problem of happiness evoked above; for it is only when individual happiness, subjective contentment, is not positive (in the sense of ultimate satiation by the consumer's society), but rather *negative*, as a symbolic refusal of everything which that society has to offer, that happiness can recover its right to be thought of as a measure and an enlargement of human possibilities.

Marcuse's work is not, however, exhausted by this description, for at the same time that it develops the vital urgency of Utopian thinking, it also lays the groundwork for the very possibility of such thinking in the first place. At the same time that it develops a new hermeneutic, it establishes the conditions of existence of hermeneutic activity in general. This theoretical foundation takes the form of a profound and almost Platonic valorization of memory, anamnesis, in human existence. Indeed, it is not too much to say that Mnemosyne occupies something of the same emblematic and mythopoetic position in Marcuse's thinking that the deities of Eros and Thanatos hold in Freud's late metapsychology.

The functional value of memory may be judged by the fact that it is for Freud the very source of conscious thought itself, the latter being "merely a detour from the memory of gratification . . . to the identical cathexis of the same memory, which is to be reached once more by the path of motor experiences."[4] On account of the diagnostic character of so much of Freud's writings, we are tempted to think of memory chiefly in terms of pain, in terms of trauma, whereas in reality memory's primary function is in the service of the pleasure principle. "The memory of gratification," Marcuse tells us, "is at the origin of all thinking, and the impulse to recapture past gratification is the hidden driving power behind the process of thought."[5]

Now the origin of Utopian thinking becomes clear, for it is memory which serves as a fundamental mediator between the inside and the outside, between the psychological and the political, whose separation we described at the beginning of this essay. It is because we have known, at the beginning of life, a plenitude of psychic gratification, because we have known a time before all repression, a time in which, as in Schiller's nature, the elaborate specialization of later, more sophisticated consciousness had not yet taken place, a time that precedes the very separation of the subject from its object, that

---

[4] Quoted, *Eros and Civilization*, p. 29.
[5] *Eros and Civilization*, p. 29.

memory, even the obscured and unconscious memory of that pre-historic paradise in the individual psyche, can fulfill its profound therapeutic, epistemological, and even political role: its "truth value lies in the specific function of memory to preserve promises and potentialities which are betrayed and even outlawed by the mature, civilized individual, but which had once been fulfilled in his dim past and which are never entirely forgotten."[6] The primary energy of revolutionary activity derives from this memory of a prehistoric happiness which the individual can regain only through its external-ization, through its reestablishment for society as a whole. The loss or repression of the very sense of such concepts as freedom and desire takes, therefore, the form of a kind of amnesia or forgetful numbness, which the hermeneutic activity, the stimulation of memory as the negation of the there and now, as the projection of Utopia, has as its function to dispel, restoring to us the original clarity and force of our own most vital drives and wishes.

The theory of memory, indeed, furnishes an unexpected theoretical justification for such a priori social models as those of Schiller, for we may say that such apparently indefensible reasoning is as it were the conceptual disguise which memory takes, and it is as though the eighteenth-century philosophers were able to reinvent the psycho-logical truth of individual existence only by imagining themselves to be in the act of deducing, through reason, the characteristics of the historical state of nature and of original human society in general. Thus, what looked most abstract turns out to be concrete on a wholly different and unexpected level, and Schiller's famous words about the objects of nature win a new and profound resonance: "They *are* what we *were*; they are what we must once more *become*. We were Nature just as they are, and our culture must lead us back to Nature along the path of Reason and Freedom. They are therefore the representation of our lost childhood, that which will eternally remain dearest to us; for that reason, they fill us with a certain sadness. At the same time, they symbolize for us our highest possible completion in the realm of the Ideal, and for that reason they awaken in us the noblest exaltation."[7] But what Schiller took to be the hypothetical origins of humanity itself turns out to have been but reason's way of misinterpreting the prehistory of the individual psyche.

---

[6] *Eros and Civilization,* p. 18.
[7] *Philosophische Schriften,* p. 210.

Marcuse's position with respect to Freud is in many ways markedly similar to that of Schiller in the face of Kantian critical philosophy. The latter had set itself the task of exploring the conceptual preconditions of what already exists, of formulating the necessary conditions of possibility of the experiences of sense perception and of beauty, of free will. Schiller, as we have seen, continues to deduce conditions of possibility: but these are now the preconditions not of an existing but of a hypothetical state. Schiller wishes to determine, in other words, how man's psyche would have had to have been constructed for a genuinely free and harmonious personality to become one day a real possibility; but in the very terms of this argument, there remains the logical alternative that such a being does not and can never exist.

In much the same way, where Freud's instinctual theory is designed to explain the structure of real and existent mental phenomena, of hysteria and the neuroses and psychoses, Marcuse's use of that theory has a more speculative and hypothetical cast: for it aims at describing the conditions of possibility of a society from which aggression will have been eliminated and in which libidinally satisfying work will be conceivable. Thus, for example, the ingenious hypothesis of a "maternal super-id"[8] is designed to show how in a Utopian future the apparently contradictory claims of the pleasure principle and of some form of social morality might be harmonized and justified by the topology of the instincts themselves.

To be sure, there is always the possibility that such a society is precisely impossible: and this final alternative, which the a priori model leaves open for us, is itself the source of Marcuse's realism, of his insistent reminder that salvation is by no means historically inevitable, that we do not even find ourselves in a prerevolutionary, let alone a revolutionary, situation, and that the total system may yet ultimately succeed in effacing the very memory of the negative, and with it of freedom, from the face of the earth.

---

[8] *Eros and Civilization*, p. 209.   This is perhaps the psychic equivalent, for Marcuse, of Marx's and Engels' valorization of the stage of matriarchal communism in social development.

The Therapeutic as Narcissist —

BY MICHAEL BELDOCH

It is only a handful of years since Philip Rieff published *The Triumph of the Therapeutic,* but evidently decay proceeds at an exponential rate. Completed in the mid-sixties, Rieff's complex socio-logical surgery exposed a patient who, in the last words of his book, was approaching "a human condition about which there will be nothing further to say in terms of the old style of despair and hope." Now, the operative sutures hardly in place, there is no longer any doubt about the accuracy of what Rieff, his patient laid bare to the bone, revealed; metastasizing moral cancer in the Western world has left us all terminally ill.

But accuracy of description, while essential to any diagnostic procedure, is not sufficient. And Rieff, evidently fearing to be too easily understood, uses his elegant language in such an oblique manner that we are left with a portrait which at one and the same time we can recognize as correct, and also terribly confusing. Just who the "therapeutic" really is, and how he came to be, is more than difficult to understand.

That we are left with the confusion is in part a function of Rieff's heavy reliance on irony, and his insistence on using words in such an idiosyncratic manner that their meaning sometimes comes around a full 180 degrees from their starting point. Thus, the "triumph" of the therapeutic is not a triumph at all, and the "therapeutic" — or "psychological man," as Rieff also calls him — turns out to be badly in need of help.

From the sociological point of view, the emergence of this character type is quite obviously of more than passing interest. As Wright and Mejia[1] put it, "If the dominant character type of the twentieth century is really what Rieff calls 'psychological man,' the consequences for

---

[1] G. Wright and A. Mejia, Jr. (eds.), *An Age of Controversy: Discussion Problems in Twentieth-Century European History* (New York, 1963), pp. 416-417.

western society are quite incalculable." And reading Rieff's *The Triumph of the Therapeutic,* which he describes as a "calculus of the incalculable," is not a happy experience, for we already know that the man Rieff describes, who can manufacture need faster than he can gratify it, is in skyrocketing ascendancy; what we *don't* know (and here the psychoanalytic point of view may be helpful), is why this is so, or, indeed, what (if anything) we could or should do about it.

Rieff's thesis, once extricated from his complicated use of language, is that it is the triumph of the therapeutic that he has become "autonomous from the compulsions of culture." The compulsions of culture he describes as those that "bind and loose men in the conduct of their affairs with reasons which sink so deep into the self that they become commonly and implicitly understood." In other words, culture, as Rieff reads it, can be seen as the social equivalent of what the psychoanalyst sees as the personal super-ego, i.e., as that which permits and prohibits, that which approves and disapproves, and that which tells the self what properly belongs to it — and what belongs to others, i.e., to the community.

But in fact Rieff's psychological man, far from being autonomous, is a man who has replaced a potentially flexible relationship to the authority of the community with an addict's obligation to fulfill the demands of his own desires. From a psychoanalytic point of view such a man is anything *but* autonomous; he is rather the captive and the victim of his own narcissism.

When Rieff describes the death of a culture as beginning "when its normative institutions fail to communicate ideals in ways that remain inwardly compelling," he identifies an individual as well as a cultural problem. When the individual's personal normative institution, i.e., his super-ego (and especially that aspect of his super-ego called the ego ideal) has failed to communicate ideals in a way that has remained inwardly compelling, a disordered personality is the inevitable result.

It is a particular kind of disorder that results when the essential communications between a culture and its members break down, a disorder that Rieff has the poet Yeats[2] describe for him in these familiar lines:

> Things fall apart; the centre cannot hold;

---

[2] William Butler Yeats, *Collected Poems* (New York: Macmillan Co., 1924).

> Mere anarchy is loosed upon the world,
> The blood-dimmed tide is loosed, and everywhere
> The ceremony of innocence is drowned;
> The best lack all conviction, while the worst
> Are full of passionate intensity.

But the brooding portrait Yeats caught a half-century ago, emerging only now in sharp relief like a photographic enlargement taking on stark blacks and whites under chemical developer, is a group portrait, and inevitably one in which we can see individual faces only poorly. So too with Rieff's emergent type; it, too, is a group portrait, a sociologist's study, meant to provide a useful *Gestalt,* but inevitably somewhat at the loss of the subtle shading that the perspective of the psychoanalytic clinician permits. Both perspectives are useful; but each reveals something the other misses, and what Rieff has missed is that his "therapeutic" is a pathological narcissist.

The portrait the psychoanalyst assembles is a composite, a montage, a series of daily accumulated superimpositions, built up the one on the other until a viable and palpable dimensionality results. In the case of someone suffering from a narcissistic character disorder for example, i.e., someone whose pursuit of his self-interest has cost him his ability to pursue the needs of others, it may be the portrait of a superficially "normal" — i.e., a socially "competent" person, but one for whom mere competence is insufficient. It may be in fact the very signs of success that first reveal the extent of the pathology. In such an instance the sociological point of view may not reveal the subtle complexity of the disorder.

Those who today seek out the special skills of the psychoanalyst are likely as not to be suffering from pervasive feelings of emptiness and a deep disturbance of self-esteem, both of which are painful representations of defects in their sense of inner cohesion and continuity. Despite the possibility of an outer facility, and ample evidence of the signs of success, there may be a marked inner emptiness, as if each victory over reality falls through a false bottom in the self and must be compulsively repeated. This "insufficient consolidation of the self" has been well described by the analyst Heinz Kohut in *The Analysis of the Self,*[3] and identifies in individual terms what Rieff understands to be the problem of an Age.

---

[3] H. Kohut, *The Analysis of the Self, a Systematic Approach to the Psychoanalytic Treatment of Narcissistic Personality Disorders* (New York: International Universities Press, 1971).

Of course it is more than curious that Rieff chooses such an ironic title for his work. His "triumph" of the therapeutic represents what is in reality a serious if now ubiquitous flaw in normal development; it is a complex, subtle and pervasive flaw which requires the most complex, subtle and consummate therapeutic skill to overcome. What Rieff describes as his emergent type in fact describes those who suffer from an addictive and unrelenting narcissism. As the archetypal pathology of our age, it is sociologically and historically relevant, and informs us about the age in which it has become dominant. But it is badly misleading to attach the notions of "triumph" and of the "therapeutic," however ironically conceived, to what can in fact be nothing but severe psychopathology.

Rieff himself offers no detailed historical perspective for the evolution of his character type, and he certainly does not celebrate the arrival of the therapeutic. But the insistent (if incorrect) implication of his work is that the responsibility for the emergence of psychological man falls in part to the developments in psychological science itself, and especially to the brilliant reorganization of thinking about the nature of man that is psychoanalysis. According to Rieff it is as if it has been "the proper study of mankind" itself that has left us all in jeopardy.

Perhaps Rieff has suggested such a reading of recent history because psychoanalysis has focused interest and attention on the "inner" man in a manner never before attempted. Before Freud, feelings had been largely the province of the poets. But since the Enlightenment, and especially (until recently) in this century, man has begun to believe that reason (science) might be a sufficient tool with which to redress the unfair advantage held in human life by the passions. With the discovery of psychoanalysis, a first attempt at a "science of the feelings" was born. But despite Freud's warning that "it is not easy to deal scientifically with feelings,"[4] expectations were aroused that now, finally, man would no longer have to remain the pawn of his unknown inner self. As Rieff sees it, man turned away from his essential allegiance and commitment to the authority of the community, and in its place moved towards the pursuit of his own inner well-being, supported on this internal crusade by the honest but dangerous example set by Freud and his school.

[4] Freud, *Civilization and its Discontents*, The Complete Psychological Works of Sigmund Freud, Vol. XXI (London, Hogarth Press, 1961).

The psychoanalyst, of course, cannot claim any special objectivity when it comes to opinions about the general use or misuse of psychoanalysis in the world at large.[5] Although he can lend his special understanding to historical issues, as he increasingly does in his role as psychohistorian, he no more has the right to claim objectivity in this regard than has anyone else. However, the psychoanalyst *can* attempt to understand sociologist Rieff's "psychological man" in psychoanalytic terms, and this means to understand him not as someone who has made good social use of his deepened knowledge of himself, but as someone suffering from a narcissistic commitment to himself which has come at the cost of his ability to commit himself to others i.e., at the cost of his ability to love.

To attempt this understanding it will be necessary to deal at least briefly in what follows with the meaning of narcissism, with the problem of the transformation of early narcissism and its relation to the process of idealization, and to the problem of "values" in general. Then, as an extended illustration of these definitions and processes, it may be helpful to look at the way in which these issues become dominant and focused (as under a psychic microscope) in the transference that occurs in the psychoanalysis of people who suffer from an unusually heavy burden of narcissism.

* * * * *

What hysteria and the obsessive neuroses were to Freud and his early colleagues in the psychoanalytic exploration of man at the beginning of this century, the narcissistic disorders are to the workaday analyst in these last few decades before the next millenium. Today's patients by and large do not suffer from hysterical paralyses of the legs or hand-washing compulsions; instead it is their very psychic selves that have gone numb or that they must scrub and rescrub in an exhausting and unending effort to come clean.

Narcissism is still another of those many words which are shared by the common language of every day and the scientific language of psychoanalysis. The common reading has it that the narcissist is in love with himself, as in the famous myth which saw Narcissus wasting away from self-love. Psychoanalytically, the meaning is similar, except that it is understood that normal development proceeds from the stage of pure narcissism in infancy to a stage of emotional

---

[5] I will return later in this essay to the general problem of the attempt to use psychoanalysis in pursuit of a *Weltanschaaung*.

maturity in adulthood in which much of the original narcissism (not all) has been outgrown in favor of the ability to love others.

The need for narcissistic gratification forms part of the core of every man; without it we would not get out of bed in the morning. It is in some very real sense true that there is a narcissistic element in every human act, although quite clearly there is a difference between that which is done *only* for the self and that which it pleases the self to do for others.

We all began as narcissists; we were that before we were anything else. But in the community of two in which we received our first sustenance we began to learn that all is not I. We learned that first and foremost dichotomy of our lives when we learned that there is a world beyond our fingertips, when we learned that there is an Other.

All the rest of our lives there will be the Self and the Other. It is inevitable that we learn this, for only in death and autism are there exceptions. For the autistic as well as for the dead, there is no "other." As for the rest of us, once we have begun to learn this first painful lesson of separation, we see the proof of it everywhere about us. We will even learn to split off pieces of ourselves, to become foreign bodies still within the self, more or less permanent and troublesome aliens ready to stand as scapegoats in moments of crucial embarrassment: "I don't know what got into me," we say, or, "I'm just not myself today." We would like to think that a "foreign element" had just then invaded the self, but clearly it was there all along, a denied part of the very same self, treated now as an "other."

In our early years this idea of "other" is over-learned; little children (as well as older primitives, and psychotics and dreamers of every age), like to think that the tree droops because it is "tired," or that the thunder pounds because the clouds are "angry." Only later do we begin to understand that there is also a third condition of being in the world — an "it" — which is neither I nor Thou.

Still later the world takes on even richer dimension, as pure ideas and concepts occupy our imagination. The flowering of man as truly unique in the world (B. F. Skinner notwithstanding) is nowhere more evident than here in the capacity for abstract thought. A double-edged virtue to be sure, responsible for neurosis as well as for art, but a singular achievement in the phylogenetic scheme of things. But all of these others, the Thou, the It, and the Idea can each (and to some extent *must* each) carry the burden of the shadow of the self cast upon it. Our ideas, no less than our lovers and our possessions, are pieces of ourselves. The most exquisitely rewarding and excruciatingly painful example of this inevitable fact of human life is in our relations with our own children. These are not merely "other"people to us, or even those who act simply as a genetic or legal bridge between our past and our future. These pieces of ourselves are in some very real sense our most exposed flesh; a hurt to them can be unbearable far beyond our own corporeal pain; joy in who they are can lift us far beyond reason.

And, of course, from the other side of this Janus-faced coin, the view is equally over-invested. The child's conception of the parents, especially once that conception is internalized and consciously forgotten, will later crucially affect the nature of his relations with all subsequent authorities. It becomes clear that it is in the crucible of the family that our narcissism is first dislodged from its omnipotent position, and it is in our relations with our future families — writ large as community, creed or nation — that the vissicitudes of that narcissism will be re-experienced.

How interesting then to note that the family is just now under considerable attack. The work of Laing and Cooper in England, the women's liberation and gay liberation movements in this country and elsewhere, the massive attempts to reverse the population explosion, the increasing interest in imitations of unisexuality, all of these are part of a still larger trend that seeks to make more optional the previously obligatory sanctity of the nuclear family.

It is as if the intensities of the nuclear family have turned out to be too painful to bear. One mother, one father, one set of siblings, the whole of a child's emotional life dependent on too few and, as it has turned out, too unreliable "others" for safe keeping.[6] What was once the essential and sufficient modality for learning about life in civilization — the family — has in some respects become an inefficient teacher. Perhaps this has occurred in part because the teachers (the

---

[6] It is interesting that in the treatment of some very regressed psychotics it has recently been thought to attempt to "split up" the intensities of transference (and countertransference) between two therapists. The rationale here is that the patient cannot tolerate all that he feels being focused on one person and that the strong reactions such patients may evoke when all of their feelings are focused on one doctor may be too much for the doctor, too. Similar reasoning may underlie the resurgence of interest in a wide variety of group therapies in this country; the emotional impact of the one-to-one is diluted by being spread around among the group members.

parents) are no longer genuinely available for the constancy and intensity of effort required, and have themselves set out for career or club for a replenishment of their own narcissistic supplies, leaving the young to learn the painful lessons of reality from essentially disinterested and/or hired hands.[7]

Even the resurgence of interest in the extended family, defined here as commune or kibbutz, can be seen as part of the larger disenchantment with the nuclear family itself. It is as if the psychologically internalized fibres of the nuclear family have come apart, leaving its children foreswearing allegiance to family, party and nation. The children of today's nuclear families are keeping their narcissism to themselves, and despite the fervor with which they make and sing of love, they trust no one and no thing too much. In this regard they show some of the characteristics of Rieff's emergent type, Psychological Man, whom Rieff describes as "living his life with a minimum of pretense to anything more grand than sweetening the time."

* * * * *

Analysts are just now (in the last dozen years or so) beginning to set down the clinical considerations that follow from the theoretical understanding of the narcissistic personality disorders. As so regularly happens in psychoanalysis, the original and most fruitful seeds for this understanding were sown long ago by Freud himself, in this case in his papers On Narcissism[8] (1914) and in Group Psychology and the Analysis of the Ego,[9] in which he wrote that the ego ideal "is the heir of the original narcissism."

The ego ideal is a concept at once easier and more difficult to understand than that of the super-ego, of which it is thought by some analysts to be a significant part. In its simplest form the ego ideal has to do with values, and is that image of the self to which we aspire, and against which we measure ourselves. When life is lived

---

[7] I mean to include here, of course, the ubiquitous television, as well as the baby-sitter and the mother's "helper." For a penetrating view of the consequences, since the advent of mass industrialized society, of the abdication of the father's protective authority, and the concomitant release of instinctual drive and the breakdown of cultural norms, see Alexander Mitscherlich's Society Without the Father.

[8] S. Freud, On Narcissism: An Introduction (1914). Standard edition, Vol. XIV (London: Hogarth Press, 1957), pp. 73-102.

[9] S. Freud, Group Psychology and the Analysis of the Ego (1921). Standard edition, Vol. XVIII (London: Hogarth Press, 1955), pp. 69-143.

in harmony with that ideal, John Murray[10] points out, the present and the future hold much of promise. But when that ideal is so narcissistically based that it remains infantile and socially unrealistic, no satisfaction can follow.

The ego ideal originates in (but is not limited to) the earliest identification, i.e., in an identification with our parents (and perhaps still in this last age before cloning, primarily in an identification with the mother). In that sense, the ego ideal precedes the development of the full super-ego, which occurs only later, in the crucible of a rivalrous competition with one parent for the exclusive possession of the other. The super-ego, as conscience, finally demands nothing less than the renunciation of this precious infantile wish, a demand which, when denied, supports an urgent and life-long struggle with guilt.

But guilt already presupposes a "self" which can feel it; it implies a more or less cohesive personality organization which lends itself to the kind of symptomatic psychopathology with which Freud was more familiar than is the typical psychoanalyst in these difficult times. Hysterical symptoms, obsessions, phobias, these are the badges of those walking wounded who have already won significant developmental battles. The narcissistic personality disorders, on the other hand, while not in any case short of obvious and overt symptomatology, have wounds indicative of still earlier battles, fought and lost.

The difficulty in adequately understanding the ego ideal, which seems so much a matter of common-sense, belongs in considerable part to the fact that it begins to develop as one of the first transformations of our narcissism. But the ego ideal, a representation of early and important figures in our lives, is not necessarily an identification with who those people actually *are*. Its first dimensions are formed before good cognitive capacities have developed, and are as much based on phantasy (later on idealized reconstructions), as they are on the reality that a "proper" (i.e., developmentally more mature) perspective would permit.

But one cannot simply say that the ego ideal demands that one should be who the parents in fact *are*. Who one would be, and the values and ideals one aspires to, originally have more to do with who

[10] J. M. Murray, "Narcissism and the Ego Ideal," *Journal of the American Psychoanalytic Association*, XII (1964), pp. 477-511.

one *experienced* the parents as being, and more, as who one would have *had* them be. Here is the meaning of Hartmann and Lowenstein's [11] "the ego ideal can be considered a rescue operation for narcissism," or, as Murray[12] put it, "it is born of an effort to restore the lost Shangri-La of the relations with the all giving primary mother."

What we would accomplish with our idealizations (it is at the heart of every dream) is to restore in outer form that original and archaic sense of our inner selves which preceded even the awareness of the all giving mother, and which once knew no limits and accepted no disappointments; what we would accomplish is in fact to make viable an infinity of the self. Of course, reality will not allow it — reality does not even owe us happiness, let alone infinity. The painful introduction to reality, experienced in the erratic flow of things right and not right, of pleasure and of pain, of processes beyond our control, is followed by the attribution of all this would-be power to the significant Other. It is then this "other" that becomes omniscient and omnipotent; this "other" — this idealized self, we think — can do what the self *would* have done but could not.

Here is the genesis of the slow-dying dream of immortality and eternity, of Utopia and of God. The archaic core of the ego ideal, as against the more mature and reality-based ego ideal, which, unless frozen, continues to evolve throughout growth and development, is nothing but the subtle transformation of the original narcissism; it is the least concession to reality the early infantile omnipotent self can make and still have reality hold sway.

It is interesting to note that in later moments of stress, when reality is too harsh, a demand is made upon the psychic organization that can strain it to the point of producing "symptoms." A symptom — i.e., a psychological symptom — is in fact a compromise solution between a wish and a fear — a compromise between what our grandiose and infantile self would wish (really demand) that we do, and an over-elaborated fear that all the (potentially nay-saying) power resides outside of ourselves. On the other hand, we call those people healthy who can "deal" with reality — i.e., those who can wind their way

[11] H. Hartmann and R. M. Lowenstein, *Notes on the Superego: The Psychoanalytic Study of the Child*, XVII (New York: International Universities Press, 1962), pp. 42-81.
[12] Murray, *op. cit.*

between the powerful wishes of the self and the powerful demands of reality without denying the truth of either.

Even those who produce symptoms (and it does no rude injustice to the truth to include us all) retain a balance of power in the psychic world by that creative act. To produce a "normal" symptom is to give both reality and the self their due.[13] It is when the symptoms no longer "work," when they cost more than they purchase, that we begin to call the result a sickness. It is the special sickness of those with narcissistic disorders (that Rieff has mistakenly called a triumph) that they cannot settle for mere symptoms. The symptomatic impotence of the ordinary neurotic, for example, may mean that what he would have his penis do is more than his conscience feels it *ought* to do; he is then free to suffer the failed erection, and in that failure keep alive the hidden wish that he *could* have had more than he otherwise feels he is entitled to.

The man with a narcissistic character disorder, on the other hand, may maintain an erection almost as good as gold. His penis is not merely the agent of his sexual desire; it must stand for more than sexuality — perhaps for the very existence of the self. It is an attempt to keep alive an illusion that should long ago have been surrendered, an illusion of permanence, of wholeness, of the immortality of the self. It is as if in keeping his penis erect (feeling more pride than sexuality) he can keep his soul afloat. Such a man has yet to accept the transient nature of all things. He has become an exquisite imposter of a real man, but he does not feel himself real enough to risk losing himself in a genuine intimacy with another.

The narcissist has not yet made that compromise with reality that would let him actively pursue those goals that *can* be reached. The idealized, perfect self (or those utopian goals which stand for that perfect self) is the minimum he can accept; compromise is defeat, and reality too painful a prospect. He must struggle to make his personal ideal a reality in order to rescue his narcissism from humiliating defeat.

In earlier times, such a man could assign to others, e.g., to Gods, those personal goals of immortality that he could not himself make come true. But the Gods having failed him, he now turns to science

---

[13] I use the word "symptom" here in a somewhat enlarged way to include *all* that is a compromise between the instinctual needs of the organism and the form in which civilization allows its appearance. I am aware that this usage stretches the definition too far and at the cost of its original shape.

to fulfill those archaic personal wishes that things be better than they ever turn out to be. B. F. Skinner's insistent, dogmatic utopia is a clear example: "It is Science or nothing" according to Skinner.[14] But to mis-use science in this fashion, i.e., to over-invest in it the narcissistic residue of the infantile self, is in fact to stand the whole notion of science on its head.

The language of science, as distinct from the language of faith, is not revelatory but analytic. Science largely confines itself to the observable and the replicable, while it is left to the language of faith to find its *raison d'être* in addressing itself to that which is otherwise not observable. However, this has not prevented man from using science in the service of his considerable Need-to-Believe. This regular fact of psychic life helps to explain in part what has happened to the complex relationship between psychoanalysis and our cultural life; it has been inexorably swept up in the need to find a reason for existence, and a suitably modern *Weltanschauung*.

Despite the clarity with which Freud warned against the attempt to use analysis in this way, many people, analysts among them, have turned to psychoanalytic science for relief from existential distress. Of course at the moment that they do so they become more active moralists than Freud ever intended, replacing part of their commitment to pursue the knowledge of "what is," with exhortations in the service of what they feel "ought to be."

Psychoanalysis cannot tell what "ought to be." It can, however, provide a fairly good understanding of the unconscious and genetic sources of any given "ought," some knowledge of the consequences for the self of the achievement of (or of the failure to achieve) that "ought," and even something more general about man's need to posit "oughts" in the first place, as well as something about the nature of the disturbances he may suffer if he fails to achieve this uniquely human stage of development.[15] About the burden these "oughts" may cause men to suffer, each man already knows quite well for himself, although he may turn to a personal psychoanalysis in order to better understand their origins in himself and the ways in which he can make them a more tenable and integrated part of his life.

That man has a need to believe — to some extent independent of *what* he believes in — seems hardly in need of proof. But it is one of

[14] B. F. Skinner, *Beyond Freedom and Dignity* (New York: Knopf, 1971).
[15] See, for example, Heinz Hartmann's *Psychoanalysis and Moral Values* (New York: International Universities Press, 1960).

the most interesting paradoxes that identify the human condition that the *relativity* of values implicit in the knowledge that man needs to believe in "something," must in each individual instance be transcended by the *absolutist* quality of each individual's belief system. Although, in an attempt to resolve (really avoid) the heart of this paradox, we may *say* that we can believe in something "as if" it were true, these are in fact mutually contradictory states of mind. At the moment that we *believe* in something it *is* true; the moment that we add *as if*, we cease to believe and become rationalist "hedgers" and religious imposters.

Although this is clearly a problem about which philosophy and epistemology may have more to say than psychoanalysis, the psychoanalyst has a unique opportunity and vantage point from which to observe and study this singularly human paradox. The psychoanalytic situation demands from the patient (among other things) that which is technically impossible. The patient is asked to engage in a process which, if successful, will inevitably lead to the analyst's being perceived *as* the mother (father, brother, lover, sadist, rescuer, etc.). It is in this transference to the analyst, that is, in the resurrection of pre-existing feeling states originally directed towards others and now experienced in relation to the analyst as a *reality in the present,* that the infantile past is recreated in a setting that permits the adult ego, with its capacity for reality testing, delay of gratification and balanced reason to be brought to bear on it.[16]

At the same time that this transference takes place, or (and this is a crucial qualifier that makes analysis possible), at *almost* the same time, the patient is expected to know that his perception of his analyst is incorrect, that it is only "as if" his analyst were his mother, father, etc. It does not seem to be possible for there to exist at the very *same* moment the full transference distortion of the analyst, *and* the therapeutic (or working) alliance (which correctly perceives the analyst as who he is — a cooperative and concerned partner in a deeply well-meant research into the psychic origins of the patient's present life). In actual analytic practice there are vacillations from moment to moment and from session to session of transference and

---

[16] The essential manner in which the psychoanalytic situation permits cures by insight alone is based on the fact thtat what may have been an impossible situation for the child, resulting in neurotic symptom formation, may be a bearable one for the adult unencumbered by his past. It is as if an opportunity were presented to reexperience the unfair dilemmas of childhood with the strengths of the adult.

working alliance; at one moment the analyst *is* the punitive and/or idealized parent (or so the patient would swear) — the next moment a balance is restored and the patient is in a position to be able to understand the reasons *why* the analyst was just then so (mis)perceived. Out of this matrix of reality and its distortion something crucially useful may be learned.

But clearly, for transference to exist, it must be a distortion (at the least an exaggeration) of reality. If the analyst is *in fact* punitive (or seductive, or delighted, or bored) and the patient perceives this, there will be (in that instance) nothing to learn other than that the patient can adequately perceive reality and what his characteristic response to that particular reality will be. It is primarily when the patient has feelings toward the analyst that the analyst, by his behavior, did *not* earn, that there is something special to learn, i.e., to analyze.

As can be seen, the situation for the patient in analysis (although obviously not one solely confined to analysis) is one which touches on the paradoxical heart of the matter of knowledge and belief. If the patient has too much the feeling that the analyst is only an "as if" representation of his past, his analysis may well result in rather dry, sterile intellectual formulations about himself; the analysis will have no emotional reality.

On the other hand, if there is a serious limitation in the ability of the analysand to take some psychic distance from the manifestations of his transference reactions, that is, if he cannot recognize at *some* point that the analyst is *not* who he has been perceived as being, the analysis will also fail. Intense manifestations of transference may occur in any analysis, sometimes of such dramatic nature that they may be called "psychotic" transference reactions. But if there is to be a viable analysis, then these "intensities of belief" not supported by present realities must be understood for what they are, as shadows of the patient's past now thrown across his present path; seen as such they set the stage for inevitable benefit to the patient's emotionally valid (as against simply intellectual) self-knowledge.

What a psychoanalysis ideally does, then, is to set in motion a process which recreates in the emotional present aspects of those early and formative times in a person's life when his very first systems of knowledge, belief and values were laid down. A classical psychoanalysis offers a unique opportunity (to those who can avail themselves of it) to walk an almost invisibly fine tight-rope between knowledge and belief; it requires, of course, an exquisite sense of balance. But, when successful, it permits one to see the early sources of one's belief systems, the role that the nature of belief plays in one's life, and how one has come to respond to instances of belief confirmed or denied. One learns not only *what* one believes in, but the extent to which one will go in an attempt to get life to "prove" the validity of one's beliefs.[17]

* * * * *

To return now to the notion of the ego-ideal as one of the first transformations of narcissism, we can see that what happens is that we invest in that first significant other in our lives (it will most regularly be the mother) not only all that she in fact is, but also all that we would *wish* her to be. Knowledge (that is, reality) tells us only who she *is*; our need to believe — that is, our need to *transcend* reality — makes her over into whatever we would have had her be. Since who we would at first have had her be is all that we would have the self be (i.e., omnipotent and omniscient), an immediate tension is set up between aspects of the self that govern the relations between what we discover the world to be (our sense of reality) and the way we would rather insist that it be (our beliefs).

Although there is probably no such thing as an "easy" analysis, it can easily be seen that the psychoanalysis of persons with narcissistic personality disorders is especially difficult and trying (for both parties). This is because such an analysis, in order to be successful, must partially recreate those very conditions when such relations between belief and reality were *first* experienced.

In the transference in any analysis, the analyst temporarily becomes the repository of all that is good as well as all that is evil in the patient's world. But in the analysis of patients with narcissistic personality disorders, he must carry the burden of the patient's ambivalent and insistent demand that the analyst actually *be* the patient's

---

[17] Life is ordinarily malleable enough for a man to be able to find in it that which will confirm his most precious notions about himself. If, for example, he needs to see himself as a victim, he will surely be able to arrange it so that life does him one bad turn after another. It is even possible that he will manage to find his way to analysts who cannot help him uncover the masochist core of his need to suffer, thus leaving repeated, but uncomprehended and essentially intact, an early determined pattern, and in the process adding one more instance of "proof" of his outrageous fortune.

self, even as the patient once placed all that ambivalent power in the person of the mother.

In such analyses the analyst is idealized in the deepest sense of that term. He *becomes* the ideal, *the* respository of all that by the nature of reality he cannot be. Obviously, despite the patient's desire, the analyst can only be real.[18] Yet the patient insists that he be more. When the patient learns that his demands cannot be met, his narcissistic rage can be of extraordinary proportions. If the analyst will not be all that is good (and immortally good) then he is nothing at all. For a while in such an analysis, the analyst may be experienced as worthless, psychically impotent, dead. The patient can feel that he has once more been deceived by life, and that reality is inadequate to his immortal purpose. It is a crucial time, and requires artful understanding and the judicious balancing of "doses" of reality and of transference for the patient to be able to discover that he *can* let the analyst be who he is, someone who is neither everything nor nothing, just as in the reality of the patient's earliest life the important figures were also only mortal.

* * * * *

It seems we live in a real world, not an ideal one. This simple fact, daily taught and retaught, is regularly forgotten (in psychoanalytic terms, denied). But the values and ideals to which we aspire must be better than those the world of reality can make come true. It is the nature of values and ideals that they represent the unobtainable; in that regard they have more to do with belief than with simple reality. It is a just measure of our mental health that we can accept this paradoxical state of affairs without a loss of self-esteem; it means that we can perceive values and ideals as autonomous, and not just as transformations of our narcissism. In that event we can continue to work toward ideals without falling into easy depression when they cannot be achieved.

Rieff's psychological man, like those with narcissistic character disorders, cannot accept the notion of working toward absolute values that can never be reached. He can neither surrender his values (the psychological solution of the psychopath, whose "wisdom" it is that

---

[18] In this regard the analyst differs crucially from the religious or faith-healer, who cures by agreeing to be *in fact* the magical and all powerful figure the patient demands that he be. I will not here go into the interesting question as to just how ubiquitous such religious (i.e., transference) "cures" are in what originally set out to be cures by understanding—i.e., by insight—alone.

there is no meaning worth pursuing), nor surrender reality (the solution of the psychotic, who remakes reality in his own archaic image).

The narcissistic character would solve his dilemma by establishing as the only valid activity the pursuit of his self interest. As Rieff describes him, "psychological man takes on the attitude of a scientist, with himself alone as the ultimate object of his science." He is a man alone: "Psychological man can continue to work efficiently without permitting his feelings to be entrapped." "The therapeutic, even in erotic action, can do without attachment . . . the therapeutic treats love instrumentally."

Rieff understands Freud on a very sophisticated level, and he understands that what the "therapeutic" has done is to mis-read and mis-use Freud. But nevertheless Rieff aids him in this misunderstanding by some of his own mis-reading: "The therapy of all therapies, the secret of all secrets, the interpretation of all interpretations, in Freud, is not to attach oneself exclusively or too passionately to any one particular meaning, or object." And: "The best one can say for oneself in life is that one has not been taken in, even by that 'normal psychosis,' love." This is not what Freud would have thought. Freud's definition of "meaning" in life included "to love and to work." He would have judged the capacity to love, with its full commitment to a valued other (an other valued as *more* than just a transformation of the self), as a necessary expression of fully human development.

To be able to love is to be able to believe in reality. Those who deny reality completely we call psychotic; but those who treat reality "as if" it exists, while actually experiencing it as only a transformation of their own narcissistic self, can only imitate love.[19] They love only themselves as they can experience it in the other; they love their ideals and their values *only* as representations of themselves. When they cannot win their love, or make their ideals come *fully* true, they suffer severe narcissistic blows and become acutely depressed, withdrawing from the work of life altogether, or else they

---

[19] The psychotic actually believes, but it is in his own reconstructed reality, in which we can find little truth of a general nature. However, it is interesting that in those extremely rare instances when someone shows us a new version of reality that is sufficiently compelling, we will surrender our own version, call the result progress, and call him a genius who has shown it to us. Genius and psychosis are not at all the same thing, but they share in common an ideosyncratic view of reality.

immediately seek a "new beloved" to replace the old. Thus they are more interested in *being* in love than in the ongoing process of loving. And they are more interested in being *committed* to a belief system than in the actual substance of what they believe in.

Perhaps this helps to explain such regular phenomena in our current social life as the rapid "switching" of allegiances from one charismatic leader to another, and the rapid proliferation of temporary sexual and other partners in today's "Now!" life style. As the fly-leaf of Rieff's book states it: "[the therapeutic] is the true unbeliever, and postulant of an anti-creed, using *all faiths or none* in the systematic pursuit of his sense of well-being" (my emphasis).

Curiously enough, Rieff states that "representing Freud as a prophet of non-culture contradicts his own highest intentions," and yet he lays the responsibility for the emergence of the therapeutic most significantly to this mis-reading of Freud. Of course, no one can blame Freud for the way he is mis-read any more than one can blame Mozart for the way he is mis-played; but Rieff's analytic description of psychological man might well leave the reader thinking that it is the goal of a successful analysis to produce just such a type as psychological man.

Nothing could be further from the truth. The goal of any analysis must be to increase the self-knowledge of the analysand. To know more about oneself is also to know more about what it means to be a human being, and to know more about the paradoxes that the human condition inescapably entails. Humans are the only species with self-consciousness, and, consequently, the only ones who must face the duality of their need to posit values at the same time that they must know that to posit values may be madness.

The great poets have always known this, their capacity to see within being greater than that of the rest of us: "Life's but a walking shadow, a poor player/That struts and frets his hour upon the stage/ And then is heard no more; it is a tale/ Told by an idiot, full of sound and fury,/ Signifying nothing."[20]

What we will believe in may make no ultimate difference when the planet finally grows cold, but lest we become too cold while we are still here, we will have to confront the depth of our capacity to believe in a reality that exists outside of ourselves. The first reality is always that of the mother, and then later in those enlargements

---

[20] Shakespeare, *Macbeth*, Act V, Scene V.

and modifications that constitute the family and the community. It is in the achievement of the uniquely human task of accepting both the value of the other and the separate value of the self, without diminishing either, that we can become fulfilled. For the narcissist, who is interested in those others and those ideals only as they can re-establish the primacy of his own narcissism, only an imitation existence can be had. There can *never* be enough gratification to fulfill the narcissist's perenially empty self; only in the reality of the "other" can the self be real.

Puerilism

BY J. HUIZINGA

EDITOR'S NOTE: The following is a chapter of Huizinga's 1936 volume *In The Shadow of Tomorrow*, a work by the great Dutch historian that deserves to be better known than it has been in this country. In "Puerilism," though he speaks to conditions associated in his mind with particular European upheavals in the thirties, he describes a phenomenon that is surely a prime aspect of our current situation. The phenomenon is at least in part attributable to what Huizinga in another chapter calls "The Decline of the Critical Spirit," a decline that calls to mind Rieff's contention that the cultural elite have already "become spokesmen for what Freud called the instinctual mass." Huizinga seems to me an early practitioner of the kind of cultural history we have designed this volume to consider, impressed with the problems of value and the "excessive concentration on self" that are central to the project. — R.B.

With a word whose depth surpasses all logical understanding, Plato once called men the playthings of the gods. To-day one might say that man everywhere uses the world as his plaything. Though the latter statement is much less profound, it is yet more than a superficial lamentation.

Puerilism we shall call the attitude of a community whose behaviour is more immature than the state of its intellectual and critical faculties would warrant, which instead of making the boy into the man adapts its conduct to that of the adolescent age. The term has nothing to do with that of infantilism in psychoanalysis. It is based on the observation of evident cultural and sociological facts. We shall not attach any psychological implications to it.

Examples of current uses demanding the qualification of puerilism abound. The *Normandie* makes its maiden voyage and returns from its triumphal journey with a certain blue ribbon. Noble rivalry of nations, astonishing achievement of science! Shipbuilders, shipping companies, maritime specialists all agree that giant liners are impracticable in every respect. In winter the *Normandie* is laid up; it would not pay to run her. Thus one returns to the practice of early mediæval shipping. The sailor's heart sickens to think that this floating palace should be called a ship. That the power of creation embodied in this achievement is impressive, yes, even inspiring, no one with any eye for modern culture will be able to deny. In the tremendous dimensions lies a beauty like that of the Pyramids; beauty there is also in the refined internal efficiency. But the spirit who commanded all this did not strive to express majesty or eternity. All that man has achieved here in calculated transformation of nature merely goes to serve an empty purpose, to play a game which has nothing in common with culture or wisdom and which lacks the high values of play itself because it refuses to be taken as such.

Or take that other game masquerading as business, that game of political ninepins, of continually overthrowing governments on purposely elicited conflicts of party intrigue whereby some great countries, entangled in the rules of a parliamentarianism whose true nature they have never grasped, deprive themselves of the chance of a real purification and strengthening of their system of government. Or think of the renaming of old cities after national figures of the day like Gorki and Stalin.

Let us make only a passing allusion to that spirit of drilling and parading which has engulfed the world. The multitudes are massed together, no square is large enough to hold them, a whole nation stands rigidly at attention like millions of tin soldiers. Even the foreign onlooker is unable to escape the fascination of this spectacle. This seems greatness, power. It is childishness. An empty form creates the illusion of a serious and worthy purpose. Those who can still think know that all this has no value whatever. It merely shows how closely the popular shirt-and-arm heroism is related to a general puerilism.

The country where a national puerilism could be studied most thoroughly in all its aspects, from the innocent and even attractive to the criminal, is the United States. Only one should be careful to approach it with an open mind. For America *is* younger and more youthful than Europe. Much that here would deserve to be qualified as childish is there merely naïve, and the truly naïve guards against any reproach of puerilism. Besides, the American himself is no longer blind to the excesses of his youthfulness. Did he not give himself Babbitt?

The modern puerilism shows itself in two ways. On the one hand, activities of a professedly serious nature and universally regarded as serious, like those mentioned above, come to be permeated with the spirit of play and to bear all the characteristics of play; on the other, activities admittedly of a play-character come to lose the true quality of play because of the manner in which they are carried on. To these latter belong the hobbies and pastimes which assume the weight of international interests with congresses, special newspaper columns, professional experts, manuals, and theories. They should, of course, not be considered on the same level with that particularly striking but superficial symptom of general puerilism, the so-called crazes with their rapid world-wide popularisation like the cross-word puzzle of a few years ago.

It goes without saying that in speaking of these hobbies and pastimes we are not thinking of sport. It is true that physical exercises, hunting and athletic contests are pre-eminently manifestations of youthfulness of human society. But this type of youthfulness is a different thing from puerilism. Without competition there can be no culture. That our time has found in sport and sporting events a new international form of gratifying the ancient agonistic impulse is perhaps one of the factors which may contribute most towards the preservation of our culture. Modern sport is in no small measure a gift to the world from England, a gift of which this world has learned to make a better use than is the case with the other things that England gave, such as parliamentary government and trial by jury. The new cult of physical strength, of skill and courage, for both sexes, is in itself a positive cultural factor of the greatest value. Sport gives vitality, zest for life, balance and harmony, all of inestimable worth for culture.

This should not blind us to the fact that modern puerilism has also found its way into sport. It is present wherever athletic rivalry assumes proportions tending to push intellectual interests into the background, as is the case at some American universities. It threatens to creep in with over-organisation of sport and with the disproportionate place which the sporting page and the sporting magazines have come to occupy in the mental diet of untold numbers. It shows itself in a particularly striking form where national passions impede the observance of fair play in international contests. In general, sport is capable of temporarily effacing national antagonisms. It is only too well known, however, that this rising above the desire for national glory is not always what it should be, as for instance in those cases where the fear of public commotion curbs the arbiter's independence of judgment. With the acerbation of national feeling the chances of such degeneration become progressively greater. Being a bad loser has always rightly been called childish. A whole nation which shows itself a bad loser deserves no other qualification.

If modern society must indeed be held to exhibit a marked degree of puerilism the question arises whether it shares this characteristic with earlier civilized periods, and if so, whether it compares unfavourably with these latter in this respect. It could easily be shown that erstwhile society often conducted itself in a manner which can only be qualified as immature. There would, nevertheless, appear to be a difference between the immaturities of the past and the childishness of to-day.

In the more incipient phases of civilization a large part of social life is carried on in the form of play, that is to say, within an artificial mental sphere governed by rules of its own and temporarily encompassing all conduct in a voluntarily accepted system of action. A conventional proceeding takes the place of the direct pursuit of utility or pleasure. Where the play is holy this activity becomes a cult or a rite. Even if the rites or contests involve bloodshed the action still remains play. All such play requires a local limitation, the creation of a playground shut off from the world outside. Ordinary life is excluded from these precincts for as long as the play lasts. The old Greek *temenos*, the lists of tournament, the stage of a theatre, the ring, are such sacred circles of play. The reality outside the playground is forgotten, there is a general surrender to the common illusion, free judgment is set aside. All true play still bears these features.

The most fundamental characteristic of true play, whether it be a cult, a performance, a contest, or a festivity, is that at a certain moment it is *over*. The spectators go home, the players take off their masks, the performance has ended. And here the evil of our time shows itself. For nowadays play in many cases never ends and hence is not true play. A far-reaching contamination of play and serious activity has taken place. The two spheres are getting mixed. In the activities of an outwardly serious nature hides an element of play. Recognised play, on the other hand, is no longer able to maintain its true play-character as a result of being taken too seriously and being technically over-organised. The indispensable qualities of detachment, artlessness and gladness are thus lost.

To a certain extent something like this contamination has been present in all cultures as far back as we can see. But it is the dubious privilege of modern Western civilization to have given this diffusion of the two spheres of life its greatest intensity. With great numbers of both the educated and the ignorant, the play-attitude towards life of the adolescent has become permanent. At an earlier stage we have already alluded to the prevalence of a state of mind which might be called one of permanent adolescence. It is characterised by a lack of sense of decorum, a lack of personal dignity and of respect for others and the opinions of others, and an excessive concentration on self. The general weakening of judgment and of the critical impulse has prepared the soil for the spread of this attitude.

Now it is both interesting and disquieting to note that the emergence of this state of mind is facilitated not only by a decreased desire for individual judgment, by the standardising effect of group organisations providing a set of ready-made opinions, and by the ever-available opportunities for trivial diversion, but also by the marvellous development of technical facilities. In his world full of wonders man is like a child in a fairy tale. He can travel through the air, speak to another hemisphere, have a continent delivered in his home by radio. He presses a button and life comes to him. Will such a life give him maturity? On the contrary.

In making mention of the contamination of play and seriousness in modern life, we enter upon a fundamental problem of culture which cannot be investigated here. The phenomenon shows itself partly in a semi-serious attitude towards work, duty, fate and life, partly in the attribution of great importance to what a clear judgment would qualify as trivial, and in the treatment of truly important things with the instincts and gestures of play. Political speeches of leading figures which should properly be described as mischievous pranks are not rare.

It would be interesting to investigate how in the different languages the words for play continually overflow into the sphere of the serious. American English would offer an especially promising field for a study of this kind. The American reporter speaks of his profession as "the newspaper game." The politician who, though by nature honest, finds himself forced to howl with the wolves of corruption, offers as his justification that he had "to play the game." The customs official is implored to close his eyes to an infringement of the prohibition law with the words "be a good sport." It is clear that far more is involved here than a mere question of popular speech. It is a fundamental change of a moral-psychological nature.

The semi-serious attitude towards life is characterised by the use of *slogans* as a means of persuasion. In the comparatively recent past the Americans gave to the old Scottish-Irish word for the battle and rallying cry of the clans the meaning of a political password or motto. A slogan, one might say, is a party adage of which those using it know perfectly well that it is only half true and that its purpose is to help the party to power. It belongs to the realm of play.

The Anglo-Saxon peoples, with their highly developed play-instincts, enjoy the privilege of remaining capable of distinguishing the element *fun* and *game* in their actions. Not all races have been equally blessed. The Latin, the Slavonic, and the continental Germanic peoples often seem to be far less well equipped in this respect. What else, for instance, is "Blood and Soil" but a slogan, a maxim which with a suggestive image veils all the defects of its logical foundation and the dangers of its practical application? The slogan, however, which is not recognised as such and instead is made a part of even the official and scientific language of a nation, necessarily becomes twice as dangerous in its potential effects thereby.

The slogan belongs to the field of publicity, whether commercial or political. Now it is one of the fundamental features of all modern publicity, that hypertrophic product of our time, that it is based on this attitude of semi-seriousness characteristic of overrefined civilizations. It is perhaps to be viewed as a symptom of old age. Puerilism is the proper word for it.

This widely prevalent attitude of semi-seriousness at once explains the close connection between heroism and puerilism. The moment the motto becomes "Let us be heroes" a great game has started. It could be a noble game if it were consummated entirely within the sphere of Spartan matches of youths, or the Olympic games. But as long as it is played in the form of political action, in parade and national drill, in oratorical bombast and "officially inspired" newspaper articles, and with all this yet takes itself seriously and demands to be take seriously, it is truly puerilism.

The confusion of play and seriousness which lies at the bottom of all that was here classified as puerilism, is no doubt one of the most important aspects of the malady of our time. There remains the question as to how far puerilism is connected with that other trait of modern life, the glorification of youth. The two should be clearly distinguished. Puerilism knows no ages, it attacks young and old alike. The adoration of youth, superficially a sign of fresh strength, may also be viewed as a symptom of old age, an abdication in favour of the coming heir. While most strong cultures have loved and honoured youth they never cajoled or exalted it, and they always demanded from it obedience and respect for its elders. Typically decadent and puerile were the quickly evaporated movements which called themselves Futurism. One cannot say that youth was to blame for them.*

---

* Two manifestos recently given out by the well-known founder of Futurism, F. T. Marinetti, may be recommended as an interesting illustration of what has here been said about puerilism. They can be found, in translation, in the Oct. 1935 and Nov. 1935 issues of the publication *The World* (London), as well as in the *Hamburger Monatshefte für auswärtige Politik*, Nov. 1935, p. 7.

Rieff's "Fellow Teachers"

BY NORMAN O. BROWN

Editor's Note: In April and May of 1973 Norman O. Brown had occasion to spend some time in Saratoga Springs. He had shortly before read and very much admired Philip Rieff's long essay "Fellow Teachers" in the Summer-Fall 1972 issue of SALMAGUNDI, and had determined to make some public observations on Rieff's text. To this end, Robert Orrill and I met with Norman O. Brown in the television studios of the N.Y. State Education Department in Albany, N. Y., under circumstances arranged by Empire State College. Our purpose was to discuss "Fellow Teachers" in a video-tape that would subsequently be used by students in a variety of disciplines. What follows is an edited transcript of a more or less extemporaneous address made by Norman O. Brown, at the start of that taping session, with the assistance of note-cards and various other jottings. The text we've put together speaks for itself, of course, but I might say that it does engage issues raised by Rieff in a way we had not ourselves considered, and should interest readers of SALMAGUNDI for a variety of other reasons as well.—Robert Boyers.

I met Philip Rieff a long time ago: at Herbert Marcuse's wedding to Inge Neumann, in fact. Around the year 1959 there were three books published on the subject of Freud, all of them attempts to get at the social implications of psychoanalysis. One was Herbert Marcuse's *Eros And Civilization,* another was Philip Rieff's *Freud: The Mind of the Moralist,* and a third was the one I wrote called *Life Against Death.* Since then we've gone separate ways. But I'm reminded of the philosopher Heraklitus: the unseen harmony is stronger than the seen. In fact I find myself now greatly impressed and deeply stirred by Rieff's latest piece, addressed to "Fellow Teachers." The publication this fall (1973) in book form of *Fellow*

*This text is published with the permission of Empire State College and the State University of New York.

Teachers will coincide with the publication of a new book of mine called *Closing Time*. Perhaps my reaction to his piece as it appeared in SALMAGUNDI in the fall of 1972 will throw light both on his work and on mine, and on the question to which we are both addressing ourselves, namely, what time is it?

What time is it? The title of my book, *Closing Time,* is symbolic of what time I think it is. I take the structure of the book from a philosopher of history whom, strangely enough, Philip Rieff does not mention — Vico. To oversimplify the Viconian system of thought beside which I want to place Rieff's, let me say that Vico in a great panoramic view says the history of the world goes through four stages. First there is the age of the gods, then there is the age of the heroes, then there is the age of men. This is followed by an interlude of dissolution into barbarism, followed by a cyclical renewal and a return of the age of the gods.

The first thing to be said about "Fellow Teachers" is that it anticipates the return of the gods: Rieff rediscovers the necessity for the category of the sacred. As is appropriate, the gods make their presence felt in mysterious and ambiguous language. He says: "Only culture-less societies can exist without presiding presences."* And then, just in case you might think "presiding presences" are things like Presidents of the United States, he says in another passage, "In our authority figures, the absence of any reference beyond themselves to a presiding presence is fatally weakening to their position as authority figures." These presiding presences are referred to later on as "God-terms," God-terms "that will not be treated as mere heuristic devices," "God-terms that must have binding authority."

In Rieff, as in Vico, the great historical process in a long-range view is a process of secularization, or profanation. He sees America "edging nearer and nearer to a condition of life entirely free from the sacred and its prohibitions." This is what (in Rieff's terms) the triumph of the therapeutic means: instead of souls we have neuroses, instead of sacraments we have shows. There is an almost Viconian summary of the process of secularization: "Therapy is that form which degrades all contents, for use by those who will succeed the late 19th and early 20th century psychologizers, themselves successors to moralizers, themselves regular successor types to all primitive

---

*All quotations from Philip Rieff's "Fellow Teachers" included in this essay by Norman O. Brown are drawn from the text published in *Salmagundi* (Summer-Fall 1972, pp.5-85). They do not make reference to the later, revised and much expanded book version which was not yet available in the spring of 1973.

spiritualizers." In the beginning there was primitive spiritualization — Vico's age of the gods.

In his meditations on the process of secularization, Rieff makes some very interesting observations about Marxism. He describes Marxism as "the last major credal effort to reorganize western society," the last major effort to draw on its religious roots, to transform or transcend itself: Stalin is seen as putting an end to that last major effort by transforming credal discipline into organizational discipline. The final obituary is given in the form of a quotation from Hannah Arendt: "The consistent elimination of conviction as a motive for action Hannah Arendt considered a matter of record, since the great terror under Stalin." It would be interesting to ask Rieff to comment now upon Maoism in this context.

But this piece of Rieff's is addressed to fellow teachers. What does he have to say to us? There are some confusing and irrelevant invocations of traditional notions of the highly specialized objectivity of the professor. There are contradictions in Rieff: he says for instance that teachers are not preachers: but he preaches. The real preachment, the real position, though, is that the university is the temple of intellect, the last sacred institution in our culture; if a university is not the temple of the intellect then it is not a university at all. In the university we teachers are called upon to represent the god-terms, and Rieff does not hesitate to call our role priestly. Also, as in Vico, our priestly role is inherently aristocratic — we are a priestly elite. All knowledge, the kind of knowledge we can pass on, is privileged. What Rieff sees around him is the destruction of all aristocracies of feeling intellect.

The priesthood of professors has two main functions: the restoration of the authority of the past and the reinstatement of the law: "The role of the professor is to be an interpreter of the interpreter, and thus to form a great link in the chain of interpretations by which higher culture is held together." We are not ourselves prophets, we should produce nothing new, no breakthroughs — breakthroughs are seen as destructive. We can only work to confirm or disconfirm but not to originate. Originality in thought — he has a phrase which he repeats, "the endless expressional quest" — is in his categories both transgressive and orgiastic. The maintenance of the tradition, the authority of the past, is our primary sacred responsibility; the act of teaching becomes interpretation, and the interpretation of preceding interpretations, thus forming that great link which is a tradition.

Against those breakthroughs that have characterized the "intellectual rhapsodes," as he calls them, of modern times, against these breakthroughs and their celebrants, revolutionary enthusiasts, we need a science of limits, or what Rieff calls an interdictory order. Interdicts are the main constituents of god-terms; to go back to the Old Testament, God said "No" before He said "Let there be light." God's first word was "No." Against our democratic orgiasts, Philip Rieff calls for a revival of a severe code of laws. These interdictory restraints are integral to the reinstatement of the process of soul-making, and to the rediscovery of that sense of guilt without which, says Philip Rieff, there can be no culture.

Thus the teacher, in Rieff's presentation, emerges finally as the equivalent of Dostoyevski's Grand Inquisitor. I am fully aware of what I'm saying and how terrible that vision is. According to Rieff our duty as teachers is "the enforcement of intellect on ourselves and reluctant students." We must be masters of guilt and of the knowledge of guilt, he says. Commenting on the novelist John Barth, he writes that "All giftedness, like Barth's, signifies guilt — although all guilt does not signify giftedness, for to become gifted, guilt must take on the form of privileged knowledge. This is to say: our guilt must be instructed. For a true culture, there must be masters of the knowledge of guilt." The stern severity with which he pursues the logic of the Grand Inquisitor is shown in another passage: "The human being is born a criminal. To praise the infantile is to praise criminality. You and I, fellow teachers, are the real police, whether we like it or not. No culture can survive without police of our sort — priests and teachers." The deeper chords of Rieff's meaning are struck when he says "fear is not a bad teacher of certain elementary lessons." *Principium sapientiae timor dei* — the beginning of wisdom is the fear of the Lord. (So also Vico.)

Although Rieff explicitly abjures prophecy, he's a great apocalyptic prophet in this piece. He sees the return of barbarism which is the final stage of the Viconian cycle. He begins and ends where George Steiner begins and ends his book *Bluebeard's Castle*: with T.S. Eliot's *Notes Towards The Definition of Culture*. All these men see the phenomenon of hostility to culture in any form — I think correctly — as a distinctly modern phenomenon. Rieff's elaborations of this theme are full of insight, showing the many ways in which we are

experiencing the return of barbarism: "Our desire for permanent
revolution is for a permanent barbarism." By permanent revolution
he means the cult of innovation in all spheres of culture, not just in
politics. For example, science is not forgotten, perhaps the most
energetic barbarizing activity in our culture. "Without a science of
limits" — rooted in godheads — "the domination of science implies
a cultureless society ; we are bound to become the world's first
barbarians."

In the same spirit he has sharp remarks to make about what is
journalistically called the counter culture, and to which many of us
teachers, in touch with the young, have mixed or even sympathetic
feelings. Among the paradoxical and extreme formulations which he
risks in this piece you find the following: "Immediately behind the
hippies stand the thugs"; "transgressive succeeds remissive." I think
he's very suggestive, perhaps just plain right, on the complicity of art
and intellect and politics in the spread of violence. Let me just refer
you to his basic definition of the cult of violence: "By *cult of violence*
I mean that critical openness to possibility in which nothing remains
true; in this original of all cults, all oppositions are welcomed as if
life could be an endless experience of political, technological or interpretative breakthroughs, against orders recognized only for purposes
of disestablishment." Now anyone who lives in a university would
have to say that critical openness to possibility has been recognized
or even praised as the proper atmosphere. What a variety of types
(including myself) are linked in common responsibility for the cult
of violence by such a formula as this: "What destructiveness is implied
in our desire to make life extraordinary."

Rieff has insights and aphorisms probing the interchangeability
between terror as an artistic phenomenon and terror as a political
phenomenon. Burckhardt in his praise of the Renaissance used the
term "terribilita," as something that could be applied equally to the
sculpture of Michelangelo and the politics of Cesare Borgia. Philip
Rieff looks at Hitler and sees some further consequences, some further
twisted horrors down that path. Hitler he calls the failed artist or
the armed bohemian, and this is exactly what the American university
is turning out in excessive quantities: "The American universities are
now producing tens of thousands of failed intellectuals and artists of
life; this mass production may lead to the destruction of culture in
any received sense."

Now the return of barbarism is not a subject to joke about. In my

book *Closing Time* I try to face the truth that Rieff here has painted
with such dazzling darkness, and yet situate our time in a different
perspective. Engels, in *The Origin of the Family, Private Property
and The State* — one of the Marxist classics which I consider relevant
to our time — is quoted in *Closing Time* as saying: "Only barbarians
are capable of rejuvenating a world laboring under the death-throes
of unnerved civilization." Engels may have had only the limited
political idea that the socialist revolution that he and Marx expected
would not come from the advanced industrial civilization of the west
but from some barbarians further to the east instead: the Russians
for example, or from some barbarians even further east. My guide
Vico has a more fundamental and necessary affirmation of the principle of the necessary renewal through barbarism. In the Viconian
cycle we go from the age of gods to the age of heroes to the age of
men, and then into a second barbarism. But only barbarians are
simple-minded enough to recognize gods. That is to say, only barbarians can acquire that second innocence which is necessary for the
return of the gods. Let me read from section 1106 of Vico's *New
Science*, which is strange to put beside Philip Rieff, and leaves much
to think about that I cannot spell out. Vico contemplates the return
to barbarism as he sees it in his own age, which is 1740, and he speaks
as follows: "But if the people are rotting in that ultimate civil disease
and cannot agree on a monarch from without, and are not conquered
and preserved by better nations from without, then providence for
their extreme ill has its extreme remedy at hand. For such peoples,
like so many beasts, have fallen into the custom of each man thinking
only of his own private interests, and have reached the extreme of
delicacy, or better, of pride, in which like wild animals they bristle
and lash out at the slightest displeasure. Thus, no matter how great
the throng and press of their bodies, they live like wild beasts in a
deep solitude of spirit and will, scarcely any two being able to agree,
since each follows his own pleasure or caprice.

"By reason of all this, Providence decrees that, through obstinate
factions and desperate civil wars, they shall turn their cities into
forests and their forests into dens and lairs of men. In this way,
through long centuries of barbarism, rust will consume the misbe-
gotten subtleties of malicious wits that have turned them into beasts
made more inhuman by the barbarism of reflection than the first men
had been made by the barbarism of sense. For the latter displayed
a generous savagery, against which one could defend oneself or take

flight or be on one's guard; but the former, with a base savagery, under soft words and embraces, plots against the life and fortunes of friends and intimates. Hence peoples who have reached this point of premeditated malice, when they receive this last remedy of providence and are thereby stunned and brutalized, are sensible no longer of comforts, delicacies, pleasures, and pomp, but only of the sheer necessities of life. And the few survivors, in the midst of an abundance of the things necessary for life naturally become sociable and, returning to the primitive simplicity of the first world of people, are again religious, truthful and faithful. Thus providence brings back among them the piety, faith, and truth which are the natural foundations of justice as well as the graces and beauties of the eternal order of God."

There is a difference in time perspective between me and Philip Rieff: how close we are, how far apart we are. We share a feeling of the barbarism of our present interlude, but Vico's cycle moves forward to a fresh beginning with a fresh age of the gods, which Rieff cannot see. And so Rieff has to draw back into the posture of restoration — restoring the authority of the past, reinstating the old law. To Philip Rieff I have to say that it is later than he thinks. If the university is our last sacred institution, we who are in it know that the temple is in ruins. The leopards have broken into the temple and drunk of the sacred chalice. Let us say it openly — Western civilization is over. Rieff himself says it openly: "In particular, I have not the slightest affection for the dead church civilization of the West. I am a Jew. No Jew in his right mind can long for some variant of that civilization." But there is a very strange fellow walking through the pages of Rieff's paper; he appears in the next sentence as "the Jew of Culture." In another strange passage Rieff tries to align what he calls "the proud elitist culture of Israel" on the side of Nietzsche and against the democratic, rancorous tendencies which he derives from Hellenism, and against the Christian principle of love. This principle he sharply caricatures: "Nothings would be instant everythings by imposing a love that was entirely mendacious." And Rieff's Jew of Culture turns out to have a strange symbiotic identity with Western culture as a whole — at the end of the essay he is finally revealed as "Lionel Trilling, superior teacher and leading American Jew of Culture." Now Rieff speaks sharply and clearly about religion, and we too have to speak sharply and clearly. Lionel Trilling, the Jew of culture, is the Jew whose Moses is Matthew Arnold.

Rieff, who is very self-aware, immediately recognizes the ironies of the position he has drawn: "For us pedagogically inclined Jews of culture, England was Zion, the fantasy fatherland; perhaps it was only the Pax Britannica, seen from the top of Magdalen tower." With the same ambiguous irony he signs this whole message as written from the Codrington Library, All Souls College, Oxford.

We are talking seriously about religion, and we must take seriously Rieff's involvement with Judaism. Rieff's sense of Moses as the presiding presence of Judaism is very strong, omnipresent throughout the essay: "Jews cannot exist without that Mosaic presence." He picks up and repeats what he has learned from his life-long study and interpretation of Freud as the 20th century Jew: "The Mosaic revolution is the formative event in Freud's primal history." Therefore he can now come forward with that final appreciation of the tragic and overpowering significance of Freud's book *Moses and Monotheism*: "It is in Freud's last testament to his own prototypical history, *Moses and Monotheism*, that we discover the ultimate murderer of Moses, Freud himself." Freud himself, who has been in *The Triumph of the Therapeutic* ambiguously distinguished from the therapeutic tendencies which succeeded him, is here seen as the father of the therapeutic and the murderer of Moses.

It is no surprise, if you remember his picture of the teacher as Grand Inquisitor, that the Moses of Rieff is the Moses of the Ten Commandments only, "a supreme interdictory figure." Moses at no point appears as the Moses who led the children of Israel out of bondage in Egypt, Moses the liberator. He is simply the author of the Ten Commandments, an interdictory figure. Even Jesus — we are still speaking of Jews — even Jesus is transformed by Rieff into an interdictory figure: "Jesus is a tremendous reviver of the interdicts. He came explicitly to deepen the law, not to abolish it." There is, from my point of view, a misquotation here, a mistranslation. The word in the New Testament text says that Jesus came to fulfill the law; Christian theology interprets the passage as meaning that by fulfilling the law, ultimately by the crucifixion, he paid off in full the debt owing to the angry father figure, and thus liberated the sons from the angry father figure and the Grand Inquisitor. In an uncanny moment in Rieff's address he amends the seven last words of Jesus on the cross as truthfully he says a Freudian would have heard them spoken, not as a Jew of culture would hear them spoken: "father, father, why have we forsaken thee?" From the Christian point of view we must return from this blasphemous alteration of the text to the original "father, father, why hast thou forsaken me?" It is his moment of liberation.

Whereas Rieff says we should be grateful for our sense of guilt, Jesus came to preach forgiveness. There is no forgiveness in Rieff that I can see. Jesus preached remission of sins, but Rieff uses the word remissive as if it were permissive, anarchic, orgiastic, a bad word. I do note a qualification at one point; Rieff has been speaking of the necessity of no's and thou shalt nots, and he says: "*No* has to be studied and interpreted almost without break, although it too must exist in a sense heavily qualified, under the sabbath rule of remissions." I would like to hear more from Rieff about the sabbath rule of remissions. To speak as sharply as he speaks, there is no forgiveness in Rieff. In my view he stands condemned out of his own mouth. There are a number of passages in which he rejects American civilization as rancour: "our rancorous civic religion"; "a culture organized by contempt and rancour." One has to register that Philip Rieff's address to fellow teachers is rife with rancour.

Rieff's Judaism has no Messiah. I guess the first appearance of the Messiah in Judaism is in that Moses who led the children of Israel out of Egypt into the promised land. Christians have always seen Christ as some kind of reincarnation of that Moses. We need a new Moses to lead us in a new exodus, an exodus out of western civilization into that world civilization that has been promised to us. There is no world to be preserved; there is a world to be made or to be remade. As James Joyce says in *Finnegans Wake*: "We are once amore as babes awondering in a wold made fresh where with the hen in the storyaboot we start from scratch."

For me it comes to a collision between Rieff and *Finnegans Wake*. In my book *Closing Time* I have tried to compress Vico's *New Science* and Joyce's book, asking those two authors the same question — what time is it? — and making a collage of their answers. Joyce's answer is as different from Rieff's as Vico's is: as Rieff calls us to a return to tragedy, Joyce announces and enacts a return to the satyr play, that original goat-story out of which those siamixed twins, as Joyce calls them, tragedy and comedy, by separation arose; you know the word tragedy in Greek just means goat song. For Rieff, "the most original figure of lightness and play is the satyr, who opposes the Jew of culture." I should like to ask Philip Rieff what he thinks of this quotation from Nietzsche's *Ecce Homo*: "What does that synthesis of god and goat in the satyr mean? I estimate the value of human beings as races according to how necessarily they cannot understand the god apart from the satyr." Rieff should have discussed in "Fellow Teachers" not Barth's *End of the Road* but *Giles Goat-Boy* where you have precisely an obscene reincarnation of a satyr born from a goat mother and sired by a computer father. Barth over-elaborates his ideas, but this work does include a marvelous parody of Sophocles' *Oedipus the King*, transformed into farce taking place on an academic campus. From *Finnegans Wake* — I'm still an interpreter of texts — I get the message to go back, back, back to a time before Moses and before Jesus, when gods were appearing in the form of beasts. Earlier we mentioned Rieff's solemn contrast between the Jew of culture and the satyr. But marvelous inconsistencies crop up in Rieff; there is an extraordinary passage in "Fellow Teachers" which is straight out of a satyr play. It reads: "This reminds me of a little book for humans, titled *My Thoughts*, written down by my wife and myself at the command of our Dandie Dinmont terrier, Darcy, that unfailing, decent and comic representative of what a presiding presence must have been like. You are aware of what *dog* is, spelt backwards." Such madness is only given to Dionysian spirits. One of Rieff's strengths is his knowledge of Nietzsche, who recognized his own style of exaggeration and aphorism as the style of decadence and destruction. I don't know whether Rieff knows how deeply he has been bitten.

It is perhaps another way of saying the same thing to say that we have to reconsider another key religious term in Rieff's analysis — orgy. In Rieff, orgy is the enemy against which all interdicts are directed. "Orgiasts produce new experiences," he tells us. "Note that orgy is the one, only and original totally democratic institution." Ezra Pound has a line somewhere in the *Cantos* where he says, confusion, source of renewal. Mircea Eliade in his studies of comparative religion has taught us to see in the orgy the form in which over-rigid structures have to be periodically dissolved in order to be renewed. In Freud's *Group Psychology and the Analysis of the Ego* there is a passage in which he recognizes the possibility that the separateness of the separate ego must be periodically dissolved in ritual orgy or saturnalia, festival orgy, so that it can be renewed or emerge again restored. Freud says: "It is quite conceivable that the separation of the ego ideal and the ego cannot be borne for long, and this is indeed shown by the institution of festivals which in origin are nothing more than excesses provided by law and which owe their cheerful character to the release they bring." Freud mentions the saturnalia of the Romans and the essential feature of their festivals as their ending in debaucheries of every kind, in transgressions of what were at other times the most sacred commandments. Thus, he says, as a result of the temporary abrogation of the ideals — Rieff's interdicts — the orgy may be regarded as a magnificent festival for the ego. It is possible that we have to extend the notion of orgy from being an institution which individuals need to being also an institution which history needs. That is to say, great historical periods may end, or have to end, in that orgy out of which they can be reborn.

Perhaps I speak as a Christian when at this point I use the category of rebirth, or second birth. The category was introduced into psychoanalysis by Erikson in his book *Young Man Luther*, where he drew on William James' distinction between the once-born and the twice-born. The chosen young man like young man Luther — notice the analogy between the chosen young man and the Jews as the chosen people — who has suffered catastrophic loss of objective identity and total alienation from the roles in which he finds himself, may have to go through a regression which in Freudian terms would take you back to birth, or before birth, in order to be reborn. I give you a summary of this idea not from Erikson but from a more orthodox psychoanalyst, H. Lichtenstein: "Thus the danger arises that instead of maintaining a sense of identity that the reaction to a depersonalized social role may empty the sense of identity and create the danger of alienation. Under such circumstances a return to earlier mirroring narcissistic experiences will again become necessary, leading even to a temporary object loss. At other times it may indicate a second birth in the sense in which Erikson, following William James, has used this term." I have the feeling that second birth is precisely what is happening to Philip Rieff. Hence the violence: as I said in *Love's Body*, birth is bursting, and it is a knife that cuts open the womb. I feel in the whole text of "Fellow Teachers" a shaking of the foundations taking place in Rieff's mind; one says, as Shakespeare says in such moments, is it a birth, is it a death? This piece of writing feels as if it were an explosive birth of a nova, a new star which sheds light all over the place. What will come of it?

I'd like to end with the question of language. Vico had those three stages of history — the age of the gods, of the heroes, of men — and he had three correlative languages — of gods, heroes, and men. With

the return to the age of the gods we would return to the language
of the gods. What that could mean is a question which I think we
clerks, we professors of humanities, who have a particular responsibility to the language, should ask ourselves. What can we do to
prepare for the return of the gods to the language of the gods? Rieff
acknowledges, to me very movingly, the way his language and himself are trapped in the language of critical intellect. Some of his
more formal didactic statements are quite terrifying. At one point
he says that he rarely allows his students to read living authors.
Students advance under his tutelage to "something like late Jamesean
sentences." Then they advance possibly to Proust and "to Chardin
and still life." I say that still life is still born. Vico is never tired of
pointing out that language began with the poets; that the word poet
means maker; that poets are makers and creators through being makers
of language and thus of culture and humanity. I think we must turn
from the philosophers to the poets — or at least turn philosophy, in
the manner of the late Heidegger, to listen to the poets, as Heidegger
listens to Hölderlin, waiting for the return of the gods. In this spirit
I'm releasing not a book but a set of tapes — it's possible that the
spoken or rather the singing word is closer to the language of the
gods than the written — tapes entitled *To Greet the Return of the
Gods*. They will appear simultaneously with my book *Closing Time*.
The presiding presences are not so far away. The spirit stalks us.
Inspiration lies waiting for us. We need a new language, to greet
the return of the gods.

Perspectives on the Therapeutic in the Context of Contemporary Sociology:

A Dialogue between Benjamin Nelson and Dennis Wrong

* Conducted in closed session at The New School for Social Research Graduate Faculty, March 1972.

INTERVIEWERS: ROBERT BOYERS AND ROBERT ORRILL

Q.: *One of the things that struck us in putting together the volume on* Psychological Man *is that Philip Rieff's work is really not very well known among sociologists, despite the fact that he sees himself as one who is responding to several traditional sociological concerns. I thought we might begin by asking you if you can locate Rieff with respect to any particular sociological tradition, whether you see him as furthering the necessary work of sociology in any way.*

NELSON: I do myself believe that Philip Rieff is moving towards a sociology of culture. Certainly he promises to elaborate one in future writings and I am in full agreement with his sense that sociology has unduly neglected cultural structures and sociocultural process. My bother comes with the fact that instead of proceeding as a sociologist of culture must, as — let us say — Max Weber did, or as Emile Durkheim did, Rieff chooses to rest his case upon a sociological meta-history which only rarely makes clear contact with actual documentable histories of peoples and predicaments as they occur in varied times and climes. One has the sense that the developments Rieff sets forth have a peculiar or local, even parochial, kind of reference within a fairly restricted temporal horizon. I would hope that in the works to follow this restriction of perspective will be corrected and that Rieff will, in fact, put many of the questions he has put to himself in *The Triumph of the Therapeutic* in these broader ways. Whether he will choose to do so remains to be seen.

Q.: *Rieff readily concedes that he's talking about a certain kind of man, about a more or less literate and reasonably affluent individual, in fact about a class to which he himself belongs, and which he considers of very great importance in the development of western history. He doesn't pretend that he's speaking about a wide range of people or adopting anything like an inter-temporal perspective. Do you feel that there is a place within sociology, or within cultural history, for that kind of approach, even though it isn't the kind of approach that you would think most valuable?*

NELSON: My own sense is that every people and time has its spiritual directors who get to be identified as curers of souls with particular powers and skills. This is because all societies produce their shares of varieties of men and women who — for whatever reason — cannot heal themselves, cannot exorcise their own demons, require some kind of guidance or counsel. But unless one takes the widest societal, cultural, even civilizational perspectives into account I don't see how one can escape falling into traps and excesses in telling this story. If one is going to make any sense out of the triumph or the failure of the therapeutic in our time, if we are to render the meanings of these conceptions precisely, then it appears evident we shall have to account for many intricate changes that have occurred over many centuries. By the same token, I would add we would need to talk of these changes in relation to more than a single group of men; at the very least we have to take the wide society's response, differentiated to be sure, by class, by ethnic group, by geographic location. There are empirical stories to be told, which I do not encounter in Rieff, tracing the shifting responses to, let us say, the claims of the "Therapeutes" in different countries.

WRONG: First of all, let me say I agree that Rieff is working towards a theory of culture, and I also tend to agree that this holds some promise for sociologists. Certainly such a thing is needed in sociology, which has sadly neglected the whole notion of the autonomous realm of culture. Here I think is a point where Rieff makes contact with Alvin Gouldner, who in *The Coming Crisis of Western Sociology* also points to the overemphasis on social structure in Parsons and in American sociology in general. But, to return to Ben's last remark, that's of course the risk of introducing any kind of temporary or current reference in your work. Despite Rieff's very olympian stance of cultural historian — which I should add is how I see him, as an analyst of ideas primarily, not as a sociologist — despite this olympian stance of a cultural or intellectual historian looking at two or three centuries in Western history, tempted to exclaim 'I've seen it all before,' he does try to relate what he is saying to the knife edge of the present. In doing so he runs the risk of being dated. There are references in *The Triumph of the Therapeutic* to the civil rights movement and to the new status of psychotherapy from which you could not entirely infer some of the developments, including the influence of Ronald Laing, that have happened in the last six or seven years. Now I think that it's a fascinatng subject to see how in some ways these developments confirm, though not in a direct and immediate way, many of Rieff's diagnoses. But the turning on the psychiatrists and the therapists themselves as being a pretentious, establishment oriented kind of profession, in it for their own good, is not something that he seems to have entirely anticipated. On the other hand in "doing your own thing," and in communes and encounter groups in which the leader is really simply one of the participants, there is a sense in which every man has become his own therapist, and this would be an extension of Rieff's notion of *The Triumph of the Therapeutic,* something, it seems to me, that he could absorb in his categories. One then, of course, has to ask, well, are not his categories so flexible that they could absorb most anything that happens. Mostly, though, I'm impressed by Rieff's sense of cultural tendencies. There is even a footnote at one point about the possibility of youth becoming the new elite cultural class, which didn't seem so great in the early 60's but certainly did by the beginning of the 70's, with pop youth elitists like Charles Reich looming large. Though you can obviously date Rieff here and there, I think it's a fascinating question as to whether or not some of the things that have happened in the last six years have refuted some of his most daring temporal and contemporary insights. Perhaps he even regrets having made them because, after all, what is six years in three centuries of Western civilization?

NELSON: I guess what I would say to that would be that the revolts which have occurred in recent days can by no means be attributed uniquely or even preeminently to the triumph of the therapeutic although they sometimes, of course, express themselves within the sphere of attitudes to therapy, psychoanalysis or whatever.

Our proper subject, after all, has to do with very large alterations which have been occurring for some time, recurrently, and which generate wave-like reactions, with different intensities. So much of what is happening nowadays can in fact be shown to have occurred before the 1840's in Europe, and in the U. S. And even these are parts of very much larger reactions to emergent notions of rationalization.

Q.: *Could you elaborate a bit on what you mean when you speak of these waves or currents of reaction?*

NELSON: I must at once explain that I don't mean to speak of waves in any strict sense, although I guess that some historians of cultural trends might be willing to try their hand at some kind of mathematical expression — I don't know if it would be of any use to do that. But what I would say is that over the past several centuries there have in fact occurred, intermittently, irregularly, these thrusts against highly structured systems which affected to establish the total rationality of the world and to underwrite the claims and demands of rationalism.

Let's take a simple illustration connected with Fourier. Nowadays many of those who are most intent upon getting away from the therapeutic establishment and who have, so to speak, found their way towards communities in which there is a powerful stress upon the recreation of a communalistic love ethos and a solidarity that knows no division or difference, many of them keep returning to Fourier. A striking example would be Herbert Marcuse himself. Marcuse has gone beyond Marx — and back of Marx — *to Fourier*. Fourier's stresses on associationism and the phalansteries of love have a long pre-history and do not as such have very much to do with the therapeutic unless we construe the therapeutic in such a way as to make it con-terminous with the whole of the emotional and erotic life of man.

And so I repeat: We must see the developments of our own time against a wider background that permits us to make sense of responses to crystallizations of various structures of rationalization. Only in this way can we approach the urgency of current responses to those structures.

WRONG: Well, after all, Rieff subtitled his book *The Uses of Faith After Freud* and at the time the book came out there were two other very prominent cultural figures around influencing large numbers of people who seemed clearly more "relevant", to use the student term, than the three he took, Jung, and Reich, and Lawrence. One of them, of course, was Marcuse, the other Norman Brown, and I suppose one could throw in lesser prophets like Timothy Leary and a great many others. And there is, of course, Ronald Laing. You could almost see the book in that sense as being rather prescient, coming out on the eve of the great ideological debauch, if you want to call it that, which we've been going through in the last five or six years. I'm not quite sure, Ben, if what you are saying is that all this has happened before, that there have been these currents and countercurrents throughout Western history. Well, in part of course, that is Rieff's stance, the sort of "I am Tiresias, I have witnessed all" mode; this is the tone of super-weary sophistication which he tends to adopt and in relation to which his occasional very contemporary references to Martin Luther King and the Negro protest movement and the like strike a rather clashing note. If one wants to take him now in a very literal, square way, obviously he is wrong in what he meant by the *Triumph of the Therapeutic*. Psychotherapists have not become the priests of our society, they are much less prominent now than they were ten years ago; students consider Freud "a fink" and a bore to a considerable degree. In addition the picture of a society of men who are highly privatized, who are indifferent to communal purposes, who treat their own emotions like the capital of a bourgeois (he has this cute phrase in there about how each man becomes his own eleemosynary institution and things of that kind) obviously doesn't answer to a great deal that we have lately seen. Surely it doesn't address what we see among the students, the great hungering for some kind of faith and communal purpose that has touched so many of the aroused young in the last few years. You could say simply that the book is in that sense outdated, that it wields an elaborate apparatus encompassing the cultural history of Western civilization to explain a mood in the 50's and early 60's that turned out to be rather transitory. But I think that would be doing Rieff an injustice . . .

NELSON: What I am in fact saying is that a sociologist, especially one who wanted to place stress upon sociocultural process in these wider perspectives, would, I believe, be obliged not to neglect certain kinds of phenomena. We have seen in our time an extraordinary complex of revolutions in the reshaping of our environments and ecologies, under the impact of global technologies, transport, communications, atomic energy and all the rest. Unless one is attentive to these broad developments, especially of the relations of the civil wars in the structures of consciousness to the spread of systems of instrumentalized function, one misses much about the actual ground of these revolutions, even in the sphere of the "therapeutic."

My reason for referring to the past is not so that I might pass for a Tiresias but because I want very much to throw light upon the very fundamental alterations we are witnessing. We cannot allow ourselves to think, however, that everything that is going on before us today has this very peculiar character, an eccentric quality resulting from the collapse of a prior theonomy. I just don't see that as answering to my own way of thinking about the story of sociocultural process, or even about the development of psychotherapy.

WRONG: Of course, Rieff begins *The Triumph of the Therapeutic* with two quotations which must be among the most quoted lines in the 20th century; I blush to quote them to my classes they're so quoted now. One is Yeats's "The Second Coming," which tells us that "the center cannot hold, mere anarchy is loosed upon the world" and so forth; the other quote, something which I must say I can barely refrain from quoting myself every third paragraph I write, is Weber's magnificent closing lines in *The Protestant Ethic* about "specialists without vision, sensualists without heart." In Rieff's decision to start there he announces, I think, his intention to link the effects of Freud and of psychotherapy deriving from Freud to a much larger kind of change. There is a very good chapter in Rieff's first book, *Freud, the Mind of the Moralist,* where he tries to link Freud up with other currents, not merely with Nietzsche and the German romantics, but others that were more contemporary with Freud. And we know now of course that there was a vital connection between Max Weber and D. H. Lawrence, two people whom one would not ordinarily have associated with each other — cultural historians regularly illuminate connections of this sort. Perhaps Rieff does place too heavy a burden on Freud and on psychotherapy, isolating a phenomenon that might better be viewed in a broader context. I don't know. But the really interesting question seems to me to involve the relation between sociological and psychoanalytical self consciousness. One might well write a book called the "Triumph of the Sociological" showing how awareness of what goes on, of social interaction, of norms and consensus, and roles and so forth, destroys the possibility of creating new groups that are really united in terms of consensus and shared norms and the like. Rieff quotes somewhere from Harry Stack Sullivan, to the effect that if you tell them about sublimation then they can't sublimate anymore, which sums it up very well.

NELSON: There isn't any doubt that a vast amount of experimentation is going on in the domain of consciousness, or that new symbolic designs are being woven. But I do not see this as in any way diremptive, as evidence of the fact that the center is gone and all is in chaos; I see it as a sociocultural process which is rooted in deep experiences and which may very well take us in directions we cannot right now foresee. I do not want to be pedantic about this, but it is clear that comparable developments in the history of the West were similarly difficult to foresee — in the Roman world, for example, there did occur a passage from a relatively stable rationalism to what might be called the triumph of the therapeutic. The key figures in this passage were men like Seneca and Marcus Aurelius, of course, but one would include the Church Fathers as well.

What seems to me transparently clear, bringing it all up to our own day, is that we inhabit a world in which the dominance of various rationalized images and the stress upon rationalism of various sorts is giving way to an order whose outlines cannot altogether be seen. What we know is that they will include mixes of, say, West and East, though the precise nature of the mix is as yet obscure. It seems to me that a sociologist of culture would want to speak to these issues, and resist the temptation to explain developments of this scope in terms of a fall from some sort of sacred structures or established traditions. I do not see it as especially useful to yield to a kind of pathos in describing the fate and fortune of mankind, for the process is a highly complicated one, and we have all to attend to what is passing very carefully.

WRONG: Well, I don't know, Ben, I don't think that there is anything in what you've said on this issue to which Rieff would not assent. Perhaps he has yielded to a kind of historical nostalgia — certainly it is a very powerful emotion, one I've often felt myself in the last decade or so. I suppose many of us tend to fall in love with the period of twenty years before we were born, when our parents were young. I feel closest to the late 19th century and the Victorian era in many ways emotionally, although I was born in 1923. What Rieff very nicely avoids in looking to the future, I think, is any prediction of apocalyptic disaster. The subtlety of Yeats's rough beast slouching towards Bethlehem to be born is maintained in his projection. His is really a very sophisticated version of what the world will be in the future, not a 1984 but a kind of gentle, sort of privatized, affluent kind of world, though he makes much too much of this notion of affluence, and the affluent society. The rediscovery of poverty hadn't entered into his horizons apparently. He does seem to feel that we are going through something unique and unprecedented and that the past, even the decline of Rome, doesn't give us any sure guideline to it. This is no more than what Weber and Yeats and Nietzsche understood but Rieff provides a context that is somewhat different from theirs. While I agree with all you say about the great revolutions we're going through, I can only say that people have been telling me some such thing all my life, for over 40 years, so that I'm not impressed by Mr. Toffler's notion of future shock. I'm much more impressed in fact with the idea that these changes are more than a century old and that we've worked out our own cycles of control and remission in Rieff's terms, and a way for handling them. There was a sense in which the 1960's seemed to me, as it did to many other people, to be a recapitulation of the whole history of radical thought since before Marx, and I have heard others more versed in cultural history and the history of the arts than I am say that it also recapitulated the whole history of modern art in a certain sense. Perhaps there will be a few more recapitulations until somehow the "rough beast" arrives.

Q.: *Perhaps we should try to speak more directly to Rieff's conception of the triumph, or prevalence, of a therapeutic mode of existence, a way of life in which self-concern becomes the one legitimate guide to conduct. Can the self, preoccupied with its own well-being, be at once free to pursue its own desires and bound to others in common purpose? This seems to me to be the most difficult idea in all of Rieff's work — how we can have a culture, a moral order, without some manner of personal effacement, submission to collective imperatives. Clearly the question we are asking here has to do with Rieff's notion that psychoanalysis is the first great system of therapy to remain free of some moral aim or doctrine, or I should say that he sees Freud as insisting that this should be the case. Analysis, this is to say, is a method created to help the individual withstand the impositions of, and expose the "illusion" of, the rules and beliefs of the group.*

NELSON: I'd like to speak to that if I may, and tell you it is precisely these last-stated claims that I find most problematical in Rieff's way of telling the story.

To give substance to my own sense of the backgrounds, transformations and current expressions of the therapeutic movement, I shall have to become personal. I first became concerned about the promises — and limits — of Freudian theory when I was an undergraduate. The question which I insistently put to myself had the following form: "What would a 'Freudian' theory of symbolism have to be in order to throw light upon the actual productions of men in art, science, literature, law, in short in their expressions in all the spheres of human achievement?" Without going into detail, let me simply say that my initial in-depth explorations in these spheres "turned me off." Strindberg's prefaces to his late plays, D. H. Lawrence's *Studies in Classic American Literature,* T. E. Hulme's *Speculations,* A. O. Lovejoy's essays opened vistas which were not contemplated in Karl Abraham's papers on the ontogenesis of cultural structures. The result was that I did little with issues of this sort for many years, hoping one day to have fresh power to get to the roots of my questions.

Issues in this sphere swam into my ken again about the time I was finishing my *Idea of Usury.* As I was drafting the work's epilogue, I became aware of the fact that my monograph in one sense was hardly more than a tiny footnote in a larger study which would one day focus on the problems of *conscience, casuistry* and the *cure of souls,* all issues having to do with the varied historical sources and shapes of self-images, images of the world, systems of spiritual direction, symbolic designs, and so on.

As I worked with these new frames I found myself having to hold off an over-strong renewal of interest in a Freudian theory of symbolic culture in order to deepen my probes into subjects about which little was yet known in a systematic way — the relations of "conscience," "casuistry" and the "cure of souls." Luck must have been in my favor. I soon made a string of unexpected discoveries which compelled me to think all of the issues in what I was to describe as the story of "Self-Images and Systems of Spiritual Direction in the History of European Civilization." I was launched on what was to be a central strand of my work to the present day, the comparative history and sociology of psychotherapies in civilizational perspective.

1. I discovered that the era called the Middle Ages witnessed a flowering rather than a *nadir* — of the notion of conscience. Feelings of guilt and remorse and conscientiousness had of course existed from time immemorial and were — and are — to be found almost everywhere. The centuries in which I was now concentrating illustrated new faces of conscience not before clearly perceived. Not only were there references to behaviors, attitudes and sentiments illustrating the feeling of "conscience"; there were new levels of ordered symbolic articulation, new logics and dialectics which came to be centered in the dual notion of "conscience" in multiple meanings. The notion of the moral conscience was at the root of the later expanded spheres of religious, philosophical, and spiritual consciousness.

2. The longer I worked at the attempts to resolve problems of the casuistries the clearer it became that pre-modern European men had been intensely *predicamental* in their vision of the world. Whatever the issue or the sphere of existence, they were intently concerned to try to arrive at the relevant dictate of conscience; wills and opinions being shifting and perplexing, they hammered out elaborate treatises of human acts; cases being many and various, they organized *summae* of the *cases of conscience,* setting forth the rationales of conscience and the multiple states of the conscience and consciousness. Beyond this, they perceived that in the course of all our existences all of us at one time or another, in one way or another, fall into doubt, confusion, conflict, shame, sin; they understood that we go aground and discover we may need help in one or another way. Such were the foundations on which the triangulated institution of conscience, casuistry, and the cure of souls had been reared.

I had only to ask one more question to return to my initial point of departure and to permit myself new ways of seeing into the pre-history and current shapes of psychoanalysis and the therapeutic. *What if I were to consider all the developments from the Protestant Reformation forward into the 20th century from the perspective of conscience, casuistry, and the cure of souls?* What actually happened when this triangulated structure was broken up for a variety of very good reasons, in the eyes of those who found every element and link in this structure a bar to pure religion and true reform? What happened when great numbers would no longer tolerate casuistry, since it seemed to them in every particular to be a deviation from the moral principle which presented itself with absolute clarity in Scripture or by the Inner Light or through some other source? What took the place of casuistry? And then, how was the *cure of souls* taken care of when men came to have a horror of judges in the court of conscience?

Here I must limit myself to report only a few episodes in the story of the transfiguration of the conscience and the self in the modern era. If these episodes prove anything, they prove that the story of the triumphs or failures of the therapeutic are far more complex than they have generally been made out to be.

The near demise of the older arrangements of conscience, casuistry, and the cure of souls is the indespensible background of the relentless surge forward of a series of new religious emphases since the 16th century. The most powerful among the new religions which were released by the Reformation may be described as the *religion of the transcendental self, the transmoral self beyond conscience.* Its myriad expressions are elaborated in all the spheres of existence, experience, and expression since the 16th century — its echoes will be found in all the masterworks of theology, philosophy, art, literature, and even science. Its rumblings are the sources of all the triumphs and tragedies of our collective and individual lives.

Interestingly — I have told the story elsewhere — the key notion was the concept of the spark or witness of God in the soul (*scintilla animae, syneidesis*) — itself drawn from medieval mysticism.

Modern rationalism of the Enlightenment variety owes more than most men know to Platonic and neo-Platonic mysticism. The shift from the religious to a more secular orientation occurs as early as the seventeenth century. Once the move had been made to the new notion of inner light by the dissenting groups of the seventeenth century, the medieval orchestration of conscience, casuistry and the cure of souls was undone.

Romanticism is the deification of the individual (and collective) ego and the apotheosis of the unconscious forces which have been discovered to be the ego's foundation and underside. Romanticism joins all other variants of illuminism by rejecting the contextual integration of conscience, and casuistry, and the cure of souls. Romanticism makes the emancipated feelings the sovereign legislator for each man and for all mankind; directly applies these feelings to the complicated circumstances of the daily life resolving the riddles of tangled interest by reference to the command of love and the dictate of will; relieves itself of the need for spiritual counsel by treating explosive impulse as ultimate norm. The most impressive and fashionable expression of contemporary Romanticism is Existentialism now oddly wedded in morganatic marriages to all of the most compelling constructions of modern thought: Marxism and neo-Marxism, Freudianism and neo-Freudianism, Husserl's constitutive phenomenology, Heidegger's neo-Gnostic fundamental ontology, and every sort of orthodox theology of crisis and so on.

So far as I know, few have yet thought to wonder about the paradox: Is it possible that the limitations upon the confessional in Protestant lands were too great to admit the growth of organized spiritual direction? Protestant culture tended to produce individuals who understood their responsibility and wills in ways that inhibited recourse to others. Jews and Catholics have never shared the Protestant religion of self-reliance.

The key issue here has to do with the most interesting hypothesis on this score provided by a French publicist, Raoul de Roussy de Sales. It was precisely, claims this author, because of what we are calling "instrumental activism" in American Puritanism that once it was decided to organize the overcoming of neurosis, no cultural limits were placed upon the achievement of a liberation from sin and guilt in relation to the superego. It was precisely sectarian Protestantism which encouraged the conviction that world and self could be permanently purged of imperfection and confusion. Nowhere else has there been so much conviction in the positive power of unashamed love and self-expression. The social constraints upon the triumph of any such notions on the Continent have always been very notable. America is a country in which, in Max Weber's language, the psyche was to receive its most comprehensive rationalization. If time allowed it would be interesting to trace out the ways in which the social democratic outlooks so clearly noted by de Tocqueville in the 1830's, contributed to the constructions placed on psychiatric and psychoanalytic ideas in American culture.

How understand Freud against this background? If we would

appreciate what Freud and psychoanalysis mean in our present era we need to know *to what degree Freud is the heir of the religion of the transcendental self, to what degree he meant to be its undertaker.* I have elsewhere suggested that a key to this riddle lies locked in Freud's 'Divine Comedy,' which he called by the name, *The Interpretation of Dreams.*

I find it hard to end this part of my remarks without some reflection on one of two historical paradoxes marking the relations of Protestantism, the major source of the religion of the self, and psychoanalysis, whose cultural implications are even at this moment being violently disputed. The paradoxes are:

1. Psychoanalysis did not originate in Protestant settings. It emerged in Catholic Vienna and its pioneer was a Jew.

2. The highest development of psychoanalysis to date has occurred in Protestant America.

I turn abruptly now from these seemingly remote and general horizons to speak about more proximate perspectives.

Quite apart from the existence or non-existence of all sorts of integrated directive systems, people came to Freud for some kind of aid because they were at odds with themselves and others. In some cases their problems traced their inabilities to create workable balances of the different sorts of directives needing to be linked — *eros, logos, nomos, polis* — if they were to be able to manage their life histories. Some of the people to whom Freud ministered in his special way were severely disassociated; some of them hysterics, or else caught up in obsessional phobias of one kind or another. We have the records available to us now and we are in a position to see their lives in wider contexts and to reflect upon Freud's own work.

Freud considered it a primary responsibility to assist an individual to recover the capacity for moral agency and to carry forward in a way that would be most congruent with his moral sense. What we notice, though, in studying the case histories, and in reading *Freud: The Mind of the Moralist,* is that there is virtually no mention of any moral predicaments from which Freud might have suffered. It is hard, isn't it, to think about a moralist without moral predicaments? Pascal, we know, had moral predicaments; many classical moralists admit to having undergone moral agonies and confusions. So far as the record now shows, Freud didn't really have these very dreadful moral predicaments, although doubtless he ought to have had them.

In fact, Freud was wedded to the Kantian categorical imperative. Rightly, or wrongly, he knew what he was supposed to do and felt that normal persons similarly knew what they were to do. Now this has a great deal to do with his entire understanding of the tradition in which he worked. He felt that in previous structures of cure of souls, it was always taken for granted that the person who acted as the minister or doctor or confessor or whatever could not possibly work with an individual unless that individual were, so to speak, in a positive transference and unless there was the possibility of giving him absolute direction, guidance and so on. Freud is the one man in this tradition who makes a very decisive move in a quite new direction: he considers dealing with people who, in fact, did not have quite that much positive transference, and then goes further, to the very fascinating notion that it was precisely when the individual was in the deepest transference to the analyst that he was in the neurosis that most needed to be cured. All other neuroses collapse into the transference neurosis; that is the prime resistance, it is that which has to be worked through, after which Freud felt that the individual was in a position to act with moral autonomy.

A central question that came up in the 1920's is a clue to one's unease in regard to these issues. I refer to the debate over the problem of psychosynthesis. A number of theorists and clinicians who were having very great difficulty in their treatment rooms continued to note that it was not inevitably the case that the interpretation of the analyst did put the person together in a way that somehow gave him enhanced agency to act with efficacy and to act with a certain kind of personhood in respect to the moral, social and other sorts of options that he encountered in his existence. There were analysts who saw that, and who proposed that psychoanalysis did a very great job in some regards; but there was a necessity for another part of treatment, called *psycho-synthesis*. Freud regarded this as an utterly false idea — he rejected it wholly.

Interestingly, his rejection included a revelation of what was a key to something that had hitherto been concealed — not deliberately, by any means — but I suspect concealed from Freud himself, namely that he was committed to a pre-established harmony, principally with respect to those components of the complex that had been analyzed out of the complex in the course of the therapeutic situation by the act of interpretation of the analyst. He supposed that when the elements were released from the unhappy complex, they would all find their way back again to a new fusion which would be ego-syntonic as well as world-syntonic; and that the individual would now have new agency, new capacity, enhanced power to function, fresh power to constitute his world.

Q.: *I think that our problem lies precisely in Freud's manner of relating to patients. Freud would not indicate to patients the content of the choices they were to make, would not choose for them, but that is for Rieff the very essence of culture: culture makes choices for one and sinks them at an unwitting level. What we must consider is whether Rieff is getting at anything beyond this particular predicament, the one he said that Freud did not meet, whether we can find in, to use Rieff's language, a culture of total remission, some kind of ground for a new structure.*

WRONG: I also make a lot of sense out of what you just said, and you certainly do in some sense say it more proximately than does Rieff, who writes about Freud more as a moralist, as a thinker, than as a therapist. It is not surprising to find Rieff write the following: "It is significant that Freudian theory is most alive today outside the professional confines of psychoanalytic medicine among some historians, critics, philosophers and in the social sciences". Now I think this is profoundly true, but it also happens to be true, a fact that I have to confront, that the most impressive psychoanalytic therapists whom I have encountered have been people who don't write articles for intellectual journals, who don't even write articles for psychoanalytic journals and who are nevertheless very brilliant at the level of therapy, a level Rieff rarely touches upon.

Q.: *He is very critical of the psychotherapeutic movement in terms of the competition of cultural elites which he sees going on, and that is something we ought not to overlook, I think.*

NELSON: The proposition that elites are continually contesting for precedence is one that I think is undeniable. The most critical elites from this point of view, across the centuries, have of course been mediatorial elites who have at least been supposed to have peculiar access to certain intimations of wider meaning. From the standpoint, as I see it, of a sociology of culture, the central questions of issue come to be precisely to what sets of social urgencies, predicaments, to what breaks as it were in peoples' own experiences, to what do these elites speak? Are they merely subserving their own purposes as elites or are they also, so to speak, in a contest to subserve some set of wider purposes? I would just like to emphasize this, I think it is beyond doubt that in the history of the psychoanalytic movement there have been conflicts and struggles having to do with the competition for relative influence among those who might be accessible to their influence. So I don't see that that is itself a very critical kind of question.

My own feeling is that there are more vital issues, having to do with attempts of younger people to forge structures in which they will at once attend to their own individual needs even while creating forms of community which will involve fewer ravages than they now think they undergo. I'm not saying that they're going to succeed, or that the world's history will have all that much to tell them about their prospects, but I am deeply impressed by these developments, by the need to consider them in the broadest contexts we can bring to bear. In so doing we'll inevitably have to consider the various forms of the therapeutic in different areas of the world. In China, for example, one finds a highly organized and consolidated treatment structure connected up with elaborate systems of collective confession and self-criticism and so on. As we look at the situation there, we come up with a slightly different sense of the consensualist motifs that have been elaborated within the framework of culture. The stress which I should like to place is on the wider backgrounds of the histories of the appearance of the self, the person, individuated out of all kinds of collective structures. Perhaps Rieff will deal with such matters in widened perspectives in the future. I don't know.

WRONG: I'm struck by your mention of China, particularly in light of various journalistic reports coming out of Nixon's visit there, reports of a simple, faithful, even puritanical people whom the journalists would literally laugh off stage if they turned up back home. I suppose this attests, once again, to our nostalgia for the primitive, to our uncertain longing for a faith in spite of the corrosive effects of Freud's insights, and the insights of others. What Rieff sees quite clearly is the effect of sociological self-consciousness, the tendency of so many groups to rush out and create a community because they have discovered that men need community, and to encourage a sense of participation because men need to participate. This is to make means of ends, and though Rieff actually discusses these things he never quite gets specific enough because of his determination to remain aloof and ironical.

Q.: *What might these communities constitute — that is precisely what bothers Rieff, as he is bothered by the tendency of therapeutics to rush out and build them without having any clear sense of what they are about. Rieff's notion of Americans understanding quintessentially Fitzgerald's image of the green light — one need only commit himself to keep moving regardless of what the direction might be — is central to his critique of contemporary society. What I should like to know is whether either of you can conceive speaking of contemporary man as a certain kind of character type? This question would appear to lie at the root of the problem Ben Nelson has with Rieff, the sense that his reliance on a limited typology reduces the complexity of socio-cultural reality to manageable proportions and in so doing violates it.*

NELSON: I can't help but look at societies as being in the midst of flows. I see cultural and social elements continually undergoing transformations of one or another sort. And they need to be studied as though they were — in truth they are— geological sites with the help of geo-historical methods applying more or less archaeological perspectives such as those Michel Foucault has powerfully illustrated in our time.

It seems to me an error to say that there is only a single structure which is absolutely dominant in a culture and that all individuals are completely at home in that structure. Anybody who wants to know how weak the triumph of the therapeutic has been has only to take himself some miles out of the main metropolitan centers to observe that, in fact, the therapeutic hasn't really gotten very far with vast numbers of people, including those who are in very great need of some kind of aid or assistance. There is nothing that so terrifies many people in American society as having to be in a situation with a therapist or anyone who pokes around in their heads — they'd rather have electrodes put in them any day of the week, and this is really an odd fact to which not enough attention has been paid.

Along the same lines, I would suggest that we cannot speak of a character type as being in any sense uniformly distributed across our country or any other country, although there's no question that we do have shifting balances of ascendancies. At the present moment we are at a very critical turn with respect to the degree of dominance of what might be called the structures of rationality. What has been called into question is the very notion of justification for any given action or the truth of any opinion. But to deal with such matters as a sociologist one has to speak very specifically about the values that are being transformed and about the underlying structures of consciousness that are equally in flux.

WRONG: There is a fundamental ambiguity in Rieff's work that has much to do with the way in which he uses the term culture. Of course he means high culture much of the time, but he pretends to mean culture in the sense in which anthropologists and sociologists talk about it and of course in that sense you can go ten miles outside of New York and find people who are untouched by the triumph of the therapeutic. He's really talking about the culture of highly literate, educated urban intellectuals, namely himself and others, and he may in part be correct in the sense that often such people, ourselves included, cannot believe or affirm in the same simple way that we could before. That does not mean that other people may not be able to, of course, and so the character type has only a limited validity, at best.

Q.:   *Are you making a kind of general statement about typologies, that they do not constitute a viable mode for dealing with major socio-cultural issues?*

WRONG: Well, Rieff doesn't really have a typology, in the sense even in which David Riesman has one in *The Lonely Crowd*. Riesman after all went about establishing his in a much more conventional sociological way, trying to indicate that there were a variety of character types to be found in a single culture. And he tried to establish the specific class milieux in a much more precise way than Rieff does. So that there are different kinds of typologies, you see.

NELSON: There is a very grave risk, it seems to me, that those who don't know these issues in any depth will indeed suppose that all structures of consciousness, all actions can be properly described by reference to the alleged uniqueness or exclusiveness of one or another stress of character or experience. For example, Rieff has described the ancient Greeks as Political Man, the men of the Middle Ages as Religious Man, the men of our era as Psychological Man. This strikes me as great simplification which hardly does justice to any of the complex realities of the periods under consideration.

The Greeks were political men but they were also religious men; they were also psychological men and there is no telling their history unless one gives due weight and prominence to mixes of these elements. It just makes no sense, in my view, to talk that way any more than it makes sense to talk of the man of the Middle Ages as Religious Man because many medieval theologians paid a great deal of attention to theology. It turns out that men of the Middle Ages were at that very time, when they were presumably all caught up in theology, intensely engaged in political activities, often quite revolutionary, in transformations in government, urban centers, the generation of new liberties, new constitutions and so on. If you're going to do any close work in sociology of sociocultural process, changes in the structures of consciousness, you've got to differentiate the levels and not use the image of character type in Rieff's sense at all.

WRONG: I couldn't agree more with what you're saying, Ben, and I have attacked on many occasions just such abstract views of men and suggested that sociologists would do well to avoid these glib generalizations such as man the status seeker, and so forth. But I do think, to be fair to Rieff and to the valuable work he has done, that he has quite obviously decided not to describe the concrete ways men were but to describe the images of men that prevailed among the more articulate intellectuals in various periods and that have been passed down to us in the present. He is speaking of certain dominant images the Greeks have left us, or that the men of the Middle Ages left behind. Again, he's acting as an intellectual historian primarily, not as a sociologist describing concrete men, and the real problem which he comes to, and which does finally give him some claim to be considered a sociologist and not just an intellectual historian is how these images reproduce themselves and shape themselves by becoming what C. Wright Mills called vocabularies of motives that lots of people pick up beyond the circle of the creative intellectual elites.

Q.: *In a sense, I suppose, Rieff is arguing that the whole range of moral casuistries has passed from the hands of theologians into the hands of psychologists. New casuistries of moral conduct have in turn been developed by the therapists as they have elaborated their therapies. And in terms of typologies, the issue we've been arguing here, would it be fair to say that in any given period one representative group in the society has it as a special burden to elaborate*

*the moral casuistries, and that this group becomes in a certain sense
a model for the society as a whole? If this is so, there might be some
point in referring to this as the era of Therapeutic Man, since the
therapists, in Rieff's view at any rate, have assumed the peculiar
burden we've described.*

NELSON: True, psychology has furnished a good deal of the
vocabulary we in America use in the situation of motives, and it is
clearly operant in the communications of those who are now active
in ordinary experience and organizing action. I can't really see that
that can be questioned, but my own stress has been on the need to
consider these matters in societal depth.

Suppose we turn, though, to an illustration of a particular transformation that may assist us to focus what we've been saying. I'm
speaking now of a change in the very image and notion of the cardinal
principle of reality. Now I have undertaken a great number of essays
and papers in which I have sought to ascertain how people did indeed
come to perceive their own existences and to define reality. And as I
looked through developments in the last two centuries I observed a
number of changes in the image of reality, changes, I might add, not
motivated particularly by any sort of psycho-therapeutic school.

My difficulties started when reading Marcuse — I found myself
at a loss to understand how he could read *Civilization and Its Discontents* as he did. Eventually I saw that he had made only a bare
beginning in his redefinition of the Freudian notion of reality so that
recently I decided to look into Freud himself, very closely, to see
whether in some manner or other one could find some basis within
Freud for understanding this transformation. I think I have found
such a basis. At one point when Freud talks about "the Two Laws
of Mental Functioning" he first discusses the reality principle in
terms of outer reality, contending that the mark of the psychotic is
that he simply doesn't perceive clearly the common reality of the
physical world, which is the reality each of us must encounter.
In the very same essay he oddly shifts ground and begins to talk
about the phases in the psycho-sexual life history of the organism,
and it suddenly appears that the notion of reality principle doesn't
any longer refer to any outer world to which all have to render some
kind of homage, or at least whose existence has to be acknowledged.
By reality principle he now means something quite different, which is
the maximization principle, namely, that reality consists in the activity

of the ego, in mediating between the pleasure principle and those wider understandings which propose that we maximize pleasure if we postpone immediate gratification.

In this regard Freud asks a whole series of questions concerning the extent to which art, science and the like subserve the reality principle, and ascertains that they do in the last analysis promote the wider enhancement, so to speak, of pleasure. In this way he prepares a new conception of reality, and it is in this context that we ought properly to think of the triumph of the therapeutic, a context that is somewhat restrictive, I suppose. In these terms we see that the key to reality is the enhancement of the ego in its activity of organizing the pursuit of pleasure. Now one can take this in at least two different ways, ways Freud thought he had managed to unify in his own approach, by the way. This is hardly clear, I think, though we can say that Freud consistently moved towards an emphasis upon the psycho-genetic examinations of the phases in a patient's life history. Within the history of the psychoanalytic movement as a whole there were those who wished to confine themselves to the therapeutic framework as a special arena, involving a kind of special task that the analyst actually accomplished; he didn't set the world straight, he didn't necessarily proceed towards the delineation of all objects and structures in the world, but he did render some kind of assistance to an individual in coming into a greater capacity to act in accordance with the maximization principle. Now there I think you do have a bridge offered to those who wish, as it were, to knock out these other sorts of structures, ontological structures, social structures. Now we know that there is in Freud the idea of three blows to man's narcissisism, represented in the figures of Copernicus, Darwin, and Freud himself. What these blows portend is that the ego is not master in its own house. Confronted by this idea, Freud took a particular direction in his work, and I think we do need to say that Freud didn't give enough stress to the notion of a *social-reality principle,* to the reality that comes into existence through the interaction of all of those who constitute society in whatever shape or form. It is precisely this dimension of a social reality principle that Marcuse, Brown and a whole lot of other people miss. Clearly, given its due, it does have to be declared a *fourth* blow to man's narcissism.

WRONG: I'm not sure I like your idea entirely, especially as you relate it to Marcuse and Rieff. While I agree that Norman Brown has

been so opposed to the existence of any society that he puts forward
an entirely solipsistic, almost a psychotic vision, I think it safe to
say that Marcuse writes in a much more established and conventional
tradition. In spite of the heavy Hegelian-Marxist influence he feels
always compelled to ask the question, can one overcome the "needs"
of society, can one transcend the limits they set to human possibility?
But Rieff is not really to be grouped with these fellows, surely not
in any sense with Brown. Though he suggests the possibility of a
de-sacralized kind of society with increasing privatization among the
citizenry, we cannot really say that the social dimension, a "social
reality principle" in your terms, is lacking. So pervasive are the
nostalgia and irony in his work that it is hard to be sure what he is
after, but I feel rather certain that what he has in mind would
out-date many of our sociological categories. This despite the sense
that we are dealing with a kind of culture religion in Rieff, a religion
he himself anatomises and that he finds in more orthodox figures
like T. S. Eliot, for instance. And surely we can see the connection
between this and the desperate search to find old faiths that we see
regularly enacted among the young in our culture.

Q.: *I think that Rieff's point of departure may be Tocqueville's*
Democracy in America, a book he refers to as "the finest and still
[the] most informative book on America, and on democracy, ever
written." Particularly he seems to have been impressed by Tocque-
ville's observation that democracy tends to encourage "downright
selfishness" in its citizens, thus increasingly cutting them off from one
another. Perhaps I should quote Tocqueville: "Thus not only does
democracy make every man forget his ancestors, but it hides his
descendants and separates his contemporaries from him; it throws him
back forever upon himself alone and threatens in the end to confine
him entirely within the solitude of his own heart." Now doesn't
Rieff see the source of American sociology in this statement, that
people like Cooley and Mead labored to understand how the
American, alone and lonely, could restore himself to community?
And isn't he making a similar effort? To be sure, he talks about this
privatized individual as you say; but isn't he also seeking the terms
in which this kind of person, given his confirmed self-interest, can
enter into relationships with others? What is not clear, as I said earlier,
is how a person who believes only in himself can believe in and bind
himself to interpersonal relations. Rieff says at one point that culture

without cultus appears in almost all historical cases as a contradiction in terms, and yet this is precisely what he is talking about.

NELSON: Perhaps I can get some light on these matters by recalling again the origins of my interest in Freud. I always felt I needed to understand the origins of and meaning of complex symbolic structures or universes which one finds in art or in science. As a matter of fact, I first turned to Freud and to Abraham in the hope of really finding out more about what ways there were of construing symbolic structures that got expressed in the writing of Strindberg. And as I read I saw how these symbolic structures of meaning might be used to cure people by affecting their view of reality. But I really became excited when I came to *Civilization and Its Discontents,* and it seemed to me then that Freud had immense implication as a social thinker because he had declared certain irreducible realities about the structures of experience. Clearly he saw himself as an individual who had another story to tell than most had told about the life of the mind, the history, so to speak, of the mind. He was a kind of archaeologist, his own language specifies that, and what he saw was the permanent susceptibility of the organism to retrogression. More specifically, he had discovered there was no assurance that any set of structures, however strongly based through any set of cures or however firmly grounded in any set of symbols, would not yet be susceptible to retrogression. This was the point that he made very strongly at the very outset against Charcot and Janet — this was the point he made again and again in all of his comparisons of himself to Schliemann, and so on. The importance of this point cannot be stressed too strongly in any assessment of Freud, and we see in it his sense of the vulnerability of all therapies and all social structures. A related aspect is his awareness of circumambient realities which prevent us from imagining that we are the exclusive authors of our own existences. He declares the limits of the notion that the self can create its own reality. He does not at all appear to me to be in the tradition of, let us say, German idealism, of Fichte for instance. If you're talking about the triumph of the notion that the self, you know, did actually constitute the cosmos, it isn't to Freud that we have to look. It seems to me there are other people, with no relation at all to Freud, who have had that view.

WRONG: Well let me take this just a little more particularly in the context of contemporary American sociology. My old college classmate Erving Goffman, who has recently received a lot of publicity, wrote a book called *The Presentation of Self in Everyday Life* which deliberately echoed, of course, Freud's *The Psychopathology of Everyday Life*. While Goffman is an extraordinarily original thinker, he is in the self-linked psychological tradition which takes its point of departure in his case from George Herbert Mead and has led to a school in our field called symbolic interactionism. There was a time when any purely self-linked psychology did not seem to me, as it does today, superficial, even though, curiously, I recall Goffman himself contending this when we were both students in our late teens and he was criticizing neo-Freudians such as Horney and Fromm. By now, though, I can hardly look at social psychology except in Freudian terms, and feel I can boil down the essence of Freud's contribution to three very simple propositions that Freud took quite seriously and quite literally and explored the implications of in a way that nobody had done before or since quite as fully. These would be, first — "life begins at zero"; second — "in the beginning is the body"; third — "the child is father to the man." I simply am unable to see any other psychology that presents itself as competitor as adequately taking these propositions with the literal seriousness that Freud did and following their implications for the whole growth and development of human character structure. Obviously the self only appears in experience around about the third or fourth year of life, or with the learning of language in Meadian terms. Obviously the self becomes an object which captures an enormous amount of emotion, an entity in which a great deal is invested, but those emotions have had an existence that antedates the self and have sent out feelers, or have cathexed, in Freudian terms, objects that then have turned back upon the self. So a psychology for which the maneuvering of the self and its "presentation in everyday life" is central cannot be a fully adequate psychology in these terms — this is the way that I've come to look at it, though it's not the way that I was brought up to look at it.

NELSON: Well, Dennis, though I greatly appreciate what you have just said, the supposition that the *self* — which I would distinguish from the *ego* — does in fact emerge at age three appears to me a very doubtful supposition on which to base a responsible social psychology. There are other things that appear to me to require mentioning. If we were to look at the case in the terms of a man you've criticized but wouldn't altogether reject, if you look at the issue of the *self* in somewhat Durkheimian terms, the fact is that all societies do not really present or constitute *structured selves;* the self is an intermittent emergent within the history of societies, and Marcel Mauss in his magnificent essay, *A Category of the Human Spirit,* has, in fact, told a very great deal about all of the complex social transformations that have to occur before the self can emerge.

It seems to me that Freud didn't altogether allow himself to look deeply enough into the sociocultural-historical process, or he would have known that the way in which he defined many terms, the ambit he gave them and so on, would need to be modified, for the fact is that in the wider sociohistorical process the self is relatively late to appear and to be a dominant pivot or hinge for any set of social structures.

Further, with respect to Mead, may I add that it was never his intention to make "self" primary or for that matter to give as much stress to the particular image of social interaction and small-group exchange as have been ascribed to him in contemporary sociology and social psychology.

What happened is that Mead thought of himself as a person who was helping to build the wider community — he says so all of the time — his whole existence was devoted to a kind of religious conception of the coming of the kingdom through the emergence of the wider community and the breakdown of all of those boundaries and barriers, you see, to these wider communities of discourse and acceptance which he thought essential.

Now recall that Mead lived in Chicago in a time of very dramatic alterations, and what he saw was that people weren't relating to one another — for him the stress on communication was preliminary to a picture of communion. There's just one question about this — others have very much the same stress, including contemporaries like Royce and Dewey and so on. Now the horror of all of this is as follows from my point of view — that these authors who have simply shaved away Mead's fundamental stress and his fundamental sociology and have preserved this very limited, restricted horizon within the two-person situation, or the very small group, have missed Mead's emphasis and have kept us from having a much wider awareness of what really was working in his mind.

WRONG: I agree with what you say about Mead, but for not

entirely the same reasons — I agree he was not a social psychologist or a sociologist — I think he was a philosopher, fundamentally, asking philosophical questions — the basic thing being of course an attempt to solve the mind/body problem — and also to account for the Aristotelian problem of the *differentia specifica* of man, why man was different from the rats that behaviorist psychologists studied. I think he said quite plainly many times that the self is a purely cognitive structure. Now what the symbolic interactionists have often done is to smuggle motivations and emotions into our attitudes towards the self, and in that sense I do not see Mead as in any sense contradicting Freud, let alone creating the basis for a different and competing kind of psychology — they complement one another very beautifully. I think Freud presupposed that man possessed language and the capacity to be an object to himself, and many of the mental processes Freud describes such as identification or projection are unthinkable without this assumption. Mead himself may have had these larger interests, but when you say that the self only becomes important later on I can agree provided we have a similar notion of what self we are talking about. The self which has been culturally invested with great value and what forms a basis for "cult of individualism" is a specifically modern thing as Durkheim referred to it. Surely there is another idea of self which we cannot totally ignore. I remember once having an argument with a lady anthropologist and I said — well, of course the self is universal, the self is a given; language and self consciousness are universal human properties and we've learned that most fully and most adequately from Mead in the sense that he isolated the specific mechanism whereby language creates a sense of selfhood. The woman denied it — she said no, there were cultures in which there was *no* self consciousness, and she and I were obviously just not communicating. It turned out that what she means was that she had studied Indian villages and that the Indians did not have the great sense of value attached to self, the great competitiveness and status consciousness of which Durkheim was an early analyst, such as exists in the West. But not that Indians lack self consciousness, obviously, in the Meadian sense — I think Mead really did isolate what is a generic and peculiar human attribute and one that must be assumed to make sense of a lot of what Freud is talking about. But not one that provides a basis for an adequate developmental social psychology, which must be a motivational psychology, which must deal with the emotions as well as with cognitive processes and which must start at birth. So we come back to "life begins at zero" and "in the beginning is the body," all of which antedate the emergence of the self. I've been talking about the individual's social experience, while I think you're talking about the cultural importance attached to the self in Western Civilization, and that is of course Rieff's theme in *The Triumph of the Therapeutic*, taking the question in the larger cultural-historical sense. So I don't know that we really disagree . . .

NELSON: You use the phrase consciousness, and of course it is possible for people to have selves without there being a word for consciousness in a given language. But I am deeply sensive to the fact that the notion of conscience that we all take for granted and which Freud treats as though it were generic and universal is indeed not found in vast numbers of languages and cannot really be located within their cultures. It is not the agency to which everyone generically across the world turns as some kind of source of directive in the arrival at decisions. This very funny notion is actually of relatively late date, and I am not at all convinced there are functional equivalents for the notion of conscience even in Chinese civilization. As you try to tell the story of the emergence of the modern idea of self across millenia, you discover that there could have been no conscience, no consciousness as we know it, if there had not occurred individuations in society which allowed, encouraged, compelled men to see themselves as the center of agency. And when they saw themselves as the center of agency — this wasn't as a result of the triumph of the therapeutic or anything else — when they saw themselves this way they had no alternative but to ask questions of themselves, to ask: What am I directed to do? What is right? What is wrong? Do the Scriptures tell us the true story?

If you want to test out some of these notions I can recommend nothing better than the writings of Abelard, surely among the most thrilling documents I have ever looked at, demonstrating how a self is somehow required to see the nature of alternatives offered by a culture, or to understand precisely what are the disjunctions in that culture. Now the self has many questions to work upon once it comes into existence, but we know that the recognition of the sacred in a culture is a central event for that self, regardless of the other questions it may ask. And what we have to see about the sacred is that it is not, as some people want to suppose, simply given, somehow to be entertained through all time, or made to order in some fashion or other. And there is no easy and quick way of getting back to it. In time we see a continuous necessity for the sacred to be recreated. There is never a time when the sacred is not, in fact, being sapped at its foundations in one way or another, and we have no right to read history as if this were not the case. Too many of us fancy that if we are to understand where we are to go we must have a right to declare the nature and character of the universal on the basis of what we ourselves happen to feel. I think everyone who's now talking about conscience and consciousness in fashionable ways must have this idea.

So I shall say that it is most unlikely that in the West, at least, there will be a total dismantling of certain central elements of the structures of consciousness associated with the rationalist tradition. Anyone in the West who has confronted the very problem of the dissolution of all solidarities in communities and communions and who turns towards some possibility of a newer and wider kingdom established, if you will, on some new foundation, in the last analysis will prove to turn to universal symbols. These symbols will have some kind of universal meaning, or universal bearing, or universal claim upon us that are somehow expressed within, let us say, such structures as science or art. Isn't this what Durkheim does in the *Elementary Forms of Religious Experience* when he traces the breaking down of the structures of collective conscience, the structures of sacro-magical consciousness. Before the book is ended, he is on the road to exploring what are the phases of our days in time, what hope there is, so to speak, for some future sacred, and it turns out that the future sacred is oddly connected in his mind with the emergence of all of those structures of awareness which do link us to something universal, because he sees the social ground changing. He sees that we can't talk about persevering in structures of faith for which the ground no longer really exists. So I ask you, what kind of ground are we really talking about when we talk about the future of faith?

Q.: *Rieff seems to me to be discussing the same story that you're talking about — of the self trying somehow to win its way back to solidarity, communion, community, whatever — in an age of peculiar and severe symbolic impoverishment in which the ground has changed, to use your terms. But no matter, where are we to go with the problem?*

WRONG: Listening to Ben just now I could not help thinking of Eliot's, "after such knowledge; what forgiveness?" And it does seem to me this is a part of our problem, as is the progressive psychologisation and sociologisation of experience. Right now, the notion that reality is socially constructed, is somehow man-made, is very "resonant", to use Gouldner's favorite term, among sociologists. A book by our erstwhile colleagues here at the New School, Peter Berger and Thomas Luckmann, *The Social Construction of Reality,* is really almost a sacred text among many students because they think that if reality can be constructed, it can be reconstructed. But can it be done in such a self-conscious way, I wonder? When we have taken the psyche apart to the degree that Freud did, can we find a faith that transcends our understanding of the ways in which the psyche works? And particularly, if we're talking, as Ben has been, of a kind of universalist faith connected with science and art in which presumably scientists and artists will be the culture bearing elites, resembling the great culture bearing elites of the past, this is a difficult question. Yet I see no reason, as I said before, why Weber's "iron cage" should not be sociologically viable. I mean, a world of "specialists without vision, sensualists without heart" may be perfectly tenable even if you and I, living at the tag end of the great tradition of Western society, may find it something to be unhappy about. And as to the social-reality principle Ben earlier mentioned, I'm not sure I really understand just what it means. I'm a sociologist first and not a cultural or intellectual historian and to me his concept simply suggests the notions, documented perhaps rather prosaically by a good many sociologists, that there are certain conditions that must be met, certain "functional imperatives," if any societies are going to survive in their prevailing form. I mean, in some sense or another societies require subordinations and sacrifices of individual interests, all spelled out in rather tiresome and verbose detail by people like Talcott Parsons, but really in a much simpler way in *Civilization and Its Discontents,* surely one of the most important books ever written on Western culture. If that is what the social reality principle means, well, o.k., but then a society of "specialists without vision, sensualists without heart" may be perfectly viable by any of the sociologists' criteria even though Weber and Rieff and you and I might regard it as a

syncretistic horror, just as we might regard the kind of ersatz world
religion that Toynbee at one place dreams up in *The Study of History*,
where you make prayers to Buddha and to the Holy Ghost and so
forth, with comparable horror. So this question is really one that
seems to me to be quite distinct from the question of the social reality
principle.

NELSON: As Dennis well knows, our difficulty here is compounded
by the fact that various sociologists with whom we would both disagree have promoted a version of what I call social-reality principle
in a manner that is altogether misleading. Others pretending to use
the language of sociology are not talking about society of any shape
or form — they are in fact spinning out theologies of the self, or at
best variant theologies of two-person universes. Nonetheless, these
continue to be called sociologies.

Beyond this, I do not think that the one prospect before us is a
society regulated by "specialists without spirit, sensualists without
heart." I see the horizons before us in a rather different way. It
appears to me that we are living in a time when, you will forgive the
metaphor, the *world* — as distinguished from the earth — is waiting
to be born and the anguish is awful and there are no midwives
around. In the course of recent centuries, East and West, there have
been efforts made, not always deliberately, to constitute centers of
orientation that would maintain at least minimal structures in the
service of possible wider faiths. This is not the sort of thing that we
can afford to ignore if we are to get along in this world. Nor is it an
issue that I alone feel — I can tell you that Chou-en Lai feels it,
and there is a very remarkable statement he wrote on the reform of
language in which he explains why they chose for example, to
proceed to the Latin alphabet and not to the Cyrillic alphabet. He
had in mind the question of civilization, obviously, of the wider
acceptances we shall need to discover.

Perhaps it is true that culture without cultus is meaningless, that
culture religions are not viable notions, but it seems to me we have
got to nourish some idea of these wider acceptances. Maybe a further
point will help. There is a distinction to be made between what I
would call *rationale structures* and *rationalization processes*. The fact
of the matter is that we have witnessed in our time the continuous
pollution of all kinds of complex rationale structures that have been
elaborated across time in the interest of achieving the most rational

kinds of arguments and acknowledgments on the part of all, without respect to their point of origin or to their color or creed or whatever. These wider rationalities have doubtless now, in many places, come to subserve the interest of rationalized activities which pay no attention to these wider purposes. Now my thought would be — anyone who asserts that it is completely pointless to preserve some confidence in and work in the hope of a further development of these rationales is, in fact, not serving the cause of a wider humanity. When I say this I know full well that I say it against all sorts of people who consider the point of view very odd. Many people after all suppose that all rationale structures do by definition subserve these very limited parochial interests and cannot possibly serve any wider principle. So that I may provide suitable answers to these people I have in recent years been working intensively in all questions that have to do with the character of civilizational complexes and the sorts of things that happen in the course of their encounters. We are today, I think, at a point of the most incredible abrasiveness of such structures, for there is a kind of continuous interaction between them. What's up for grabs is whether there will or will not prevail some sort of structures I would describe as a *minima moralia* with respect to the "moralities of thought" and the "logics of action."

Q.: *Rieff speaks about such matters as well, it seems to me, though in somewhat different terms. For him, the minima moralia in our past always proceeded from a statement of the kind: you may not do this or that, except in so far and in what way the rules of the group permit. Now, however, he argues, that any new moral structure, if it answers to present circumstances, must begin from the statement: do as you please.*

NELSON: I have difficulty in replying to this point; it doesn't seem to me to offer a sufficiently inflected, orchestrated picture of what the ruling moralities have in fact been at every level of differentiation within societies. I keep coming back all of the time to the same sort of point of view . . .

Q.: *I'm speaking of the notion that you appraised earlier, the notion of taking upon the self the responsibility for developing rationale structures. Now Rieff seems to suggest that the therapeutic at his most fully elaborated is precisely liberated from that responsibility which no previous man has ever been so fully liberated from. That is, the therapeutic need not renounce, in the way that Freud suggests men in civilization must.*

WRONG: He's suggestng that everybody may do his own thing without having to elevate his own thing into a universal law, or a categorical imperative . . . Sure, there may be something in this. That wonderful line from *Mr. Sammler's Planet* keeps coming to mind here, what is it, "Liberty, Fraternity, Equality, Adultery," or some such thing.

NELSON: I agree that there are certain corners of the society which at times do in fact exhibit this kind of effect but I, perhaps oddly, continue to think of the world, the whole world, as my horizon and when I do I am overwhelmed by the high probability that the disinhibitions to which references have been made have many more complex sources and meanings than has been suggested. I don't altogether see the issue in terms of interdictions and remissions, though in a way the issue does have something to do with family management, with intimate personal operations and remissive structures emerging at these levels. But it appears to me that at the wider societal levels the issues we have been discussing take on a different color, and one has to ask whether there will occur movements in a direction of more-or-less universalistic kinds of rationales. This is a matter of the extremest urgency, for what I think we see occurring now is a passage across the world of certain peculiar combinations of socialism and nationalism which are marked by an intensive readiness to abandon any references to received rationale structures and to treat them as being irrelevant to what is called *praxis*. I refer to the enormous attacks that have been going on everywhere against the idea of any kind of reality principle, social reality principle, or against the uses of reason. This strikes me as, in the last analysis, being in the service of options that mustn't carry the future. At least I hope they won't.

WRONG: Well, I find it very hard to cope with discussion at this level because, as Weber saw it, whether there will be new prophets or mechanized petrifaction is something that absolutely cannot be foreseen, and this is why, in a way, a sociology of culture is something that positivistic American sociologists have tended to veer away from. Karl Popper's point that to anticipate things like new prophecies or new scientific discoveries is already in a sense to have made them is well taken, I think. Of course, much of what Rieff and Marcuse and others are saying is at a level which cannot be identified with the concrete historical world in which all of us now live. Really we do not know whether the future will be an iron cage or whether the iron cage will simply settle certain problems for mankind so that we can discover cultural rythms and a kind of cultural creativity that is not bound to rising and falling classes — Rieff does, to some degree, touch upon this, and surely we are able now, while much of the old and of the past still survives, to anticipate the kind of complete upset and reversal of categories that the future will likely bring. Take the ordinary political categories of right and left, the right associated with the established classes and the left associated with the deprived and rising classes. It may very well be — we've had a foretaste of it in the last decade — that the established classes will become the critics and the revolutionaries and the challengers of the order while the classes that have in the past been the carriers of social change will become the conservatives and upholders of the present structures of society. Certainly I don't think anybody before the fifties anticipated this possibility, but it has become, if not quite a commonplace, certainly something which people must cope with — the dissociation of right and left ideological attitudes towards the existing order from the positions of classes and groups in the distribution of worldly goods. So I find it very hard to envisage what a world might look like in which universal abundance, peace, and some degree of international solidarity, are established in some sort of relatively secure way. What we do have to deal with as a present reality is the revival of passionate group attachments since the middle sixties. And there is the fact that spokesmen for woman's lib or gay lib or whatever more and more assert their claims in terms of universal rationales, though their specific appropriate context has to do with limited sexual role and group identities. What all of this seems to violate is precisely the notion that the self is relentlessly privatized. What we have is the unfolding of a new kind of dialectic, though I do sense a strange kind of continuity in the current revival, a continuity with much earlier modes. The new legitimacy of ethnic groups surely seems like a return to something very old, as many people have pointed out. At the same time one recognizes the quality that Rieff talks about, the quality of self indulgence that is a part of recent proclamations of group attachment and loyalty, as though one were proclaiming the *right* to ethnicity, or to have pre-marital sex, or to smoke pot. There is involved here an assertion of self, in other words, that is

quite striking, though expressed in collective terms, and that needs
to be better explored sociologically.

Q.:   *Rieff sees all of these movements — whether it be women's lib or
youth movements or hippy movements — all of them as therapies —
and claims that despite the proclamations of commitment uttered by
adherents, they are really at base committed to nothing at all. In a
very interesting passage he claims that world culture is changing
already into a symbol system unprecedented in its absorptive capacity
— nothing much can oppose it really and it welcomes all criticism, for
in a sense it stands for nothing. That is the basic sense of it. Does it
make sense to you?*

WRONG: This is terribly complicated. It is so easy when one is
older and world weary and has lived through as much history as we
have to talk as if nothing really amounted to very much at all. As I
walk through the halls of The New School or NYU and see the kids
sitting at tables and the posters announcing meetings I feel that
none of it is new or important, that it's a repeat of something that
I've seen before and at a lower level — a cruder and more strident
level. And then I think of Marx's words about history repeating itself
— "once as tragedy and then as farce." But this is a very generation-
centered perspective. I mean, young people are born into the world
who are new and haven't known these things, and they are as new
and passionate and real to them as they were when we were young.
I know this is obvious, but I think it useful to remember, and also
to remember that Rieff writes with a special kind of vision, from the
Olympian vantage point of Western cultural history. This doesn't
mean that he can't see what's happening, to the contrary, I think
he's quite astute when he speaks of these various movements as play-
acting and the like. The question is, of course, could it be that young
rhetoricians and militants of all sorts only seem to be acting, that
their gestures are not play-acting for them? Obviously, one cannot
lump all of the new militant movements that have sprung up in
the past few years together, however. In spite of the posturing and
self-indulgence of a few of its more publicized spokeswomen, the
Woman's Liberation movement really speaks for an idea whose time
has not only come but is long overdue. With the exception of the
black movement as a whole, it is likely to have deeper and more
permanent effects on our lives than any of the other movements
asserting group claims that we see and hear around us. From the

standpoint, however, of Rieff's notions of the "triumph of the therapeutic" and the "privatized self" what is odd about so much of the
new political rhetoric is that, in spite of its assertion of collective and
communal goals presumably demanding sacrifices of self-interest and
personal hedonism, it seems quite continuous in its self-indulgence
with individualistic demands for the right to "do your own thing,"
have a full sex life, resist all forms of authority, et al. Even where
group rather than individual claims are being asserted, it all still
seems part of the outlook that Irving Howe characterized critically
some time ago as the "psychology of unobstructed need" and thus
very remote from Rieff's concept of cultural control systems making
new moral demands that subordinate the claims of the self. Even a
true politics in the narrower sense is surely "a slow and hard boring
of strong boards requiring not only passion but perspective," to quote
Weber again, which demands sacrifices, compromises, a sense of the
claims of the future reaching beyond here-and-now grievances and
alienations. The lack of this is why the notion of play-acting seems
applicable to much of the rhetoric of the new movements.

NELSON: I don't myself see these things as play acting, nor for
that matter do I altogether accept the cultural epigram of Marx that
history repeats itself for the first time as tragedy, for the second
time as farce. I think we are indeed at a radical turn with respect
to many critical structures, and it seems to me that much of the
consciousness politics of our time is something quite different and
new. At least it was not a decisive element in recent years, in the
thirties or forties, for instance. It involves new attempts to effect
reconciliation of *eros, logos, polis,* civilization, or at least to strike
some new sort of vital balances in the ingredients of existence and
polity. A critical element in the demand is that the world be made
over in response to certain clamorings of the transmoral self. Again
we are faced with the necessity of recalling the very muddled history
of the self. The contemporary self hasn't come into existence purely
as a result of disinhibition, or of remissive patterns in families, but
for a variety of deeply imbedded reasons. At the point, though, at
which the self could conceive that it constituted the world, and
insisted upon this fact, we began to have what must be called
pathologies of the self. This has evidently come to pass in our time,
with what results we cannot really tell.

I have a continuing conviction that it is of the utmost importance

for the comparative, depth-historical study of the social-cultural
processes, the utmost importance for our understanding of our structures of consciousness as they elaborate across time, the utmost
importance for our hopes of being moral agents in very wide senses
— that we address ourselves to the whole range of questions that
chance to be encapsulated in a form often anachronistic, the histories
of the structures of conscience, casuistry and cure of souls. In short I
am now persuaded that we need to work our way back through
questions of this sort if we hope to make progress in developing
basic foundations for comparative studies integrating sociology, history, psychology, anthropology and the other social sciences and
humanities.

Some may say that we do not lack — we already have — a comparative-historical sociology and psychology of the changing structures of
consciousness and conscience across times and places. I would deny
this claim. The structures we need for a proper starting point have
yet to be forged. Even the great pioneers in the "cultural sciences"
fell short of giving us the supports we need. Freud's metapsychologies
and metahistories have yet to generate proper points of departure for
a wider cultural historical psychology. Weber made enormous contributions to that end but he shied away from questions of the sort
we are discussing here. Durkheim knew and said that consciousness
and conscience were very decisive spheres to relate to, but his ventures
were limited to comparative-historical analysis of the phenomena in
this sphere. Marcel Mauss and some others — notably Jane Harrison,
Johan Huizinga, and a number of more recent investigators — do
offer some aid.

The fact remains, however, that a massive amount of work remains
to be done if we are to get anywhere near a satisfactory understanding
of the tumultuous sociocultural processes exploding across our 20th
century world, insofar as these have roots and expressions in the
civil wars now raging in the structures of conscience, consciousness,
the muddles in our casuistries and cures of souls.

It is against these larger horizons that the work of Rieff needs to
be appreciated.

Mental Illness *Is* Illness

BY PETER SEDGWICK

I am going to develop some thoughts which have arisen out of a study I am at present conducting into the work of the distinguished anti-psychiatrist (or ex-anti-psychiatrist), R. D. Laing. I do not propose to take up the specific questions raised by the work of Laing and the school of thought around him (which is in any case very desultory and unsystematic). Instead I am going to face squarely the central issue raised by all the sociological or quasi-sociological "revisionists" of the idea of mental illness. It appears to me that none of them have begun by asking the question: What is *illness*? Only in the light of an answer to *this* question could we determine our answer to the question: Is mental illness really illness in the 'medical' sense?

Let me begin by identifying who I am talking about. Not all of the "revisers" of mental health are sociologists; and not all sociologists working in mental-health problems are revisers. The influential work of Thomas Szasz, the Professor of Psychiatry at the State University of New York, rarely contains any material from the deviancy experts of the sociological profession (though it is braced by many striking allusions drawn from political science, law, economics, fiction and medical and psychoanalytic literature).[1] Michel Foucault, whose book *Madness and Civilisation*[2] has become deservedly famous in studies

NB: Notes are given in abbreviated fashion; the title of a work will be presented only once, and in subsequent references mentioned by an initial form (e.g., MMI for *The Myth of Mental Illness*), followed by the number of the footnote in which the full title is given.

[1] *The Myth of Mental Illness* (New York, 1961) deals mostly with hysteria and malingering. *Law, Liberty and Psychiatry* (New York, 1963) is Szasz's fullest treatment but draws most of its examples from the forensic field. Szasz nowhere presents a comprehensive theory of mental illness which closely examines the different typologies of psychiatric diagnosis. *Ideology and Insanity* (New York 1970) is a collection of essays repeating old themes and suggested reforms of psychiatric practice. *The Manufacture of Madness* (New York, 1970) largely consists of an extended analogy between psychiatry and medieval witch-spotting.

[2] New York, 1965.

of the cultural relativism of psychiatric concepts, is a historical analyst
of ideas in the social and natural sciences who appears to have worked
in complete independence from the academic specialism of sociology,
in either its American or its European branches. On the other hand,
the bulk of 'medical-sociological' writing in the subject-matter of
psychiatry merely represents a parallel with the developed science of
'epidemiology' in the prevalence and incidence of physical diseases
by different social classes, age-ranges, cultures and other social vari-
ables: these researches take it for granted that 'mental illnesses' exist
as facts of life (to be correlated with other social facts) and do not
discuss the logical status or the social nature of either diagnosis or
therapy in the psychopathological field. Even the more advanced and
closely focussed studies of 'family process' or 'psychiatrically-induced
mental disorder' which are characteristic of the best work in British
and American social psychiatry begin their analysis at a very late
stage of the *total possible analysis* of mental illness. Chronic mental
patients deteriorate, we are told, through spending long years in over-
crowded locked wards: but what, pray, is a 'mental patient'? How
does such a person come to exist, in terms of his own definition "I am
a mental patient", the definitions of others, to the same effect, and
the relations between these ascribed and self-ascribed identities?
Family pressures, according to the American schizophrenia-researchers,
impel susceptible people into severe breakdowns which necessitate
their treatment in a suitably equipped clinical institution: the problem is to discover how the illness began, so that once again our very
notion of a mental illness is never posed as constituting any kind of
problem. That trend in the sociology of psychiatric classification
and treatment which, on the contrary, takes 'mental illness' and its
'treatment' as being problematic, to be analysed as value-laden *social
constructions,* is an unpopular trend in psychological medicine —
though it dominates the teaching of deviancy-sociology in many
American colleges. We have a contrast, in brief, between what might
be called an *exterior* sociology of mental illness and an *immanent*
(or in-dwelling) sociology of 'mental-illness-as-a-social-construct.'
The same contrast, as a matter of fact, is visible in the sociological
treatment of several social-problem areas outside the aetiology of
madness: prostitution, homosexuality, drug addiction and criminal
delinquency are all topics which can be discussed in the literature
either via an external sociology analysing pathological 'givens' or

from an immanent, critical perspective which sees the official counts and categories of deviancy as mere projections of society's formal or informal control-process, and performs an imaginative entry into the deviant's own actions, viewing these as an attempt to manufacture significance for his life within and against a rejecting, 'labelling' world.[3]

Immanent theorists of mental illness, whether in sociology or outside it, have usually had to begin by denying the validity of a natural-science perspective on psychological abnormalities. Thus we have Szasz, Leifer and Goffman drawing a sharp distinction between the natural-scientific, value-free language of physical medicine and the socially and politically loaded language of psychiatry. Szasz believes that, in physical illnesses, "the notion of a bodily symptom is tied to an *anatomical* and *genetic* context" as distinct from the social or ethical context which informs psychiatric judgments: our description of the norm of physical health (a deviation from which constitutes a physical illness or disease) is just a description, which "can be stated in anatomical and physiological terms".[4] Leifer, while thoroughly aware of the social grounding of medicine as a profession, insists that in physical diagnosis and treatment "the term 'disease' refers to phenomena that are not regulated by social custom, morality and law, namely bodily structure and function"; psychiatric concepts of disease refer, on the contrary, to "behaviour, which is subject to the regulation of custom, morality and law".[5]

Erving Goffman, the most influential sociological theorist in the 'anti-psychiatry' tradition, offers in different works a number of quite distinct approaches in the demarcation of physical from psychiatric disorders. One of his most readable books, *Stigma*, applies a careful phenomenological and interpersonal analysis to the victims of physical handicap and disfigurement, with a method very similar to that adopted in his celebrated study of "The Moral Career of the Mental Patient".[6]

Thus far, Goffman would appear to be using a unitary schema in

---

[3] See Earl Rubington and Martin Weinberg, *The Study of Social Problems: Five Perspectives* (New York, 1971), especially Chapters 6 and 7, for a good presentation of the differing vantage-points on deviancy problems.

[4] Thomas S. Szasz, "The Myth of Mental Illness", *The American Psychologist*, February 1960.

[5] Ronald Leifer, *In the Name of Mental Health* (New York, 1969), p. 35. Leifer is a disciple and systematic expounder of Szaszian doctrine with a much more sophisticated use of sociological theory than Szasz has.

[6] *Stigma* (New York, 1961); *Asylums* (New York, 1961), pp. 125-70.

which the division of the patients' case-files into 'psychiatric' versus 'physical' categories would contribute nothing to our further understanding of the difficulties experienced by the subject in his various social settings and encounters. Elsewhere, a more definite distinction between physical and psychiatric symptom construction is propounded. At one point, the 'political' vested interests surrounding the procedures of mental medicine are contrasted with the presumably apolitical practices of ordinary doctoring: thus, decisions concerning behavioural (psychiatric) pathology "tend to be political, in the sense of expressing the interest of some particular faction or person rather than interests that can be said to be above the concerns of any particular grouping as in the case of pathology". There is an assumption here that the language of body-pathology works within a unanimously common culture, rising above the historically-evolved social formations whose notorious diversity has been an important traditional beginning-point of sociological investigation; we shall have occasion later to question this assumption and to provide a few examples of wide cultural variation within man's conceptions of physical illness. Even in the strange sense of 'political' whereby politics means only open dissent among factions (so that, e.g., there could be no such thing as the 'politics' of a successfully manipulated consensus), it is extremely sweeping of Goffman to announce that decisions about physical pathology never involve conflicting interests between different parties to the situation. It is perhaps not surprising that, in his most recent exposition of the difference between 'mental' and 'medical' symptom-patterns,[7] Goffman falls back on an unsophisticated Szasz-type contrast between the purely biological, value-free substrate of medical classifications and the socially-determined character of judgments about mental symptoms.

"Signs and symptoms of a *medical* disorder presumably refer to underlying pathologies in the individual organism, and these constitute deviations from biological norms maintained by the homeostatic functioning of the human machine. The system of reference here is plainly (*sic*) the individual organism, and the term "norm", ideally at least, has no moral or social connotation . . . biological and social norms are quite different things. . . ."[8]

The position of the Laing School is different again. Unlike Szasz

---

[7] In the Appendix, "The Insanity of Place", to *Relations in Public* (London, 1971), pp. 335-90.

[8] RP (No. 7), pp. 345, 346.

and Leifer, Laing does not give a general endorsement to face-to-face psychoanalysis as the method *par excellence* for dealing with disturbed patients in an ethically acceptable (because non-medical) framework, but instead devotes much effort to the critique of psychoanalytic and psychological explanations of human pathology, on the grounds that they do not, with the exception of his own perspective, do justice to the actual experience of persons.[9] The argument is extended by David Cooper in a distinction between "two types of rationality" within the range of scientific knowledge. The study of humankind is to be conducted through a *dialectical rationality* which uses a historical-biographical method modelled on Sartre's interpretation of Jean Genet's life. *Analytic rationality* is the method of the natural sciences, which works for 'inert' data in physics, biology, etc., but is inapplicable to the study of people.[10] It is not clear where this leaves the role of medical science. Cooper concurs with Szasz and Goffman in assigning physiological descriptions of human bodily states to a sphere that lies outside the proper understanding of people. Physiological explanation amounts to a 'reductive analysis', the misuse of analytic rationality in an area (the science of persons) for which it is inappropriate. But learning-theory and psychoanalysis, at any rate in the Freudian form, are equally 'reductive analyses', and just as bad as physiology. However, the Laingian classification of the sciences still has room for the medical role in the treatment of patients. Laing refers to himself as a physician and a psychiatrist,[11] and Cooper offers similar identifiers, complaining only that other doctors should deal with the physical ailments of schizophrenics and that non-medical administrators should attend to the procedural paraphernalia that are at present left to hospital psychiatrists.[12]

To sum up these rather complex alignments of position: it looks as though Laingians deny the applicability of a natural-science method to human investigations but claim that psychiatry (or else anti-psychiatry — which must be 'anti' only in the sense that the Anti-Popes were rivalling the Popes) can still be scientifically based within a suitable Sartrean methodology. There is no special division

[9] See, eg *The Politics of Experience* (London, 1967), pp. 17-18, 41-44; *The Divided Self* (London, 1960), pp. 19-25; *Interpersonal Perception* (London, 1966), pp. 6-7, 40-41.

[10] *Psychiatry and Anti-Psychiatry* (New York, 1971 edition), pp. 7-14.

[11] See, for example, his *Intervention in Social Situations* (London, 1969), p. 17.

[12] David Cooper, "The Anti-Hospital: An Experiment in Social Psychiatry", *New Society*, March 11, 1965.

between the study of bodily states and the study of people: wrong forms of people-study are on one side of the divide, along with the psychiatric misuse of physiology and body-science generally, while the other brighter shore is occupied by a Laingian 'science of persons' which is admittedly still being developed. Szaszians, in contrast, allocate the natural sciences to an area dealing with medically reputable complaints (those referring to diseased organs of the body) and then set up another, non-medical autonomous zone for what is at present called psychiatry; concepts and methods are admitted rather eclectically to this liberated territory, on the sole proviso that psychiatric practitioners must see themselves as consultants responsible to their clients rather than as social agents programming the mentally ill. The 'scientific' status of Free Psychiatry is left indeterminate: Szasz writes at one point as if it had a descriptive, empirical foundation in the cataloguing of developmental levels during social maturation, but more recently has celebrated the 'moral science' of a liberated psychiatry which refuses any classification of persons — including (one may take it) a classification in terms of their level of social development.[13]

The position of the cultural historian Michel Foucault is hard to compare with any of the above theoreticians of present-day psychiatry. Foucault is not concerned to destroy the concepts of psychiatric diagnosis and treatment, but wishes only to point out that each age of civilisation, from the medieval period to modern times, has had its own view of madness which closely reflects the general social and logical preoccupations of the time. Psychopathology is not independent of social history, for each age has drawn the split between madness and reason at a different point and in a fundamentally different fashion. Still it is permissible to seek a psychodynamic or a genetic or an existential account of an individual patient's behaviour, so long as we do not "make these aspects of the illness into ontological forms", real essences which then require "a mythological explanation like the evolution of psychic structure, or the theory of instincts, or an existential anthropology" to support them.[14]

Psychological descriptions of insanity "are not to be suppressed by some explanatory or reductive principle which is exterior to them", but simply situated within the forgotten social-historical framework

[13] MMI (No. 1), pp. 143-5, II (No. 1), pp. 234, 210-11.
[14] *Maladie Mentale et Psychologie* (Paris, 1966), p. 101.

which has given them birth. It is possible, for example, to speak of the psychological state of 'regression' (i.e., of a resumption of infantile patterns) only in a society which has separated infancy as a pre-adult refuge: "neuroses of regression do not display the neurotic character of childhood, but incriminate the archaic nature of the institutions which are concerned with children". Thus, unlike the sociological and other re-definers of mental illness, Foucault does not *eliminate* the psychological and the medical enterprises: instead he brackets them, and shows the text of other human meanings which lies just outside the thin bounds of the parenthesis. And, while for other critics the present world may have room for a liberated region of psychiatry — Szasz's "moral science" for neurotic life-problems or Laing's existential therapy for schizophrenia — which will be immune from the deceits and compulsions of the orthodox medical tradition, there is no such sanctuary in Foucault's psychiatric universe. The moral tyranny and cultural bondage of the Reasonable Man's superior confrontation with Unreason are just as manifest in the psychoanalyst's consulting-room as in the locked wards of the asylum: they are no less implicit in our social attitudes towards neurosis than in our dismissal of the madman's rantings. The images of psychoanalysis, with their percipient charting of defense-shields, traumas, anxieties and other embodi-ments of conflict, do not (as the analysts imagine) reveal the true workings of an inner psychic machinery, but rather reflect "how mankind has made mankind into a contradiction-laden experience", hag-ridden by the theme of "competition, exploitation, group-rivalry and class struggle". Normal social structure is always the hidden truth of the psychology of the abnormal: so that if we may believe that one day, perhaps a genuine communion between Reason and Unreason can be restored, it will be within a new form of society which will see, as one of its natural consequences, the liberation of human thought from psychology.[15] In the here and now, we are left with no hopes for a reformed or even radicalised psychology of madness, and no choice, in working with patients, except to use the psychologised descriptions which have been bequeathed to us as the deposit and the disguise of social classifications made by previous centuries.

The various 'immanent' theorists of mental illness thus diverge, radically in theory and drastically for practice, in the same breath

---

[15] ibid, pp. 102-3, 96, 97-8, 89.

that they converge, as criticism and as negation, upon the established doctrines of psychiatric medicine. Immanentist theory does not present itself as a solid, cumulative mass of concepts which can be wielded as a single heavy weapon against the institutions of psychiatry. The prickled barbs of its various critiques project and tend in so many opposed directions that any attempt to grasp them for use as a unitary whole will wound the critic to the bone of his own logic. It is quite erroneous to speak, as one journalistic enthusiast has already done (in a manner which would be applauded by many other devotees), of a "school of thought" including Szasz, Goffman, Bateson, Cooper and Laing, "which offers this radical reformulation in our ideas about the true nature of mental illness, with its corresponding subversive critique of the established society and culture".[16] Not all of these theorists have expressed beliefs about "the true nature of mental illness": the views of Laing and Cooper (and Bateson) are confined to schizophrenia alone, and Goffman's theory of mental illness comes from quite a different "school of thought" from that of Szasz. Neither Goffman nor Szasz offers any "subversive critique" of larger social institutions, and indeed it appears that these two authors offer an explicitly conservative vision of societal process, founded in Goffman's case on a total immobilism of micro-structures and a total indifference to macro-structures, and in Szasz on the glorification of private medical practice at the expense of social welfare and on an anti-collective individualism which savors far more of America's 'radical-libertarian' Right Wing than of any revolutionary social philosophy. Foucault, as we have seen, is some kind of Marxist, sceptical of the neo-Freudian and existentialist perspectives on humankind that are favoured by the Laing school. Other immanentist writers like Scheff and Lemert are quite silent on the general nature of American (or of capitalist) society, being content to apply, within the special field of mental illness, the concepts of a 'labelling theory' that have been developed by their school of sociology for many types and settings of social deviancy. We have not got here a colony of 'subversives', or even the theoretical base for an 'anti-psychiatry' which would be able to agree on some working alternatives — conceptual or tactical — to the current dominant framework of psychiatric treatment.

What we do have is a consistent and convergent *tendency of*

---

[16] From the Editorial Text to the "Sanity-Insanity: Madness: Violence" issue of *Peace News*, May 19, 1967.

opposition directed against *positivist method* in the study of abnormal
human behaviour. 'Positivism', for the present discussion, may be
taken to refer to an approach towards the investigation of human
pathology which, modelling itself upon antecedents which it believes
to be characteristic of the natural sciences, (*a*) postulates a radical
separation between 'facts' and 'values' (declaring only the former to
be the subject-matter of the professional investigator) and (*b*) suppresses the interactive relationship between the investigator and the
'facts' on which he works.[17] The psychiatric labels which are cata-
logues in textbooks of medicine and clinical psychology are, on a
positivist account, terms which represent, or at least approximate
towards, existent processes inhabiting an objective structure within
the individual: the structure may be his psyche, his autonomic
nervous system, perhaps even in the last resort his brain, but it
stands towards the investigator as the ultimate object of reference
towards which his hypotheses, his empirical techniques and his
standards of validation all tend. To be sure, we may remain suitably
guarded in the finality or the completeness of the claims we may
make for our disease-categories. The judgments of psychiatrists on
individual patients are notoriously prone to discordance: a fact which,
in one variant of the positivist school, has stimulated the search for
more accurate 'measurements' of the deeper dimensions on which
personality-characteristics may be said to lie. Or it may be pointed
out that we are working, at best, with hypothetical constructs of our
own devising: a confession which offers little in the way of modest
disavowal, since on the positivist account all scientific concepts
whatsoever, from atomic particles to the Germ Theory of Disease,
from chemical valencies to the mechanics of blood coagulation, are
equally the inventive constructions of the mind, provisional models
which may be more firmly based in empirical evidence and theoretical
elegance than, say, the Hippocratic humours or the nineteenth century
Ether, but are still artifacts of human production. The stance of the
scientific investigator before the categories of psychopathology differs,
on the positivist case, in no essential way from his relationship to the

---

[17] There are several very different descriptions of what 'positivism' is, referring
to quite separate philosophical tendencies. My short definition above is somewhat
indebted to Leszek Kolakowski's *The Alienation of Reason* (New York, 1969),
but has been invented purely to contrast 'immanent' sociological descriptions of
mental illness with the alternative methodological frameworks in medicine and
psychology: it is not meant to provide any clues to what 'positivism' might be
in other controversies or other fields.

categories of biological disease, to the molecular arrangements of the elements, or to the orderings of animal species suggested by evolutionary theory. Our conceptual units for the subdivision and understanding of the natural world are, if you like, solid; or, if you like, tenuous; but in any case of a muchness. The chair in which the psychiatrist sits and the motions he engages in to sign a certificate exist and function at different levels of the organisation of matter; their existence and functioning may be understood in different departments of the organisation of theory. And the categories of human disorder which he employs in making his professional decisions about patients come from yet another area of the natural sciences, clouded (it is true) by greater complexities of error and uncertainty; they refer to yet another, higher level of the organisation of reality, to the precise inspection of which our instruments have not yet advanced.

Even the most advanced areas of clinical psychiatry bear, in their most basic terminology, the impress of this positivist tradition. We have the thriving discipline of 'the epidemiology of mental disorders', which has repeatedly displayed the considerable social variation, across classes and communities, in the incidence of the major psychological illnesses; yet it achieves this social insight by regarding the contours of the boxes into which its numerations fall as uncontroversial, objective boundaries, analogous to the physical disease-categories which are studied in other branches of the same discipline. ('Epidemiology' means originally, after all, the study of epidemics, that is to say of infectiously transmitted diseases like cholera and tuberculosis, and if the concept of an epidemic is nowadays commonly extended to the germless plagues of heart-disease, heroin-addiction or schizophrenia, it is still supposed to mark the occurrence of morbid conditions as distinct and unambiguous as those produced by actual bacilli.) Similarly, in the application of statistical techniques for the fresh classification of mental disorders (in an attempt to reach groupings of symptoms which will be more systematic than those drawn from clinical experience), we find a reliance on the methods of a 'numerical taxonomy' which was originally devised for the sorting of microbes according to the clustering of their objective characteristics.[18] The judgemental, valuational element in psychiatric

[18] eg C. J. Klett and D. M. McNair, *Syndromes of Psychosis,* (New York, 1963); R. R. Sokal and P. A. Sneath, *Principles of Numerical Taxonomy* (London, 1963).

assessments, in other words their *social* and cultural quality, is simply ignored in these taxonomic investigations. And the same can be said of the manifold drug-trials, behaviour-therapy studies, reports on hospital-ward reform, symptom-questionnaires and the like, which comprises the bulk of the serious journals of present-day clinical psychology and psychiatry.[19]

It is to the permanent credit of the immanentist critics of psychiatry that they have exposed the inadequacy of this positivist framework for the understanding of mental illness. Whatever exaggerations the more radical anti-psychiatrists and labelling-theory sociologists have engaged in, they have shown convincingly that both diagnoses and treatment-measures in psychiatry are founded on ethical judgements and social demands whose content is sometimes reactionary, often controversial and nearly always left unstated. Mental illness is a social construction: psychiatry is a social institution, incorporating the values and demands of its surrounding society. These conclusions, and their supporting arguments, deserve to be placed in the forefront of all teaching material aimed towards those who seek guidance on the problems of mental illness. Foucault and Laing, Goffman and Szasz, Scheff and Lemert, should be made part of the curriculum for all aspirant therapists, nurses and social workers in this field. Never again should it be possible for a lecturer to instruct his students, or the public, that 'mental illnesses may be caused by heredity, the environment, or a combination of both' or that 'outcome in psychopathology depends on a combination of exterior stress and the inner predisposition of the patient'. For such dicta, however seemingly authoritative and 'scientifically grounded', simply obscure a number of central features of mental illness and its associated agencies of treatment and care. For to say that somebody is mentally ill, or to announce oneself as mentally ill, is to attach complex social meanings to acts and behaviours that in other societies, or in different contingencies within our own society, would be interpreted in the light of quite different concepts. The accidents of heredity and the blows of environment do not add up or multiply into the social position and personal identity of being 'mentally ill', any more than in bygone years they combined sufficiently to form the status of being 'a witch', or of being 'possessed by spirits', or of being 'under the influence of

---

[19] This observation is not intended as a dismissal of these studies, whose method is often compatible with the valuational outlook on mental illness that will be developed later in this paper.

black bile' (to name a few of the alternative significations that have
been attached to the behaviours nowadays classified in the light of
'mental illness' concepts). 'Stress' and 'predisposition' are valuable
categories for the understanding of organisms and their malfunction-
ing; but we are concerned, in the understanding of human beings,
with the impact of stressful meanings as these affect the predisposition
of individuals to screen and consolidate these meanings into their
established images of self and society. Trauma and resistance to
trauma can, in the human case, be understood not on the analogy of
a physical force striking a more or less brittle object, nor on the lines
of the invasion of an organism by hostile bacteria, but only through
the transformation of elements in a person's identity and his capacity
to relate to other persons and social collectives. And what positivist
accounts of mental illness most flagrantly omit is the serious
'stress' (of socially-charged meanings, and not of physical or biological
influences) imposed on the subject-patient by the acts of diagnosis,
classification, hospitalization and (even, in many cases) 'treatment'.
As Marx criticised the Utopian Socialists for arriving at a position
which involved dividing society into two parts of which one (themselves) was seen as 'superior to society', so must the clinical positivism
of 'psychopathology' stand condemned for its stance of cultural smug-
ness, its erection of a local, twentieth-century style of assessment into
a timeless biological universal, its failure to take stock of its own
social role. The Utopians, Marx observed, were so busy trying to
educate society into Socialism that they forgot that "the educator
must himself be educated"; the clinical positivists are so involved in
uncovering the factual, objective basis of psychopathology that they
have forgotten the subjective valuations which impregnate their whole
enterprise. Sooner or later, for good or ill, the valuators must themselves be valued, and their judgments judged.

But the immanentist critique of clinical positivism (and of the
latter's ally, the purely exterior 'medical sociology') has begun the
task of this evaluation at a somewhat odd starting-point. In seizing
on the value-laden, subjective, 'political' elements of psychiatric diagnosis and treatment, they have implicitly — and sometimes, indeed,
explicitly — conceded the value-free, apolitical and 'objective' character of medicine-in-general: their dismissal of positivism in psychiatry
is founded on a contract with non-psychiatric medicine which actually
depends on the acceptance of positivism as a possible method in vital

areas of human decision-making. The split between fact and value is reinstated at a superordinate, strategic level precisely in order to attack it in the tactical onslaught against the particular medical specialism of psychiatry. Physical medicine belongs to the world of Fact, of the natural sciences, of anatomy and physiology, of objectively ascertainable disturbed conditions of the body or its 'functioning', and psychiatry belongs to the world of Value, of ethical judgements on behaviour, of factional coalitions against the unhappy victim, or covert and malignant social and political control. The immanentists *have accomplished the feat of criticising the concept of mental illness without ever examining the (surely more inclusive, and logically prior) concept of illness.* They have focussed a merciless lens on psychiatric treatment, detailing its foibles, its fallacies, and its destructiveness towards human self-respect, while at the same time maintaining a posture of reverent myopia towards the chemical, surgical and other therapeutic procedures that are directed by doctors against the many targets of the human organism that lie outside the gray and white matter of the cerebrum. For one who (like myself) has searched the sociological and critical-philosophical literature dealing in the various fields of medicine, the evidence of selective myopia is simply overwhelming. There is no sociological examination of illness, or of medical theory and practice, which corresponds to Scheff's *Becoming Mentally Ill,* or to Goffman's "Mental Symptoms and Public Order", within the psychiatric specialty. There is no popular critical review of practices and concepts in general physical medicine which in any way parallels the thoughtful anti-psychiatric writings of Thomas Szasz and Ronald Leifer: Shaw's play *The Doctor's Dilemma* (along with the searching Preface to its printed edition) remains as a classic locus in this practically nonexistent genre. *The Journal of Health and Social Behaviour,* established by the American Sociological Association as an organ for theoretical and empirical contributions in the sociology of health and disease, concentrates (at least in its more conceptually oriented articles) on the social character of psychiatric practices and institutions, to the virtual neglect of all other branches of therapy. In the anthropological study of medical practice across different cultures, the literature of the folk-medicine of physical ailments is small besides the immense bulk of reports on 'ethno-psychiatry' in the more primitive societies of the world: I know of no journal, for instance, which performs for physical medicine the service provided by the excellent journal *Transcultural Psychiatric Research,* published from McGill University, Montreal. Among critical philosophers, no book or article on physical maladies parallels, for example, Foucault's *Madness and Civilisation,* or the many reappraisals of Freudian psychopathology. The philosophers of 'ordinary language' in the post-Wittgenstein tradition have singularly refrained from any logical analysis of what it means to be ill or to seek treatment: the classic phenomenological and linguistic-philosophical discussions of the notions of pain, or of the body, always take place in a curiously non-medical context, in the logician's proverbial armchair rather than on the hard seat of the waiting-room or the Casualty Department's stretcher. Doubtless there exist substantial reasons for this chronically repetitive suspension of the critical faculty in the face of general medicine. Physical medicine and surgery have achieved, after all, extraordinary advances, to the blessing of countless millions: who wants to pick a quarrel with success, particularly with the success of a miraculous technology projected in the service of universally acclaimed ideals? Yet the problem remains: We cannot review the social institutions of mental illness independently of, or prior to, the institutions and constructions that men have elaborated for the case of plain illness.[20]

What, then, is 'illness'? It will be recalled that critical theory in psychiatry has tended to postulate a fundamental separation between mental illnesses and the general run of human ailments: the former are the expression of social norms, the latter proceed from ascertainable bodily states which have an 'objective' existence within the individual. One critic of psychopathological concepts, Barbara Wootton, has suggested that the expurgation of normative references from psychiatry is at least a theoretical ideal, though one immensely difficult of achievement: ". . . anti-social behaviour is the precipitating factor that leads to mental treatment. But at the same time the fact

---

[20] Talcott Parsons did develop an analysis of "the sick role", in Chapter 10 of *The Social System* (Glencoe, 1951), but this refers more to the status of *being a patient,* within a system of medical facilities, than to the concept of *being ill.* He has a more extensive discussion of health and illness in Chapter 10 of his *Social Structure and Personality* (New York, 1964), but for reasons too detailed to relate here, I cannot accept his terms. David Mechanic's *Medical Sociology* (New York, 1968) begins with a specification of disease which I find somewhat too general: "some deviation from normal functioning which has undesirable consequences, because it produces personal discomfort or adversely affects the individual's future health status" (p. 15). It would not be possible to distinguish illness from fatigue or bereavement on this definition, since these deviations from "normal functioning" are undoubtedly uncomfortable.

of the illness is itself inferred from the behaviour. . . . But any disease, the morbidity of which is established only by the social failure that it involves, must rank as fundamentally different from those of which the symptoms are independent of the social norms . . . long indeed is the road to be travelled before we can hope to reach a definition of mental-cum-physical health which is objective, scientific and wholly free of social value judgements and before we shall be able, consistently and without qualification, to treat mental and physical disorders on exactly the same footing."[21] Wooton's view has stimulated at least one attempt to begin the task of purging all cultural norms — with their inconvenient variability from one society to another — from the diagnosis of mental illness: Dr. Joseph Zubin has reported some work on 'culture-free' assessments of schizophrenia which involve the analysis of reaction-times, responses to electrical stimulation, and the like, among schizophrenic patients.[22] It would be fair to say that research in the refinement of psychiatric categories has been mounted with a similar perspective in mind, straining towards the physical-medicine ideal of a set of symptom-descriptions "independent of the social norms." Value-judgements and cultural stereotypes are seen as one form of 'error' coming between the investigator and his desired data, and the ultimate standard sought in the description of illness is to be taken to be a sociologically inert, culturally sterile specification of facts and processes which are grounded in bacteriology, biochemistry, physiology or perhaps some variety of cybernetic systems-theory.

But this enterprise, tending constantly towards the microscopic and molecular analysis of the 'objective' substrate of behaviour, forms only one of the ways in which we might begin to place mental and physical illnesses "on exactly the same footing". If we examine the logical structure of our judgements of illness (whether 'physical' or 'mental') it may prove possible to reduce the distance between psychiatry and other streams of medicine by working in the reverse direction to Wooton: not by annexing psychopathology to the technical instrumentation of the natural sciences but by revealing the character of illness and disease, health and treatment, as social constructions. For social constructions they most certainly are. All departments of nature

---

[21] *Social Science and Social Pathology* (London, 1959), p. 225.
[22] J. Zubin, "A Cross-Cultural Approach to Psychopathology and its Implications for Diagnostic Classifications", pp. 43-82 in L. D. Eron (ed.), *The Classification of Behavior Disorders* (Chicago, 1966).

below the level of mankind are exempt both from disease and from treatment — until man intervenes with his own human classifications of disease and treatment. The blight that strikes at corn or at potatoes is a *human invention,* for if man wished to cultivate parasites (rather than potatoes or corn) there would be no 'blight', but simply the necessary foddering of the parasite-crop. Animals do not have diseases either, prior to the presence of man in a meaningful relation with them. A tiger may experience pain or feebleness from a variety of causes (we do not intend to build our case on the supposition that animals, especially higher animals, cannot have experiences or feelings). It may be infected by a germ, trodden by an elephant, scratched by another tiger, or subjected to the ageing processes of its own cells. It does not present itself as being *ill* (though it may present itself as being highly distressed or uncomfortable) except in the eyes of a human observer who can discriminate illness from other sources of pain or enfeeblement. Outside the significances that man voluntarily attaches to certain conditions, *there are no illnesses or diseases in nature.* We are nowadays so heavily indoctrinated with deriving from the technical medical discoveries of the last century-and-a-half that we are tempted to think that nature does contain diseases. Just as the sophisticated New Yorker classes the excrement of dogs and cats as one more form of 'pollution' ruining the pre-established harmony of pavements and gardens, so does modern technologised man perceive nature to be mined and infested with all kinds of specifically morbid entities and agencies. What, he will protest, are there no diseases in nature? Are there not infectious and contagious bacilli? Are there not definite and objective lesions in the cellular structures of the human body? Are there not fractures of bones, the fatal ruptures of tissues, the malignant multiplications of tumorous growths? Are not these, surely, events of nature? Yet these, as natural events, do not — prior to the human social meanings we attach to them — constitute illnesses, sicknesses or diseases. The fracture of a septuagenarian's femur has, within the world of nature, no more significance than the snapping of an autumn leaf from its twig: and the invasion of a human organism by cholera-germs carries with it no more the stamp of 'illness' than does the souring of milk by other forms of bacteria.[23] Human beings, like all other naturally occurring structures,

---

[23] The above discussion is heavily indebted to Rene Dubos' masterly *The Mirage of Health* (New York, 1971), especially pp. 30-128.

are characterised by a variety of inbuilt limitations or liabilities, any of which may (given the presence of further stressful circumstances) lead to the weakening or the collapse of the organism. Mountains as well as moles, stars as well as shrubs, protozoa no less than persons have their dates of expiry set in advance, over a time-span which varies greatly over different classes of structure but which is usually at least roughly predictable. Out of his anthropocentric self-interest, man has chosen to consider as 'illnesses' or 'diseases' those natural circumstances which precipitate the death (or the failure to function according to certain values) of a limited number of biological species: man himself, his pets and other cherished livestock, and the plant-varieties he cultivates for gain or pleasure. Around these select areas of structural failure man creates, in proportion to the progress of his technology, specialized combat-institutions for the control and cure of 'disease': the different branches of the medical and nursing profession, veterinary doctors, and the botanical specialists in plant-disease. Despite their common concern with disease, and their common use of experimental natural science, these institutions operate according to very different criteria and codes; the use of euthanasia by vets, and of ruthless eugenic policies by plant-pathologists, departs from most current medical practice with human patients. All the same, the fact that these specialisms share the categories of disease and illness indicates the selective quality of our perceptions in this field. Children and cattle may fall ill, have diseases, and seem as sick; but who has ever imagined that spiders or lizards can be sick or diseased? Plant-diseases may strike at tulips, turnips or such prized features of the natural landscape as elm trees: but if some plant-species in which man had no interest (a desert grass, let us say) were to be attacked by a fungus or parasite, we should speak not of a disease, but merely of the competition between two species. The medical enterprise is from its inception value-loaded; it is not simply an applied biology, but a biology applied in accordance with the dictates of social interest.

It could be argued that the discussion of animal and plant pathology deals in cases that are too marginal to our central concepts of health and illness to form a satisfactory basis for analysis. Such marginal instances are of course frequently used by logicians in the analysis of concepts since their peripheral character often usefully tests the limits within which our ideas can be seen to be applicable or inapplicable. However, a careful examination of the concept of illness in man himself will reveal the same value-impregnation, the same dependency of apparently descriptive, natural-scientific notions upon our norms of what is desirable. To complain of illness, or to ascribe illness to another person, is not to make a descriptive statement about physiology or anatomy. Concepts of illness were in use among men for centuries before the advent of any reliable knowledge of the human body, and are still employed today within societies which favour a non-physiological (magical or religious) account of the nature of human maladies. Our own classification and explanation of specific illnesses or diseases is of course tremendously different from the categories that are current in earlier ages or in contemporary tribal societies, but it is implausible to suppose that the state of illness itself has no common logical features over different types of society. Homer's sick warriors were tended by magical incantations as well as by herbs and other primitive technical remedies,[24] but the avowal and ascription of illness in Homer does not set up a distance between his characters and ourselves but rather (like his descriptions of bereavement or of sexual attraction) a powerful resonance across the ages. Similarly, the meaning of illness among primitive peoples is usually sufficiently close to our own to enable them to take advantage of modern medical facilities when these are made accessible within their territories: tribesmen and peasants do not have to be indoctrinated into Western physiological concepts before they can accept help from physicians and nurses trained in advanced societies. Sickness and disease may be conceptualised, in different cultures, as originating within bodily states, or within perturbations of the spirit, or as a mixture of both. Yet there appear to be common features in the declaration or attribution of the sick state, regardless of the causal explanation that is invoked.

All sickness is essentially deviancy. That is to say, no attribution of sickness to any being can be made without the expectation of some alternative state of affairs whch is considered more desirable. In the absence of this normative alternative, the presence of a particular bodily or subjective state will not in itself lead to an attribution of illness. Thus, where an entire community is by Western standards 'ill', because it has been infected for generations by parasites which diminish energy, illness will not be recognized in any individual

---

[24] See the excellent account of Homeric medicine in P. Lain Entralgo, *The Therapy of the Word in Classical Antiquity* (New Haven, 1970).

except by outsiders.[25] The Rockefeller Sanitary Commission on Hookworm found in 1911 that this disease was regarded as part of normal health in some areas of North Africa.[26] And in one South American Indian tribe the disease of dyschromic spirochetosis, which is marked by the appearance of coloured spots on the skin, was so 'normal' that those who did not have them were regarded as pathological and excluded from marriage.[27] Even within modern urbanised nations we cannot assume that aches, pains and other discomforts are uniformly categorised as signs of illness among all sections of the community. Although little work has been done on social-class variations in the construction of what constitutes 'health' and 'sickness',[28] the example of tooth-decay is suggestive: among millions of British working-class families, it is taken for granted that children will lose their teeth and require artificial dentures. The process of tooth-loss is not seen as a disease but as something like an act of fate. Among dentists, on the other hand, and in those more-educated sections of the community who are socialised into dental ideology, the loss of teeth arises through a definite disease-process known as caries, whose aetiology is established.[29] Social and cultural norms also plainly govern the varying perception, either as essentially 'normal', or as essentially 'pathological', of such characteristics as baldness, obesity, infestation by lice, venereal infection, and the presence of tonsils and foreskins among children.

Once again it can be argued that these cultural variations apply only to marginal cases of sickness and health, that there are some physical or psychological conditions which are *ipso facto* symptomatic of illness, whether among Bushmen or Brobdignagians, duchesses or dockworkers. But there is no reason to believe that the 'standardised' varieties of human pathology operate according to a different logic from the 'culturally dependent' varieties. The existence of common or even universal illnesses testifies, not to the absence of a normative

[25] I have taken this observation from Dr. L. Robbins' discussion in Eron, CBD (No. 22).

[26] Cited by A. L. Knudsen, *The Individual, Society and Health Behavior* (New York, 1965), p. 49.

[27] Cited by Mechanic, MS (No. 20), p. 16.

[28] Knudsen, ISHB (No. 26), p. 48, quotes one New York study showing lower-class indifference to the need for medical attention for such conditions as ankle-swelling and backache. But these should still have been regarded as illnesses by the respondents, who could have had their own reasons (such as lack of cash) for refusing to consider medical treatment.

[29] There is now some doubt among dental experts as to whether 'caries' is a genuine disease-entity or an artifact of diagnostic labelling.

framework for judging pathology, but to the presence of very wide-spread norms. To be ill, after all, is not the same thing as to feel pain, or to experience weakness, or to fail to manifest this or that kind of behaviour. Rather it is to experience discomfort (or to manifest behavioural failure) in a context of a particular kind. Consider the following imaginary conversations between physician and client:

(a) *Client*   Doctor, I want you to examine me, I keep feeling terrible pains in my right shoulder.

    Doctor   Really? What are they like?

    Client   Stabbing and intense.

    Doctor   How often do they happen?

    Client   Every evening after I get home from work.

    Doctor   Always in the same spot?

    Client   Yes, just in the place where my wife hits me with the rolling-pin.

(b) *Client*   (Telephoning Doctor) Doctor, I haven't consulted you before but things are getting desperate. I'm feeling so weak, I can't lift anything heavy.

    Doctor   Goodness, when does this come on you?

    Client   Every time I try to lift something or make an effort. I have to walk quite slowly up the stairs and last night when I was packing the big suitcase I found I couldn't lift it off the bed.

    Doctor   Well, let's have some details about you before you come in. Name?

    Client   John Smith.

    Doctor   Age?

    Client   Ninety-two last February.

In the first example, the 'patient's' pain is not an illness because we expect pain as a normal response to being hit in tender places; indeed, if he did *not* feel pain when he was hit or prodded he would be taken to be suffering from some disease involving nerve-degeneration. In the second example, the patient's infirmity would usually be ascribed not to the category of "illness' but to that of 'ageing'. (If he had given his age as 'twenty-two' the case would be different.) In our culture we expect old people to find difficulty in lifting heavy weights, although it is easy to conceive of a culture in which mass rejuvenation among the aged had been perfected (perhaps by the injection of hormones, vitamins or other pep-pills into the water-supply) and where, in consequence, a dialogue of the type recounted would lead to a perfectly ordinary referral for medical treatment. The attribution of illness always proceeds from the computation of a gap between presented behaviour (or feeling) and some social norm. In practice of course we take the norm for granted, so that the broken arm or the elevated temperature is seen alone as the illness. But the broken arm would be no more of an illness than a broken fingernail unless it stopped us from achieving certain socially constructed goals; just as, if we could all function according to approved social requirements within any range of body-temperature, thermometers would disappear from the household medical kit.

This is not to say that illness amounts to any deviancy whatsoever from social expectations about how men should function. Some deviancies are regarded as instances not of sickness but of criminality, wickedness, poor upbringing or bad manners (though not all cultures do in fact draw a firm line between illness and these other deviations, e.g., primitive societies for whom illness is also a moral flaw and modern liberal circles for whom drug-addiction is categorised in medical as well as moral terms). Looking over the very wide range of folk-concepts and technical ideas about illness which exist in the history of human societies, one finds it difficult to discern a common structural element which distinguishes the notion of illness from other attributions of social failure. Provisionally, it is possible to suggest that illness is set apart from other deviancies insofar as the description (or, at a deeper level, the explanation) of the sick state is located within a relatively restricted set of causal factors operating within the boundaries of the individual human being. One may become ill as the result of being infected by germs, or through being entered by evil demons, or visited by a curse from the Almighty. Each culturally specific account of illness must involve a theory of the person, of the boundaries between the person and the world 'outside' him, and of the ways in which adverse influences can trespass over these limits and besiege or grip him. If the current theory of the person is positivistic and physical, the agencies of illness will be seen as arising from factors within (or at the boundaries of) his body; in cultures with an animistic tradition, the invasion will be one of the spirit or soul. But, however variously the nature of illness is specified from culture to culture, the attribution of illness appears to include a *quest for explanation*, or at least the descriptive delimiting of certain

types of causal factor, as well as the normative component outlined
above. It is indeed likely that the concept of illness has arisen in
close parallel with the social practice of therapy, i.e., with the development of techniques to control those human afflictions which can
be controlled at the boundaries of the individual person. It is hard
to see how the category of illness, as a distinct construction separate
from other kinds of misfortune, could have arisen without the
discovery that some varieties of pain and affliction could be succoured
through individual specialised attention to the afflicted person. In
traditional societies, of course, the institution of medicine is not
crystallised out as an applied branch of natural science: 'Therapy'
for the Greeks was simply the word used for looking after or tending
somebody, and, in Greece as well as elsewhere, a great deal of therapy
goes on either in the patient's household or in conjunction with
religious and magical specialisms. A specifically 'medical' framework
of treatment is not necessary to provide the link between illness and
practical action.

Practice and concept continue their mutual modification over the
ages. In a society where the treatment of the sick is still conducted
through religious ritual, the notion of illness will not be entirely
distinct from the notion of sinfulness or pollution. Correspondingly,
with the growth of progressively more technical and more autonomous
specialisms of therapy, the concepts of disease and illness themselves
become more technical, and thereby more alienated from their implicit
normative background. Thus we reach the position of the present day
where any characterisation of an 'illness' which is not amenable to
a diagnosis drawn from physiology or to a therapy based on chemical,
electrical or surgical technique becomes suspect as not constituting,
perhaps, an illness at all. Such has been the fate of mental illness
in our own epoch. It has been much easier for societies with an
animistic theory of the person (and of his boundaries and suscepti-
bilities to influence) to view mental disturbances on a par with
bodily ailments. Ceremonies of ritual purgation and demon-expul-
sion, along with primitive 'medical' methods of a herbal or surgical
type, are used indifferently by traditional healers on patients
with a mental or with a bodily dysfunction. Fever and madness,
the broken limb or the broken spirit are situated within the
same normative frame, within the same explanatory and therapeutic
system. Even the development of a technical-physiological specialism

of medicine, such as emerged with the Hippocratic tradition which runs in fits and starts from antiquity to modern times, does not impair the possibility of a unitary perspective on physical and mental illness, *so long as a common structure of valuation and explanation applies over the whole range of disorders of the person.* The medicine of the seventeenth and eighteenth centuries in Western Europe, for instance, was able to interpret our present-day 'mental' disorders as a group of illnesses inhabiting the embodied person on much the same plane as other sorts of malady: the insane or the emotionally disturbed patient was suffering from a fault of 'the vapours', 'the nerves', 'the fluids', 'the animal spirits', 'the spleen', 'the humours', 'the head', or the forces and qualities of the body.[30] This unitary integration of human illnesses was of course only achieved at the cost of a stupendously inaccurate and speculative physiology. But an integrated theory of illness, whether achieved within a unitary-animistic or a unitary-physicalistic doctrine of the person, has one singular advantage over a more fragmentary perspective: it is not beset by the kind of crisis we now have in psychopathology and psychiatry, whose conceptual and moral foundation has been exploded now that 'illness" has acquired a technical-physical definition excluding disorders of the whole person from its purview. Animistic and unitary-physicalistic accounts of illness both dealt in the whole embodied individual, but the medical technology of the nineteenth century and onwards has succeeded in classifying illnesses as particular states of the body only. Psychiatry is left with two seeming alternatives: either to say that personal, psychological and emotional disorders are really states of the body, objective features of the brain-tissue, the organism-under-stress, the genes or what have you; or else to deny that such disorders are illnesses at all. If the latter, then the way is open to treat mental illnesses as the expression of social value-judgements about the patient, and psychiatry's role will not belong to the disciplines of objective, body-state medicine. Instead, it will be analogous to the value-laden and non-medical disciplines of moral education, police interrogation, criminal punishment or religion (depending on how low or how lofty a view one takes of the values inherent in psychiatric practice).

This dilemma will perhaps seem somewhat to dissolve if we

---

[30] See Foucault, MC (No. 2), pp. 119, 121, 123, 129 and 151 ff. Entralgo, in TWCA (No. 24) has similar explanations collected from ancient Hippocratic medicine.

recapitulate what was previously said about the nature of illness as a social construction. *All* illness, whether conceived in localised bodily terms or within a larger view of human functioning, expresses both a social value-judgment (contrasting a person's condition with certain understood and accepted norms) and an attempt at explanation (with a view to controlling the disvalued condition). The physicalistic psychiatrists are wrong in their belief that they can find objective disease-entities representing the psychopathological analogues to diabetes, tuberculosis and post-syphilitic paresis. Quite correctly, the anti-psychiatrists have pointed out that psychopathological categories refer to value-judgements and that mental illness is deviancy. On the other hand, the anti-psychiatric critics themselves are wrong when they imagine physical medicine to be essentially different in its logic from psychiatry. A diagnosis of diabetes, or paresis, includes the recognition of norms or values. Anti-psychiatry can only operate by positing a mechanical and inaccurate model of physical illness and its medical diagnosis.

In my own judgement, then, mental illnesses can be conceptualised just as easily within the disease framework as physical maladies such as lumbago or TB.

There are several misunderstandings that might arise, or indeed have arisen, from my declaration of this position: let me try to remove these misapprehensions at once. In the first place, it does not follow from my statement that the existing 'official' diagnostic categories of mental illness are the most useful or truthful ones that we can reach. I believe, for example, that 'psychopathy' represents no more than an attempt at social labelling, for control purposes, by psychiatrists working in tandem with the judicial authorities. It is likely, also, that 'schizophrenia' is a pretty useless dustbin category for a variety of psychic ills which have little logically or biologically in common with one another. Equally, though, I have no doubt that many current diagnostic categories in physical medicine will disappear in the next century or so, and be replaced by others apparently (and provisionally) more adequate. I can see that, for example, by the year 2072 nobody will be classed as having diabetes or asthma, though they will undergo feelings of discomfort similar to those experienced by present-day diabetics and asthmatics. In the future development of our species, we can anticipate *either* that some conditions now classified as illnesses will be re-allocated to a different framework of deviancy (or, more drastically, become regarded as essentially normal and non-deviant); *or* that, on the contrary, conditions which are nowadays viewed in a non-illness category of deviancy (as sins, perhaps, or as consequences of ageing or excessive effort) will be re-grouped into the range of the illnesses or diseases. The latter prospect — the progressive annexation of not-illness into illness — seems at the moment much more likely to happen than the former, especially since the stupendous achievements of medical technology make it more and more difficult for doctors to sign death certificates under the rubric 'died of natural causes'. The natural causes of death are becoming, more and more, causes that we can control: so that the terminally ill, and their relatives, will be putting strong pressures on the medical profession to redefine the natural (and inevitable) causes of fatality, rendering them into medical (and hence controllable) pathologies which require the services of a doctor rather than of a mortician. *The future belongs to illness*: we just are going to get more and more diseases, since our expectations of health are going to become more expansive and sophisticated. Maybe one day there will be a backlash, perhaps at the point when everybody has become so luxuriantly ill, physically or mentally, that there will be poster-parades of protest outside medical conventions with slogans like ILLNESS IS NOT SO BAD, YOU KNOW? or DISEASE IS THE HIGHEST FORM OF HEALTH. But for the moment, it seems that illness is going to be 'in': a rising tide of really chronic sickness. Even despite the Canutes of deviancy-sociology.

Secondly and much more importantly, nothing in my argument confirms the technologising of illness; the specialised medical model of illness is not the only possible one, as I have already indicated. As Dubos points out in his fundamental work *The Mirage of Health* (to which this paper is merely more or less a vulgarised addendum), the greatest advances in the control of disease have often come about through non-medical measures, and in particular through social and political change. The insertion of windows into working-class houses (with the consequent beneficial influx of sunlight), or the provision of a pure water-supply and an efficient sewage-disposal, did more to clear up the plagues of modern epidemic infection than did the identification of particular microbes or the synthesis of 'medical discoveries' like the various antibiotics and antitoxins. There are

some authorities, notably Osmond and his collaborators,[31] who argue
that, since the category of illness is infinitely preferable, from the
standpoint of the mentally deranged, to any other variety of deviancy,
we have to concentrate entirely on a narrow medical model for
explaining diseases and curing them; in their view, social explanations
for the onset of illnesses like schizophrenia and drug-addiction are
incompatible with any illness-model, and so should be ruthlessly
jettisoned. But we do not need to technologise illness beyond the
point at which we decide that it is helpful to do so; even with
physical illness, the concept of a 'social disease' is indispensable in the
understanding and treatment of, for example, tuberculosis. Preventive
medicine and public medicine are bound to invoke social explanations
and social measures, to occupy a space which occurs, in short, at the
intersection of medicine and politics. My case points, not to the
technologising of illness, to the medicalisation of moral values (so
obvious in the practice of psychiatry that it needs no fresh rehearsal
here): but, on the contrary, to the politicisation of medical goals.
I am arguing that, without the concept of illness — including that of
mental illness since to exclude it would constitute the crudest dualism
— we shall be unable to *make demands* on the health-service facilities
of the society that we live in.

Those labelling theorists who like to yearn for the Lost Territories
of deviancy now occupied by the invading armies of medical diagnosis,
are committing a *sociological irredentism* quite as offensive as the
better-known bogey of Psychiatric Imperialism. Assemblies of devi-
ancy-experts remind me of nothing so much as the sad, moral-boosting
reunions of Sudeten Germans in the Federal Republic: they appear
dangerous to the Czechs, but basically such gatherings are those of
the devotees of a lost cause, joining in old songs and refurbished
regional accents in order to maintain a losing identity against the
harsh world which offers many rival opportunities for re-socialisation.
The 'demands' of the Sudeten Germans are, in 1972, a ritual, even
if they were not so in 1938. The demands of the sociological
revisionists of mental illness are not very obvious even as ritual:
they appear to want more money for their own research, and one or
two of their allies want to be left undisturbed to carry on rewarding

[31] Miriam Siegler and Humphry Osmond, 'Models of Madness', *British
Journal of Psych*iatry, 1966 Vol. 112, pp. 1193-1203; Miriam Siegler and Humphry Osmond, 'Models of Drug Addiction', *International Journal of the Addic-
tions*, 1968, Vol. 3, No. 1, pp. 3-24.

private psychoanalytic practices.[32] But theirs is a passive irredentism; after all, the sociologists never actually lived in the territories that the psychiatric colonizers have now taken over, so there cannot be very much energy in their grumbles. This very passivity is, however, highly dangerous in the present historical period when the amount of public money available for investment in the health services is so grossly inadequate. The voice of labelling sociology, including a good many of the 'immanentist' theoreticians, chimes in with the cautious, restrictive tones of the cheese-paring politician who is out to deny the priority of resource-allocation for the public psychiatric services (at the same time as he budgets lavishly for the military). Public psychiatry, as the result of the onslaughts of Szasz, Goffman and Laing and — to a smaller extent — of the other academic 'anti-psychiatrists', has become thoroughly unpopular with the general reading public. And since this middle-class public forms the great reservoir of candidates from which the officer-class of possible pressure-groups gets selected, the unpopularity of public-health psychiatry is an important factor which prevents the crystallisation of a vocal and determined lobby for the provision of intensive psychiatric facilities on a mass scale. Mental illness, like mental health, is a fundamentally *critical* concept: or can be made into one provided that those who use it are prepared to place demands and pressures on the existing organisation of society. In trying to remove and reduce

---

[32] The whole literary oeuvre of Szasz and Leifer is an attempt to justify one important way in which they earn their living: they are both psychoanalysts in private practice, accepting fees, sufficient to compensate them for the loss of time they might be spending in other work, from people who are in agony. Like any other intellectual, each of them has to justify what he is doing. They have to say: 'Well, at least it's better than what other people (eg psychiatrists in the community health services) are doing.' They also have to say: 'There is something rather important and special about this private fee-paying relationship: for example, it guarantees confidentiality and the responsibility of the therapist to the client alone, in a way which the psychiatrists in a publicly financed and organised health service, with their necessarily divided loyalties, cannot manage.' Hence their imperative need to destroy, intellectually (they cannot of course do it in practice, and would probably feel guilty if they could) the public mental-health service through attacking its main ideology, the category of 'mental illness'. There are of course serious problems, of the kind they adeptly stigmatise, in the bureaucratised psychiatric professions; divided loyalties are a fairly common fact of everyday life, but not everybody with a division of loyalties is a traitor. A psychiatrist or counsellor in a publicly financed institution is expected to be something of a double agent who can of course lay himself open to accusations of betrayal from either cause that he serves, i.e., from the institution or from the client. But being a double agent can be a perfectly honourable profession, at least before the court of honour which is the agent's own conscience. Whether other people believe that a person with divided loyalties is honourable or treacherous is, of course, a matter for *their* judgment alone.

the concept of mental illness, the revisionist theorists have made it
that bit much harder for a powerful campaign of reform in the
mental-health services to get off the ground. The revisionists have
thought themselves, and their public, into a state of complete inertia:
they can expose the hypocrisies and annotate the tragedies of official
psychiatry, but the concepts which they have developed enable them
to engage in no public action which is grander than that of wringing
their hands. Of course they do it beautifully. But the tragic stance of
labelling theory and anti-psychiatric sociology cannot be taken
seriously as a posture which is 'above the battle' for the priorities
of spending within our bureaucratised and militarised capitalism. It
is *in* the battle, on the wrong side: the side of those who want to
close down intensive psychiatric units and throw the victims of mental
illness on to the streets, with the occasional shot of tranquilliser
injected in them to assure the public that something medical is still
happening.

It may surprise some readers to hear that I, as a revolutionary
socialist and Marxist, am so desirous of stimulating effective reforms
in the mental-health field. But for a modern, engaged Marxism, the
evolution of *transitional demands* on the existing social and political
structure is essential. Just as the revolutionary exposes and pressurises
Parliamentary 'democracy' by demanding *consistent democracy;* just
as he exposes and fights the courts of bourgeois 'justice' by demanding
consistent justice: so he must expose and combat the evils of our anti-
therapeutic institutions of 'psychiatry' by demanding *consistent
psychiatry*. A transitional demand in Trotsky's classic conception, is
one which is placed on the system in the full knowledge that the
system cannot grant it: the failure of the system to deliver its declared
pledges will then expose its reactionary character before the masses.
In the present era, which is characterised by mass demands for
adequate medical treatment, *all* demands for public-health provision
(including the demand for mass psychiatric services) are transitional
in quality. The revolutionary can enter a united front with reformists
(as he does all the time, for instance, in trade-union work), to place
new pressures on the social order: if the system really can grant all
that it claims to be able to do, the Marxist will have no quarrel with
it, or with the reformists and liberals who expect it to carry out its
promises. If (as the Marxist expects) the system cannot deliver the
goods, then his liberal or reformist allies will become radicalised, and

may even join the ranks of his Marxist comrades. So a united front is always possible, and indeed must always be sought, between revolutionaries and reformers. But no united front and no dialogue is possible between revolutionaries and cynics. Cynics are, quite simply, people who have no hope, and therefore have no capacity to express any demands for the future. The sociological critics of the 'mental illness' concept are, as ideologues, deeply cynical: if they do have hope, or any possibility of formulating demands in the mental-health field, such hope is not made manifest through the ideas contained in their books and articles. And the cynic cannot really be a critic; the radical who is only a radical nihilist, or a radical tragedian, is for practical purposes the most adamant of conservatives.

I have caught, in some discussions of a draft of this paper, a certain pervasive anxiety among my audience, an anxiety which is afraid lest psychiatry may, in the service of our abominable social and economic order, succeed in 'adjusting' the mentally ill to its goals. It is as though people believe that there is only a finite pool of grievances and maladjustments available in this society for radicals to work with: the fear is that psychiatry, with its tranquillisers, hospitals and whatnot, may succeed in mopping up this limited supply of miseries, discharging its patients into the hell of the factory and the purgatory of the home as permanently 'cured' and adjusted robots. Once again; if capitalism could really 'adjust' people, through psychiatry or any other technology, who would want to quarrel with it? I myself am perfectly happy to see as many mentally-ill persons as possible treated, fully and effectively, in this society; for no matter how many maladjustments may become adjusted through expert techniques, the workings of capitalism will ever create newer and larger discontents, infinitely more dangerous to the system than any number of individual neuroses or manias. Some people in this audience have seemed to me to be wanting to hoard the existing supply of neuroses and insanities, by leaving them untreated as long as possible, in the conviction that these are the best grievances we have got, and once they have gone, where will we get any more? I can suggest plenty more alternative sources of maladjustment, within our present-day society. But I forebear from doing so; for there is no arguing with people who will not read the newspapers.

History, Discourse and Discontinuity* —

BY MICHEL FOUCAULT

(Translated by Anthony M. Nazzaro)

EDITOR'S NOTE: A few years ago, the editors of the French journal ESPRIT put to Michel Foucault a series of questions for which he was to write a series of responses. He decided instead to treat in depth one of the points raised, and by the way to bring up a number of other questions surely worthy of careful attention. The editors of this volume consider the document prepared by M. Foucault a major contribution to the consideration of problems with which we are deeply engaged. Though it does not address itself directly to the issue of Psychological Man, it represents an implicit critique of perspectives developed in this volume, and recommends to us alternative modes for getting at our central issues.

Here, then, is the question M. Foucault chose to deal with. The essay that follows is his reply. — R.B.

Doesn't a thought which introduces constraint of the system and discontinuity in the history of the mind remove all basis for a progressive political intervention? Does it not lead to the following dilemma:

—either the acceptance of the system,

—or the appeal to an uncontrolled event, to the irruption of exterior violence which alone is capable of upsetting the system?

I have chosen the last of the questions put to me (not without regret for abandoning the others):

1) because at first glance it surprised me, and because I became quickly convinced that it concerned the very core of my work;

2) because it allowed me to offer at least a few of the answers which I would have liked to give for the others;

3) because it gave expression to questioning which no theoretical work can today eschew.

* First English translation of "Réponse à une question," ESPRIT, May, 1968.

I must admit that you have characterized with extreme accuracy what I have undertaken to do, and that you have at the same time singled out the point of inevitable discord: "to introduce constraint of the system and discontinuity in the history of the mind." Yes, I recognize this almost entirely. Yes, I recognize that this is an almost unjustifiable statement. With diabolical pertinency you have succeeded in giving a definition of my work to which I cannot avoid subscribing, but for which no one would, reasonably, ever wish to assume responsibility. I suddenly sense how bizarre my position is, how strange and hardly justifiable. And I now perceive how much this work, which was no doubt somewhat solitary, but always patient, with no other law but its own and sufficiently carried out, I thought, to be able to stand by itself, has deviated in relation to the best-established norms, how discordant it was.

However, two or three details in the very accurate definition which you propose bother me, preventing me from (perhaps allowing me to avoid) agreeing completely with it.

First of all you use the word *system* in the singular. Now, I am a pluralist. Here's what I mean. (You will allow me, I think, to speak not only of my last book, but also of those which preceded it; this is because together they form a cluster of research whose themes and chronological reference points are quite adjacent; also because each one constitutes a descriptive experiment which is opposed to and therefore relates to the other two by a certain number of traits.) I am a pluralist: the problem which I have set myself is that of the *individualization* of discourses. There exist for individualizing the discourses criteria which are known and reliable (or almost): the linguistic system to which they belong, the identity of the subject which has articulated them. But other criteria, which are not less familiar, are much more enigmatic. When one speaks of *psychiatry,* or of *medicine,* or of *grammar,* or of *biology,* or of *economics,* what is one speaking of? What are these curious entities which one believes he can recognize at first glance, but whose limits one would be at a loss to define? Some of these units seem to go back to the dawn of human history (medicine as well as mathematics), whereas others have appeared recently (economics, psychiatry), and still others have perhaps disappeared (casuistry). To these units new terms are endlessly added and they are constantly modified by them (the strange units of sociology and psychology which since their appearance have not ceased to start afresh). There are units which are obstinately maintained after so many errors, neglect, so much innovation, so many metamorphoses and which sometimes undergo such radical mutations that one would have difficulty in considering them as identical to themselves (how can one affirm that economics remains the same, uninterrupted, from the physiocrats to Keynes?).

Perhaps there are discourses which can at each moment redefine their own individuality (for example, mathematics can reinterpret at each point in time the totality of its history); but in each of the cases that I have cited, the discourse cannot restore the totality of its history within the unity of a strict framework. There remain two traditional recourses. The historical-transcendental recourse: an attempt to find, beyond all historical manifestation and historical origin, a primary foundation, the opening of an inexhaustible horizon, a plan which would move backward in time in relation to every event, and which would maintain throughout history the constantly unwinding plan of an unending unity. The empirical or psychological recourse: seeking out the founder, interpreting what he meant, detecting the implicit meanings which were lying silent and dormant in his discourse, following the thread or the destiny of these meanings, describing the traditions and the influences, fixing the moment of awakenings, of lapses, of awareness, of crises, of changes in the mind, the sensitivity or the interest of men. Now it seems to me that the first of these recourses is tautological, the second extrinsic and unessential. It is by marking out and by systematizing their very character that I would like to attempt to individualize the large units which scan simultaneously or successively the world of our discourses.

I have retained three groups of criteria:

1) The criteria of *formation*. What permits us to individualize a discourse such as political economy or general grammar, is not the unity of an object; it is not a formal structure; nor is it a conceptual coherent architecture; it is not a fundamental philosophical choice; it is rather the existence of rules of formation for all its objects (however scattered they may be), for all its operations (which often can neither be superimposed nor linked together in succession), for all its concepts (which may very well be incompatible), for all its theoretical options (which are often mutually

exclusive). There is an individualized discursive formation every time one can define a similar set of rules.

2) The criteria of *transformation* or of *threshold*. I shall say that natural history (or psycho-pathology) are units of discourse, if I can define the conditions which must have been brought together at a very precise moment of time, in order that its objects, its operations, its concepts and its theoretical options could be formed; if I can define what internal modifications it was capable of; finally if I can define from what threshold of transformation new rules have been brought into play.

3) The criteria of *correlation*. I will say that clinical medicine is an autonomous discursive formation if I can define the whole of the relations which define it and situate it among the other types of discourse (as biology, chemistry, political theory or the analysis of society) and in the nondiscursive context in which it functions (institutions, social relations, economic and political circumstances).

These criteria allow us to substitute differentiated analyses for the broad themes of general history (whether it concern "the progress of reason" or "the spirit of a century"). They allow us to describe, as *epistemic* of a period, not the sum of its knowledge, nor the general style of its research, but the deviation, the distances, the oppositions, the differences, the relations of its multiple scientific discourses: the *epistemic* is not *a sort of grand underlying theory,* it is a space of *dispersion,* it is an *open field of relationships and no doubt indefinitely describable.* They allow us furthermore to describe not broad history which would carry off all the sciences in a single swoop, but the types of history — that is to say, what was retained and transformed — which characterize the different discourses (the history of mathematics does not follow the same model as the history of biology, which does not follow the model of psycho-pathology either): *the epistemic is not a slice of history* common to all the sciences: it is *a simultaneous play of specific remanences.* Finally they allow us to situate the different thresholds in their respective place: for nothing proves in advance (and nothing demonstrates after examination either) that their chronology is the same for all types of discourse; the threshold which one can describe for the analysis of language at the beginning of the nineteenth century has doubtless no counterpart in the history of mathematics; and, what is more paradoxical, the threshold of formation for political economy (noted by Ricardo) does not coincide with the constitution — by Marx — of an analysis of society and of history.[1] *The Epistemic is not a general stage of reason; it is a complex relationship of successive displacement in time.*

Nothing, you see, is more foreign to me than the quest for a constraining sovereign and unique form. I do not seek to detect, starting from diverse signs, the unitary spirit of an epoch, the general form of its conscience: something like a *Weltanschauung*. Nor have I described either the emergence and eclipse of a formal structure which might reign for a time over all the manifestations of thought: I have not written the history of a transcendental syncope [??].* Nor, finally, have I described thoughts or century-old sensitivities coming to life, stuttering, struggling and dying out like great phantoms — like souls playing out their shadow theater against the backdrop of history. I have studied, one after another, whole sets of discourses; I have characterized them; I have defined the play of rules, of transformations, of thresholds, of remanences. I have compounded them, I have described clusters of relationships. Wherever I have deemed it necessary I have allowed the *systems* to proliferate.

* * * * * * *

You say, a thought which "emphasizes discontinuity." This, indeed, is a notion whose importance today — amongst historians as with linguists — cannot be underestimated. But the use of the singular does not appear to me to be entirely suitable. Here again, I am a pluralist. My problem is to substitute the analysis of *different types of transformation* for the abstract general and wearisome form of "change" in which one so willingly thinks in terms of succession. This implies two things: setting aside the old forms of weak continuity through which one ordinarily attenuates the raw fact of change (tradition, influence, habits of thought, broad mental forms, constraints of the human mind), and stubbornly stressing instead the lively intensity of the difference: establishing meticulously the deviation. Next, discarding all the psychological explanations of change (the genius of the great inventors, crises of conscience, the appearance of a new form of mind); and defining with the greatest care the transformations which have — I don't say provoked — but

---

* Translator's Note.

[1] This fact, already pointed out by Oscar Lange, explains at once the limited and so perfectly circumscribed place which the concepts of Marx occupy in the epistemological field which extends from Petty to contemporary econometrics, and the founding character of these same concepts for a theory of history.

constituted the change. Replacing, in short, the theme of *becoming* (general form, abstract element, primary cause and universal effect, a confused mixture of the identical and the new) by the analysis of the *transformations* in their specifics.

(1) *Within* a given discursive formation, detecting the changes which affect the objects, the operations, the concepts, the theoretical options. Thus, one can distinguish (I limit myself to the example of *general grammar*): the changes by deduction or implication (the theory of verb-copula implied the distinction between a substantive root and a verbal inflexion); the changes by generalization (extension to the verb of the theory of word designation, and consequent disappearance of the verb-copula theory); the changes by limitation (the concept of attribute is specified by the notion of complement); the changes by passing to the complementary (from the project of constructing a universal and readily understood language is derived the search for the hidden secrets of the most primitive of languages); the changes by passing to the other term of an alternative (primacy of vowels or primacy of consonants in the constitution of roots); the changes through permutation of dependencies (one can establish the theory of the verb on the theory of the noun or inversely); the changes by exclusion or inclusion (the analysis of languages as systems of representative signs renders obsolete the search for their relationship which is reintroduced, on the other hand, by the quest of a primitive language).

These different types of change constitute in themselves altogether the whole of the characteristic *derivations* of a discursive formation.

(2) Detecting the changes which affect the discursive formations *themselves*:

—displacement of boundaries which define the field of possible objects (the medical object at the beginning of the 19th century ceases to be taken in a surface of classification; it is marked out in the three dimensional space of the body);

—new position and new role of the speaking subject in the discourse (the subject in the discourse of the naturalists of the 18th century becomes exclusively a *looking* subject following a grid, and *noting* according to a code; it ceases to be listening, interpreting, deciphering);

—new function of language with respect to objects (beginning with Tournefort the role of the discourse of the naturalist is not to

penetrate into things, to capture from them the language which they
secretly enclose, nor to bring it to light; but to extend a surface of
transcription where the form, the number, the size and the disposition
of elements can be translated in a univocal manner);

—new form of localization and of circulation of the discourse in
society (the clinical discourse is not formulated in the same places,
it does not have the same recording procedures, it is not diffused, it
is not cumulative, it is not conserved nor is it contested in the same
way as the medical discourse of the 18th century.).

All these changes of a type superior to the preceding ones define
the transformations which affect the discursive areas themselves:
mutations.

(3) Finally, the third type of changes, those which affect simultaneously several discursive formations:

—reversal in the hierarchical order (the analysis of language had,
during the classical period, a directing role which it has lost, in the
first years of the 19th century, to the advantage of biology);

—change in the nature of the directing role (classical grammar, as
a general theory of signs, guaranteed in other areas the transposition
of an instrument of analysis; in the 19th century, biology assures the
"metaphorical" importation of a certain number of concepts: organisms - organization; function - social function; life - life of words or
of languages);

—functional displacements: the theory of the continuity of beings
which, in the 18th century depended upon the philosophical discourse, is taken over in the 19th century by the scientific discourse.

All these transformations of a type superior to the two others
characterize the changes peculiar to epistemic itself.
Redistributions.

There you have a small number (about fifteen perhaps) of different changes which one can assign concerning discourses. You see
why I would prefer that one say that I have stressed not discontinuity, but *the discontinuities* (that is to say, the different transformations which it is possible to describe concerning two states of
discourse). But the important thing for me, now, is not to establish
an exhaustive typology of these transformations.

1) The important thing is to offer as the content of the wearisome
and empty concept of "change" a play of specified modifications.
The history of "ideas" or of "sciences" must not be the list of innova-

tions, but the descriptive analysis of the different transformations effectuated.[2]

2) What is important to me is not to confuse such an analysis with a psychological diagnosis. It is legitimate to ask oneself whether the person whose work bears such an ensemble of modifications had genius or what had been the experiences of his early infancy. But it is another thing to describe the field of possibilities, the form of operations, the types of transformations which characterize his discursive practice.

3) What is important to me is to show that there are not on the one hand inert discourses, already more than half dead, and then, on the other hand, an all-powerful subject which manipulates them, upsets them, renews them; but that the discoursing subjects belong to the discursive field — they have their place there (and possibilities of their displacements), their function (and possibilities of their functional mutation). The discourse is not the place where pure subjectivity irrupts; it is a space of positions and of differentiated functionings for the subjects.

4) What is important to me above all is to define amongst all these transformations the play of dependencies.

— *intradiscursive* dependencies (between the objects, the operations, the concepts of a same formation).

— *interdiscursive* dependencies (between different discursive formations: such as the correlations which I have studied in *Les mots et les choses* [*Words and Things*] between natural history, economics, grammar and the theory of representation).

— *extradiscursive* dependencies (between discursive transformations and others which have been produced elsewhere than in the discourse: such as the correlations studied in *l'Histoire de la folie* [*History of Madness*] and in *La naissance de la clinique* [*Birth of the Hospital*] between the medical discourse and a whole play of economic, political and social changes).

I would like to substitute this whole play of dependencies for the uniform, simple notion of assigning causality; and by eliminating the prerogative of the endlessly accompanying cause, bring out the bundle of polymorphous correlations.

As you see, there is absolutely no question of substituting a "dis-

---

[2] In which I follow the examples of the method given on several occasions by M. Canguilhem.

continuous" category for the no less abstract and general one of the "continuous." I am attempting, on the contrary, to show that discontinuity is not a monotonous and unthinkable void between events, a void which one must hasten to fill (two perfectly symmetrical solutions) with the dismal plentitude of the cause or by the suppleness and agility of the mind; but that it is a play of specific transformations different from one another (each one having its conditions, its rules, its level) and linked among themselves according to schemes of dependence. History is the descriptive analysis and the theory of these transformations.

* * * * * * *

A last point on which I hope to be able to be more brief. You use the expression: "history of the mind." In fact, I intended rather to write a history of discourse. What's the difference?, you'll ask. "You do not study the texts which you take as raw material according to their grammatical structure: you do not describe the semantic field which they cover: it is not language which is your object. And so? What do you seek if not to discover the thought which animates them and to reconstitute the representations of which they have given a durable translation, perhaps, but undoubtedly an unfaithful one? What do you seek if not to rediscover behind them the intention of the men who have formulated them, the meanings which, voluntarily or unbeknownst to them, they have deposited therein, this imperceptible supplement to the linguistic system which is something like the beginning of liberty or the history of the mind?"

Therein lies, perhaps, the essential point. You are right: what I am analyzing in the discourse is not the system of its language, nor, in a general way, the formal rules of its construction: for I do not care about knowing what renders it legitimate or gives it its intelligibility and allows it to serve in communication. The question which I ask is not that of codes but of events: the law of existence of the terms, that which has rendered them possible — they and no other in their place: the conditions of their particular emergence; their correlation with other previous or simultaneous events, discursive or not. This question, however, I try to answer without referring to the awareness, obscure or explicit, of the speaking subjects; without relating the facts of discourse to the will — perhaps involuntary — of their authors; without invoking that intention of saying which is always excessive in relation to what is said; without trying to seize hold of the inaudible when a word doesn't occur in the text.

So that what I am doing is neither a formalization nor an exegesis. But an *archeology*: that is to say, as its name indicates only too obviously, the description of the *record*. By this word, I do not mean the mass of texts which have been collected at a given period, or chanced to have survived oblivion from this period. I mean all the rules which at a given period and for a definite society defined:

1) the limits and the forms of *expressibility*: what is it possible to speak of? What has been constituted as the field of discourse? What type of discursivity has been appropriated to such and such a domain (what has been designated as the subject; what has one wished to make a descriptive science of; to what has one given a literary formulation, etc.)?

2) the limits and the forms of *conservation*: what are the terms destined to disappear without any trace? Which ones are destined, on the other hand, to enter into the memory of men through ritualistic recitation, pedagogy and teaching, entertainment or holiday, publicity? Which ones are noted for being capable of re-use, and toward what ends? Which ones are put in circulation and in what groups? Which are those which are repressed and censured?

3) the limits and the forms of *memory* such as it appears in the different discursive formations: which are the terms which everyone recognizes as valid or questionable, or definitely invalid? Which ones have been abandoned as negligible and which ones have been excluded as foreign? What types of relationships are established between the system of present terms and the body of past terms?

4) the limits and the forms of *reactivation*: amongst the discourses of previous epochs or of foreign cultures, which are the ones that are retained, which are valued, which are imported, which one tries to reconstitute? And what does one do with them, what transformations does one impose upon them (commentary, exegesis, analysis), what system of appreciation does one apply to them, what role does one give them to play?

5) the limits and the forms of *appropriation*: what individuals, what groups, what classes have access to such a kind of discourse? In what way is the relationship between the discourse and he who gives it, and he who receives it institutionalized? In what way is the relationship of the discourse to its author shown and defined?

How does the struggle for the taking over of the discourse take place between classes, nations, linguistic, cultural or ethnic collectivities?

It is against this background that the analyses which I have begun are set; it is towards it that they are directed. I am writing, therefore, not a history of the mind, according to the succession of its forms or according to the thickness of its deposited meanings. I do not question the discourses concerning what silently they mean, but on the fact and the conditions of their manifest appearance; not on the contents which they may conceal, but on the transformations which they have effectuated; not on the meaning which is maintained in them like a perpetual origin, but on the field where they coexist, remain and disappear. It is a question of an analysis of the discourses in their exterior dimensions. From whence arise three consequences:

1) Treat the past discourse not as a theme for a *commentary* which would revive it, but as a *monument*[3] to be described in its characteristic disposition.

2) Seek in the discourse not its laws of construction, as do the structural methods, but its conditions of existence.[4]

3) Refer the discourse not to the thought, to the mind or to the subject which might have given rise to it, but to the practical field in which it is deployed.

*   *   *   *   *   *   *

Excuse me for being so lengthy, so laborious, just to propose three slight changes in your definition and to ask your agreement, so that we may speak about my work as an attempt to introduce "diversity *of the systems* and the play of *discontinuities* in the history of the *discourses*." Do not imagine that I want to distort the issue; or that I seek to avoid the point of your question by discussing its terms *ad infinitum*. But prior agreement was necessary. Now I have my back to the wall. I must answer.

Certainly not the question of whether *I* am a reactionary; nor whether my texts *are* (in themselves, intrinsically, through a certain number of well-coded signs). You ask me a much more serious question, the only one, I believe, which can legitimately be asked. You question me on the *relationships* between what I say and a certain political practice.

---

[3] I borrow this word from M. Canguilhem. He describes, better than I have done myself, what I have wished to do.

[4] Is it necessary to specify again that I am not what is called a "structuralist"?

It seems to me that two answers can be offered to this question. One concerns the critical operations which my discourse carries out in its own domain (the history of ideas, of sciences, of thought, of knowledge . . .): was what it puts out of circulation indispensable to a progressive politics? The other concerns the field of analysis and the realm of objects which my discourse attempts to bring out: how can they be articulated in the exercise of a progressive politics?

I shall sum up as follows the critical operations which I have undertaken:

1) *To establish limits* where the history of thought, in its traditional form, gave itself a limitless space. In particular:

a) to challenge again the great interpretive postulate according to which the reign of the discourse would have no designated boundaries; mute things and silence itself would be peopled with words: and where no word can be heard anymore one would be able still to hear the deeply varied murmur of the meaning; in what men do not say they would continue to speak; a world of slumbering texts would await us in the blank pages of our history. In opposition to this theme I would like to substitute the notion that the discourses are limited practical domains which have their boundaries, their rules of formation, their conditions of existence: the historical base of the discourse is not a more profound discourse — at once identical and different;

b) to challenge again the theme of a sovereign subject which would come from the outside to animate the inertia of the linguistic codes, and which would deposit in the discourse the indelible trace of its liberty; to challenge again the theme of a subjectivity which would constitute the meanings and then would transcribe them into the discourse. In opposition to these themes I would like to substitute pin-pointing the origin of the roles and of the operations exercised by the different "discoursing" subjects.

c) to challenge again the theme of the indefinitely receding origin, and the idea that in the realm of thought, the role of history is to awaken what has been forgotten, to eliminate the occultations, to erase — or to obstruct again — the barriers. In opposition to this theme I would like to substitute the analysis of discursive systems, historically defined, to which one can fix thresholds, and assign conditions of birth and disappearance.

In a word, to establish these limits, to question again these three themes of the origin, the subject and the implicit meaning, is to undertake — a difficult task, very strong resistance indeed proves it — to liberate the discursive field from the historical-transcendental structure which the philosophy of the nineteenth century has imposed on it.

2) *To eliminate ill-considered oppositions.* Here are a few of them in their order of increasing importance: the opposition between the liveliness of innovations and the dead weight of tradition, the inertia of acquired knowledge or the old tracings of thought; the opposition between the average forms of knowledge (which would represent its everyday mediocrity) and its deviating forms (which would manifest the singularity or the solitude characteristic of genius); the opposition between periods of stability or of universal convergence and moments of effervescence when consciences enter into crisis, when sensibilities are metamorphosed, when all notions are revised, overturned, revivified, or for an indefinite time, fall into disuse. For all these dichotomies I would like to substitute the analysis of the field of simultaneous differences (which define at a given period the possible dispersal of knowledge) and of successive differences (which define the whole of the transformations, their hierarchy, their dependence, their level). Whereas one used to relate the history of tradition and of invention, of the old and the new, of the dead and the living, of the closed and the open, of the static and of the dynamic, I undertake to relate the history of the perpetual difference; more precisely, to relate the history of ideas as the sum total of the specified and descriptive forms of the non-identity. And thus I would like to free it of the triple metaphor which has encumbered it for more than a century (the evolutionist, which imposes upon it the division between the regressive and the adaptive; the biological which separates the inert from the living; the dynamic which opposes movement and immobility).

3) *To lift the restriction* which has been directed at the discourse in its very existence (and therein lies, for me, the most important of the critical operations that I have undertaken). This restriction consists of several aspects:

a) never treating the discourse except as an unimportant element without its own consistency nor inherent laws (a pure translation surface for mute things; a simple place of expression for thoughts, imagination, knowledge, unconscious themes);

b) recognizing in the discourse only the patterns of a psychological and individualizing model (the work of an author, and — why not? — his juvenalia or his mature work), the patterns of a linguistic or rhetorical model (a genre, a style), the patterns of a semantic model (an idea, a theme);

c) admitting that all the operations are made before the discourse and outside of it (in the ideality of thought or in the serious realm of mute practices); that the discourse, consequently, is but a slight addition which adds an almost impalpable fringe to things and to the mind; a surplus which *goes without saying*, since it does nothing else except to say what has been said.

To this restriction, I would object that the discourse is not nothing or almost nothing. And what it is — what defines its own consistency, what allows one to make an historical analysis of it — is not what one "meant" to say (that obscure and heavy weight of intentions which supposedly weighs, in the shadow, with a much greater heaviness than the things said); it is not what has remained silent (those imposing things which do not speak, but which leave their traceable marks, their black profile against the light surface of what is said): the discourse is constituted by the difference between what one could say correctly at one period (according to the rules of grammar and those of logic) and what is actually said. The discursive field is, at a specific moment, the law of this difference. It thus defines a certain number of operations which do not belong to the order of linguistic construction or of formal deduction. It deploys a "neutral" domain in which speech and writing can cause the system of their opposition and the difference of their functioning to vary. It appears as a whole group of practical rules which do not consist simply in giving a visible and exterior body to the inner agility of thought, nor in offering to the solidity of things the reflecting surface which will duplicate them. At the bottom of this restriction which has weighed upon the discourse (to the advantage of the thought-language, history-truth, word-writing, words-things opposition), there was the refusal to recognize that in the discourse something is formed (according to well-definable rules); that this something exists, subsists, changes, disappears (according to rules equally definable); in short, that, side by side with all which a society can produce ("side by side": that is to say, in a relationship which can be assigned to all that), there is

formation and transformation of "things said." It is the history of
these "things said" that I have undertaken.

4) Finally, the last critical task (which sums up and embraces all
the others): *freeing from their uncertain status* this ensemble of disciplines which one calls history of ideas, history of sciences, history of
thought, history of knowledge, of concepts or of conscience. This
certainty manifests itself in several ways:

—difficulties in limiting the domains: where does the history of
sciences end, where does the history of opinions and beliefs begin?
How are the history of concepts and the history of notions or themes
to be separated? Where lies the boundary between the history of
knowledge and that of the imagination?

—difficulty in defining the nature of the object: does one write the
history of what has been known, acquired, forgotten, or the history
of mental forms, or the history of their interference? Does one write
the history of characteristic features which are held in common by
men of one period or of one culture? Does one describe a collective
spirit? Does one analyze the (teleological or genetic) history of
reason?

—difficulty in assigning the relationship between these facts of
thought or of knowledge and the other areas of historical analysis:
must one treat them as signs of something else (of a social relationship, of a political situation, of an economic determination)? Or as
their result? Or as their refraction through a consciousness? Or as
the symbolic expression of their total form?

For so many uncertainties I would like to substitute the analysis of
the discourse itself in its conditions of formation, in the series of its
modifications, and in the play of its dependencies and of its correlations. The discourse would thus appear in a describable relationship
with the whole of other practices. Instead of having to deal with an
economic, social, political history embracing a history of thought
(which would be its expression and something like its duplicate),
instead of having to deal with a history of ideas which would be
referred (either through a play of signs and of expressions, or by
relations of causality) to extrinsic conditions, one would be dealing
with a history of discursive practices in the specific relationships
which link them to the other practices. There is no question of
composing *a global history* — which would regroup all its elements
around one principle or one unique form —, but rather of opening

up the field of a *general history* in which one could describe the peculiarity of practices, the play of their relations, the form of their dependencies. And it is in the area of this general history that the historical analysis of discursive practices could be circumscribed as a discipline.

These, then, are more or less the critical operations that I have undertaken. Now allow me to call you to witness the question that I ask of those who might become alarmed: "Is a progressive politics linked (in its theoretical thinking) to the themes of meaning, of origin, of the constituent subject, in short, to all the themes which guarantee to history the inexhaustible prescence of the Logos, the sovereignty of a pure subject, and the profound teleology of an original destination? Is a progressive politics bound to such a form of analysis — or with its being challenged? And is such a politics bound to all the dynamic, biological, evolutionary metaphors through which one masks the difficult problem of historical change — or, on the contrary, to their meticulous destruction? And further: is there some necessary relationship between a progressive politics and the refusal to recognize in the discourse anything else except a thin transparency which flickers for a moment at the limit of things and of thoughts, then disappears immediately? Can one believe that this politics has any interest in rehashing one more time the theme — I would have thought that the existence and the practice of the revolutionary discourse in Europe for more than 200 years might have been able to free us from it — that words are just air, an exterior whispering, a sound of wings which one hears with difficulty in the seriousness of history and the silence of thought? Finally must one think that a progressive politics is linked to the devaluation of discursive practices, so that a history of the mind, of conscience, of reason, of knowledge, of ideas or opinions might triumph in its certain ideality?"

It seems to me that I perceive, on the other hand — and quite clearly — the perilous ease which the politics you speak of would assume, if it gave itself the guarantee of a primitive foundation or if a transcendental teleology, if it persistently transformed time into metaphors through the images of life or the models of movement, if it renounced the difficult task of a general analysis of practices, of their relations, of their transformations, to take refuge in a global history of totalities, of expressive relationships, of symbolic values and of all those secret meanings in which thoughts and things are enveloped.

* * * * * * *

You have a right to say to me: "This is all very well: the critical operations which you are making are not as blameworthy as they might appear at first glance. But, after all, how can this work of a termite on the origin of philology, of economics, or of pathological anatomy concern politics, and be included among the problems which pertain to it today? There was a time when philosophers did not devote themselves with so great a zeal to the dust of archives . . ." To which I will answer, more or less: "There exists today a problem which is not without importance for political practice: the problem of the laws, of the conditions of exercise, of functioning, of the institutionalizing of scientific discourses. That's what I have undertaken to analyze historically — by choosing the discourses which have, not the strongest epistemological structure (mathematics or physics), but the densest and most complex field of positivity (medicine, economics, social sciences)."

Take a simple example: the formation of the clinical discourse which has characterized medicine from the beginning of the 19th century until the present, approximately. I have chosen it because we are dealing with a very definite, historical fact, and because one cannot refer its establishment back to some remote origin; because it would be very irresponsible to denounce it as a "pseudo-science"; and above all because it is easy to grasp "intuitively" the relationship between this scientific mutation and a certain number of precise political events: those which one groups — even on the European scale — under the title of the French Revolution. The problem is to give to this still vague relationship an analytical content.

First hypothesis: it is the conscience of men which has become modified (under the influence of economic, social, political changes); and their view of illness has, by this very fact, been altered: they have recognized its political consequences (uneasiness, discontent, revolts in populations whose health is deficient); they have perceived its economic implications (the desire of employers to have at their disposal a healthy work force; the wish of the bourgeoisie in power to transfer to the State the expenses of assistance); they have therein transposed their conception of society (a single medicine with a universal value, with two distinct fields of application: the hospital for the poor classes; the free and competitive practice for the rich); they have therein transcribed their new conception of the world: desacralization of the corpse, which has permitted autopsies; a greater importance accorded the living body as an instrument of work; the concern for health replacing the preoccupation with salvation. In all this, there are many things which are true; but, on the one hand, they do not account for the formation of a scientific discourse; and, on the other hand, they could only have come into existence, and with the effects that one has been able to establish, to the extent that the medical discourse had received a new standard.

Second hypothesis: the fundamental notions of clinical medicine would be derived, by transposition, from a political practice or at least from the theoretical forms in which it is reflected. The ideas of organic solidarity, of functional cohesion, of tissulary communication, the abandonment of the principle of classification in favor of an analysis of the whole body corresponded to a political practice which revealed, beneath stratifications which were still feudal, social relationships of the functional and economic type. Or else, do not the refusal to see in sicknesses a large family of almost botanical species, and the effort to find the pathological juncture, its mechanism of development, its cause and, in the final analysis, its therapeutic, correspond to the project, in the ruling social class, of no longer controlling the world by theoretical knowledge alone, but by a mass of applicable knowledge, its decision to accept no longer as nature that which would be imposed upon her as a limit and as an evil? Such analyses do not appear to me to be pertinent either, because they avoid the essential problem: what should be, in the midst of the other discourses, and in a general way, of the other practices, the mode of existence and function of the medical discourse in order that such transpositions or such correspondences are produced?

That is why I would change the point of attack in relation to the traditional analyses. If indeed there is a link between political practice and the medical discourse, it is not, it seems to me, because this practice changed, initially, the conscience of men, their manner of perceiving things or of conceiving of the world, and then finally the form of their knowledge and its content; nor is it because this was reflected at first, in a manner more or less clear and systematic, in concepts, notions or themes which have been subsequently imported into medicine. It is in a much more direct manner: political practice has transformed not the meaning or the form of the discourse, but the conditions of its emergence, insertion and functioning; it has transformed the mode of existence of the medical discourse. And this has come about through a certain number of operations described elsewhere and which I sum up here: new criteria to designate those who receive by law the right to hold a medical discourse; new division of the medical object through the application of another scale of observation which is superimposed on the first without erasing it (sickness observed statistically on the level of a population); new law of assistance which creates a hospital space for observation and surgery (space which is organized, furthermore, according to an economic principle, since the sick person benefitting from the care must compensate through the medical lesson which he gives; he pays for the right of being cared for by the obligation of being examined, and this goes up to, and includes, death); a new mode of registering, of preserving, of accumulating, of diffusing and of teaching the medical discourse (which must no longer express the experience of the physician but constitute, first of all, a document on illness); new functioning of the medical discourse in the system of administrative and political control of the population (society as society is considered and "treated" according to the categories of health and pathology.).

Now — and here's where the analysis becomes complex — these transformations in the conditions of existence and functioning of the discourse are neither "reflected" nor "translated" nor "expressed" in the concepts, the methods or the data of medicine: they modify its rules of formation. What is transformed by political practice is not the medical "objects" (political practice does not change, this is quite evident, the "morbid species" into "'lesional infections'"), but the system which offers to the medical discourse a possible object (whether it be a population surveyed and indexed, whether it be a total pathological evolution in an individual whose antecedents have been established and whose disturbances or their abatement are daily observed, whether it be an anatomical autopsied area); what is transformed by political practice is not the methods of analysis but the system of their formation (administrative recording of illnesses, of deaths, of their causes, of admissions and dismissals from hospital, setting up of archives, relations between medical personnel and patients in the hospital field); what has been transformed by political practice is not the concepts but their system of formation: the substitution of the concept of "tissue" for that of "solid" is obviously not the result of a political change; but what political practice has modified is the system of formation of the concepts: for the intermittent notation of the effects of illness, and for the hypothetical designation of a functional cause, it has allowed the substitution of a tight, almost continual, anatomical graph supported in depth, and local points of reference of anomalies, of their field of dispersion and of their eventual routes of diffusion. The haste with which one ordinarily relates the contents of a scientific discourse to a political practice hides, in my mind, the level where the articulation can be described in precise terms.

It seems to me, that starting from such an analysis, one can understand:

1) how to describe a whole group of relations between a scientific discourse and a political practice, the details of which it is possible to follow and whose subordination one can grasp. Very direct relations since they no longer have to pass through the conscience of the speaking subjects nor through the efficacity of thought. Yet, indirect relations since the data of a scientific discourse can no longer be considered as the immediate expression of a social rapport or of an economic situation.

2) how to assign the proper role of political practice in relation to a scientific discourse. It does not have a thaumaturgic role of creation: it does not bring forth sciences out of nothing; it transforms the conditions of existence and the systems of functioning of the discourse. These changes are not arbitrary nor "free": they operate in a realm which has its own configuration and which consequently does not offer limitless possibilities of modification. The political practice does not reduce to nothing the consistency of the discursive field in which it operates.

Nor does it have a universal, critical role. It is not in the name of a political practice that one can judge the scientific quality of a science (unless the latter claims to be, in one way or another, a theory of politics). But in the name of a political practice one can question the mode of existence and the functioning of a science.

3) how the relations between a political practice and a discursive field can be articulated in turn on relations of another order. Thus medicine, at the beginning of the 19th century, is at once linked to a political practice (on a mode which I analyzed in *La Naissance de la*

clinique [*The Birth of the Hospital*]), and to a whole group of
"interdiscursive" changes which were simultaneously produced in
several disciplines (substitutions for an analysis of the order and of
taxonomical characters, of an analysis of solidarities, of functionings,
of successive series, which I have described in *Les mots et les choses*
[*Words and Things*]).

4) how phenomena which one is in the habit of placing in the
foreground (influence, communication of models, transfer and meta-
phorization of concepts) find their historical condition of possibility
in these first modifications: for example, the importation, in the
analysis of society, of biological concepts such as those of organism, of
function, of evolution, even of sickness, played, in the 19th century,
the role which one recognizes (much more important, much more
ideologically loaded than the "naturalist" comparisons of preceding
periods) only in proportion to the regulation given to the medical
discourse by political practice.

Through this very long example I am anxious to show you but
one thing: how what I am attempting to bring out through my
analysis — the *positivity* of discourses, their conditions of existence,
the systems which regulate their emergence, their functioning and
their transformations — can concern political practice; to show you
what this practice can do with it; to convince you that by outlining
this theory of the scientific discourse, by making it appear as an
ensemble of regulated practices, being articulated in an analyzable
fashion upon other practices, I am not just enjoying myself by making
the game more complicated for certain spirited souls. I am trying to
define in what way, to what extent, to what level the discourse, and
particularly the scientific discourses, can be objects of a political
practice, and in what system of dependency they can be in relation
to it.

Allow me once more to call you to witness the question I ask:
Isn't this politics well known which answers in terms of thought or
conscience, in terms of pure ideality or psychological traits, when
one speaks to it of a practice, of its conditions, of its rules, of its
historical changes? Isn't this politics well known which, since the
beginning of the 19th century, stubbornly persists in seeing in the
immense domain of practice only the epiphany of a triumphant
reason, or in deciphering in it only the historic-transcendental destination of the West? And more precisely: does the refusal to analyze

the conditions of existence and the rules of formation of the scientific discourses, in what they possess both specific and dependent, not condemn all politics to a perilous choice: either to place upon a mode which one can, indeed, call, if one wishes, "technocratic," the validity and efficacity of a scientific discourse, whatever may be the real conditions of its exercise and the whole of the practices upon which it is articulated (thus establishing the scientific discourse as a universal rule for all the other practices, without taking into account the fact that it is itself a regulated and conditioned practice); or else, to intervene directly in the discursive field, as if it didn't have its own consistency, making of it the raw material of a psychological inquisition (judging what is said by the who says it), or practicing the symbolic valorization of the notions (by discerning in a science the concepts which are "reactionary" and those which are "progressive").

* * * * * * *

I should like to conclude by submitting several hypotheses to you:

— A progressive politics is one which recognizes the historic conditions and the specified rules of a practice, whereas other politics recognize only ideal necessities, univocal determinations, or the free play of individual initiatives.

— A progressive politics is one which defines in a practice the possibilities of transformations and the play of dependencies between these transformations, whereas other politics rely on the uniform abstraction of change or the thaumaturgical prescence of genius.

— A progressive politics does not make of man or of conscience or of the subject in general the universal operator of all the transformations: it defines the levels and the different functions which the subjects can occupy in a domain which has its rules of formation.

— A progressive politics does not consider that the discourses are the result of mute processes or the expression of a silent conscience; but rather that — science, or literature or religious statements, or political discourses — they form a practice which is articulated upon the other practices.

— A progressive politics, with respect to the scientific discourse, does not find itself in a position of "perpetual demand" or of "sovereign criticism," but it must know the manner in which the diverse scientific discourses, in their positivity (that is to say, as practices linked to certain conditions, obedient to certain rules, and

susceptible to certain transformations) are part of a system of correlations with other practices.

This is the point where what I have been trying to do for about
ten years now encounters the question which you are asking me.
I ought to say: that's the point where your question — which is so
legitimate and pertinent — reaches the heart of my own undertaking.
If I were to reformulate this undertaking — under the pressure of
your questioning which has not ceased to occupy me for almost two
months — here is, more or less, what I would say: "To determine, in
its diverse dimensions, what must have been in Europe, since the
seventeenth century, the mode of existence of discourses and particularly of the scientific discourses (their rules of formation, with their
conditions, their dependencies, their transformations), in order that
the knowledge which is ours today could come to exist, and, in a
more precise manner, that knowledge which has taken as its domain
this curious object which is man."

I know, almost as much as any other person, how "thankless" such
research can be — in the strict sense of the term — how irritating
it is to approach the discourses not from the sweet, mute and intimate
conscience which is expressed in them, but from an obscure ensemble
of anonymous rules. I know how unpleasant it is to bring out the
limits and the necessities of a practice, whereas one was in the habit
of seeing unfold in a pure transparency the play of genius and
liberty. I know how provoking it is to treat as a cluster of transformations this history of discourses which, until now, was animated
by the reassuring metamorphoses of life and the intentional continuity of the past. Finally I know how unbearable it is to cut up,
analyze, combine, recompose all these texts which have now returned
to silence, without the transfigured face of the author being even
discernible in it, inasmuch as each person wants to put, thinks he is
putting of "himself" in his own discourse, when he undertakes to
speak: what! so many words piled up, so many marks made on so
much paper and offered to innumerable eyes, such a great zeal to
preserve them beyond the gesture which articulates them, such a
profound reverence determined to preserve them and inscribe them in
the memory of men — all this, so that nothing will remain of this
poor hand which has traced them, of this anxiety which sought to
appease itself in them, and of this completed life which has nothing
left but them for survival? Discourse, in its deepest determination,

would not be a "trace"? And its murmur would not be the place of unsubstantial immortality? Would one have to admit that the time of the discourse is not the time of the conscience carried to the dimensions of history, or the time of present history in the form of conscience? Would I have to suppose that, in my discourse, my survival is not at stake? And that, by speaking, I do not exorcise my death, but that I establish it; or rather, that I abolish all inwardness in this outside which is so unconcerned with my life, and so *neutral*, that it does not distinguish between my life and my death?

I indeed understand all this and people's uneasiness. They undoubtedly have had enough difficulty in recognizing that their history, their economics, their social practices, the language which they speak, the mythology of their ancestors, even the fables which were told them in their childhood, obey rules which they are not aware of; they hardly wish to be dispossessed, in addition, of this discourse in which they wish to be able to say immediately, directly, what they are thinking, what they believe or imagine; they will prefer to deny that the discourse is a complex and differentiated practice obeying rules and analyzable transformations, rather than be deprived of this tender certainty, so consoling, of being able to change, if not the world, if not life, at least their "meaning" only through the freshness of a word which would come only from themselves and would remain indefinitely so very close to the source. So many things, in their language, have already escaped them; they do not want to lose, in addition, *what they say*, this little fragment of discourse — word or writing, it matters little — whose frail and uncertain existence is to extend their life further in time and space. They cannot bear — and one can understand them somewhat — being told: discourse is not life; its time is not yours; in it you will not reconcile yourself with death; it is quite possible that you have killed God under the weight of all that you have said; but don't think that you will make, from everything that you say, a man who will live longer than he. In each sentence that you pronounce — and very precisely in this one that you are busy writing at this moment, you have been answering a question so intently, for so many pages, through which you have felt personally concerned and who are going to sign this text with your name — in every sentence there reigns the nameless law, the white indifference: "What does it matter who is speaking; someone has said: what does it matter who is speaking."

75 76 77 78 79 10 9 8 7 6 5 4 3 2 1